CW01333425

BIG BAD & HEAVY

JUMPIN JACK FROST
with ANDREW WOODS

Published 2017 by Music Mondays, Unit A4, Broomsleigh Business Park, London, SE26 5BN

Copyright © **Nigel Thompson aka Jumpin Jack Frost and Music Mondays**

First published in hardback in 2017

Cover design: Josh White

Foreword: Hank Shocklee

Photo credits:

Front cover: Craig Boyko

Back cover: Sunbeatz Ibiza

Contributors: Goldie, Roni Size, Jazzie B, Congo Natty, Fabio, Bryan Gee, Nick Halkes, Tippa Irie, DJ Ron, MC Magika, Storm, Kenny Ken, Andy Swallow, DJ Empress and Chalkie White

All rights reserved. No part of this publication may be reproduced, distributed, or transmitted in any form or by any means, including photocopying, recording or other electronic or mechanical methods, without the prior written permission of the publisher.

The publishers have made every reasonable effort to contact the copyright holders of pictures used in this book. We would be grateful if the relevant people contact us directly.

A catalogue record for this book is available from the British Library

ISBN: 978-0-9934732-3-4

Printed in Great Britain, 2017, by Dolman Scott Ltd.

www.dolmanscott.co.uk

DEDICATED TO SYBIL THORNHILL

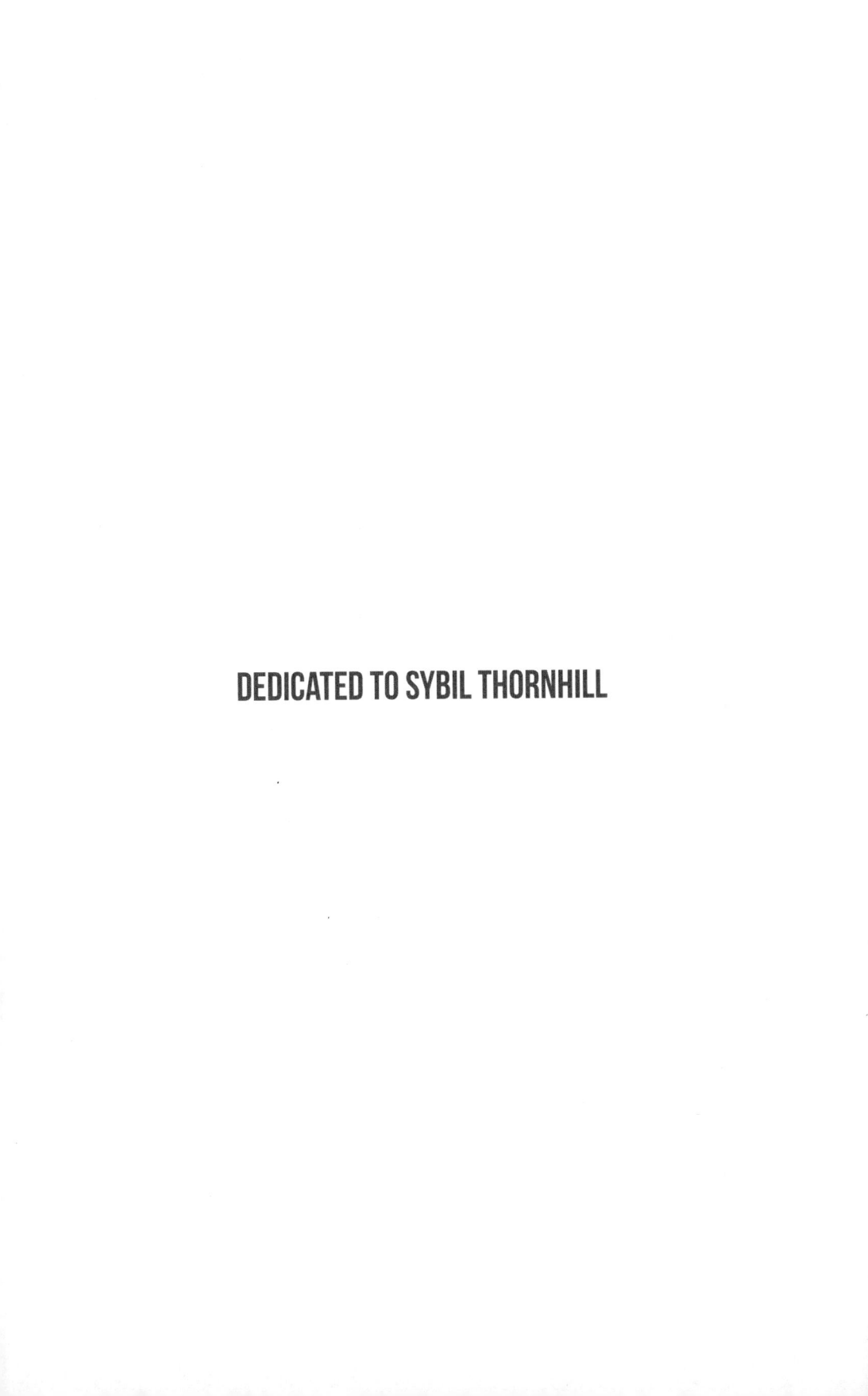

Acknowledgements

I would like to thank the following, without whom this book would not have been possible... Big love and thanks to Mum and Dad. My brothers Alvarez and Gary. My sisters Yolanda and Samantha. My kids Tanya, Ziesha, Kaya Robyn, Dante, Sion and Tori. Thanks to... Bryan Gee / Rachel Redlocks / Evil Eddie Richards / Paul Trouble Anderson / Dillinja / Tank / Jarvis / Eamon Downes / Gordon Mac / Jazzie B / Howard Hill / Jay Davidson / Andrew Nicholls / Andy Cam / Alex Hazzard / Dave Angel / Dave Lee / Delroy Stewart / Prince Duncan / Colin Marriott / Rock Smith / Donovan Smith / Christina Empress / Clayton Hardware / Mike Samuels / Joan Samuels / Shafiq / Goldie / Fabio / Grooverider / Micky Finn / Tina Bling / Robert Stush / Sarah Sandy / Corrina Kitchen / Billy Bunter / Sonya Steele / Frankie Valentine / Jeniba Amara / DJ Law / Joey Drago / Alexis Noir / Mac from Koncrete Jungle / Jaime Kalychurn / Danny Carter / Laurence Verfaillie / Wilf Prophecy / Saxon Studio / Dennis Rowe / Musclehead / Sir Coxsone / Frontline International / Jah Shaka / Mi-Soul Radio / Lightning Radio / James Joseph / Andy Swallow / Centreforce / DJ Elaine / Stewart Hawkes / Chris Music House / Leon Music House / Paul Music House / Ratpack / Levi Roots / Blacker Dread / Bikey / Sharon Swaby / Diane Small / Jon Dubaya / Laura Leroy / Spoony / Derek Moose / Tin Tin Chambers / Paul Ibiza / Tony Colston-Hayter / Jarvis / Dudley RIP / Clive Thompson / David Nassy / Robert Blake / Shirley Hutchinson / Tracey Dawkins / Mr C / Matthew B / Roger Charles RIP / Steve Goodgold / Gamal / Patrick Moxey / Simon Goffe / Guy Carlton / DJ Ruffstuff / my uncle Glenroy Emanuel and all my Brixton massive / Kerry Lady MC / Becky Full Cycle / Krust / Roni Size / Die / Suv / MC Dynamite / MC Moose / Gavin Gerbz /

Big, Bad & Heavy

The Wolf / Jenn Star / Harris / Rob Lisi / Carl Collins / Darcey Mayer / Tom Parkin / Lucy Gaynor / Dean Francis / Afeni Neville / Dan Prince / James Hyman / DJ Rap / Maxine Dunkley / Hijack / Steve Gordon/ The Dream Team / Subflow / Scooba / Rob Machete / Erin / Jodie / Sam XXXL / The LA Family / Lady Miss Kier / Towa Tei / Gavin Mills / Leon Bell at Nike…

Co-author Andrew Woods (@andrewjwoods) would like to thank Wendy Matthews for her keen eye and Keiron Bain 'the hook-up'. It was a blast! www.andrewjwoods.co.uk

Foreword by Hank Shocklee

Big, Bad And Heavy is an incredible journey through the landscape of modern music and how it synthesized and galvanized the man, the legend, Jumpin Jack Frost.

From his early childhood growing up in the tough inner city neighbourhood of Brixton, south London, to becoming one of the most respected and influential pioneers in the musical landscape, Nigel shows how you can survive and persevere as he evolved from a notorious bad boy to a drum and bass super producer and DJ.

His story is heartfelt, warm and sometimes comical as he weaves his thoughts from moment to moment providing the truth of what makes his character – a strong black man, loving father and devoted family member.

This is a story of realness. It's also a story of the power and essence of the most vibrant force in the universe... music – and how it can change lives forever.

I particularly enjoyed this book as it somewhat mirrors my own life. Being of West Indian descent myself, half of my family once immigrated to the UK. I wasn't able to be there with them to feel what it was like growing up in England, but this book filled me in on some much-needed info.

I thoroughly recommend this sincere and entertaining read to anyone who loves music. Hats off to Jumpin Jack Frost as he is BIG, BAD AND HEAVY!

Hank Shocklee. Founder and sonic architect of Public Enemy and The Bomb Squad.

Contents

Acknowledgements V

Foreword VII

1. Brixton Boy 1
2. The Wild Dogs Of Brixton 3
3. Don't Upset Toby! 11
4. Street Tough 21
5. Boarding School 27
6. Bad Boys In The Fog 33
7. Brixton Is Burning 43
8. Let's Play Hangman 51
9. You're Nicked! 61
10. Fresh Beats 67
11. Aciiiiiiiiiiiiiidddddd!!! 77
12. Jumpin Jack Frost 83
13. Frosty's Gone To Iceland 91
14. Murder 95
15. Hardcore 107

16.	Black Man In The Royal Ulster Hall	115
17.	The Ghosts Of Athens	123
18.	The Book Of Love	125
19.	Jungle	129
20.	The Old Frost Returns	137
21.	Let's Start A Label	143
22.	9mm Of Pain	149
23.	The Proper Jungle	157
24.	HMP Brixton	161
25.	Rest In Peace	167
26.	Rumbles In The Jungle	171
27.	Drum And Bass	177
28.	The Darkest Jungle	181
29.	Critical Mass	187
30.	Mercury In Our Blood	195
31.	Sex, Drugs And Drum And Bass	201
32.	White Lines And White Sand	211
33.	Party Like It's 1999	219
34.	The Boys In Brazil	227
35.	Bad Moon Rising	231

36.	A Bad Heart 233
37.	September 10th 2001 237
38.	Aftermath 241
39.	AWOL 251
40.	Rebirth 257
41.	Soul Mate 261
42.	A Promise Kept 263
43.	A Few Final Words 269

CH. 1

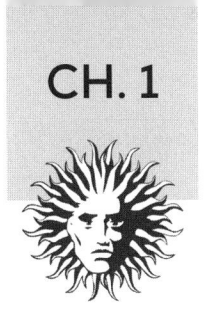

Brixton Boy

Rah!!! I'm a Brixton boy, *yeah*? I grew up on the streets of south London. For many, like myself, they were wild times back then in the seventies and eighties, yeah? Brixton can still be an unforgiving place now. But Brixton will always be my home.

Not all of the black community was like me, but I wasn't the only one who took his chances on the streets, either. I was a bit of a hustler. My boys were hustlers. We wanted something, we took it. The police would treat you like a criminal back then, anyway, whether you were walking home to do your homework or off into town to rob some shit. Growing up in Brixton could be tricky, yeah? I am not proud of these things, but nor am I ashamed. Sure, I regret some of the things I did, but that was how it played out for me.

Things were getting quite desperate for a while, but I was saved. I don't know where I would be right now had it not been for a certain turn of events.

Some of my friends from back in the day are still smiling, some are in a bad way, many are no longer with us. But I am truly blessed. I got to take a different path to many I knew and it's a journey that still surprises me today. There have been many twists and turns along the way, man.

I have tried to be as honest as I can, which is difficult when you've lived a life like mine. But here it is, warts and all. This is the story of Jumpin Jack Frost.

CH. 2

The Wild Dogs Of Brixton

There were wild dogs just roaming the streets, yeah? I remember seeing these strays hanging around the park. We were told to stay the fuck away from these scary-looking animals, but we didn't need telling. These were not house-trained dogs, you know what I'm sayin'? These were *wild* dogs. There were four or five of them and they'd howl outside the flats and fight at night. Bins would be knocked flying as they rooted for food. If the dogs came into the park, we'd leg it home. This was the seventies and rabies was a big thing back then. You didn't mess with rabies, yeah? I was a five-year-old child and I didn't know about crime or racism yet, but I knew all about rabies. The biggest source of evil in my world were those wild, abandoned dogs.

Parents were not so worried about letting their kids play out back then. We'd be out on our own at all times of day and night. I would spend a lot of time with my cousin Michael who was two years younger than me, but far more sensible. He was running around with me aged three! What the fuck?!

I have always been a little crazy. My earliest memories are of Michael and I playing with an ant nest in the front garden of our home on Palace Road, Tulse Hill. Michael and his family had the ground-floor flat and we had the top. We'd kid each other that we knew these ants by name. I called this one ant 'Supi' and would pretend to recognise him among all the others. My cousin Michael found this really funny. 'Look, there's Supi! Did you see him?'

- 'Where?! Where?! I can't see him!'

We wouldn't hurt the ants or anything, we would just watch them moving around, carrying stuff. I don't know where the name Supi came from, I just made it up, but it's something I will always remember. 'There's Supi! Wave to him!'

We would run around the streets and hang out at the local park, but we never got into any *real* trouble back then. But we were always mindful of those fucking dogs. Those strays stayed in a pack. They were *tight*, you know what I mean? You saw those dogs and you went the other way, bruv. You didn't mess with wild dogs. Especially Brixton dogs. They would chase you down the street, I'm telling you.

I was born Nigel Thompson on May 29th, 1967, in St Stephens Hospital (or Chelsea & Westminster as it is now) on the Fulham Road. We lived in Battersea until I was 18 months and then we moved to Brixton.

My brother Nicky was born severely disabled and was very ill. Nicky was in hospital most of the time and died aged two, when I was about four. Poor Nicky. We moved to Palace Road, Tulse Hill around that time. My sister Yolanda came along in October '73 just after I started at Fenstanton Primary School on Christchurch Road, Tulse Hill.

Renting flats in the same building as my mum's sister Barbara, meant I was very close to my cousin Michael. We were brothers really. We were close, you know?

I was well into motorcycle stunt king Evel Knievel at the time. I was *obsessed* with Evel Knievel, man! I liked his little action doll thing complete with the wind-up-and-go bike. When we were a little older, Michael and I would race down the hill on our bikes and recreate Evel's stunts. Michael would be on his Chopper and I would have this little Budgie. We'd make ramps and all that. People would lay down in rows on the pavement and I'd jump them. That Budgie bike really took a beating and eventually the seat snapped in half. I fixed it myself, man, with tape. That bike was a mess.

We would sometimes have a babysitter looking after us when my mum Ingrid was out at work and my dad Frankie was out doing whatever it was he did. Mrs Ojay had three sons: Hildrith, Robert and Ian, but we didn't spend too much time with them. We liked to be outside. We'd be out launching great big bits of wood into the trees to get the conkers out. We would often hang out at the church next to the park at weekends and in the holidays, or we'd go to Streatham ABC for Tufty Club, which showed films and stuff. Although Tufty was a street-wise squirrel who was always banging on about being safe on the streets, his road awareness films didn't stop me from getting hit by a car.

It was a Triumph Dolomite. I was about six years old when I got knocked flying by this car after running into the road. I twisted in the air three times before I hit the floor. I don't know if I was more embarrassed than hurt, but I just got up and walked off, feeling a bit rattled. I was left with an imprint of the car's grille on my leg for a few days after. You could tell it was a Dolomite by the shape of the indentations. It didn't seem to be much of a thing, though, getting run over by a car.

Although Brixton could be a dangerous place, my younger years were probably no different to kids growing up in the countryside. We climbed trees, picked apples and raced our bikes. I was happy.

Christchurch Road ran parallel to Palace Road and around the corner was the Martin family. There was Kim, Neil, Pamela and older brother Steve who had his own sound system (Steve went on to run 'Sir Coxone Sound' years later as Blacker Dread). I always looked up to Steve. He was so cool and although I didn't know anything about the sound systems Steve was playing with back then, I knew that this guy was *the man*. I spent a lot of time there in their house.

When the Martins' cat got pregnant, they gave me one of the kittens. I would often turn up at home with random animals; that was my thing. So, I turned up with this kitten one evening and Mum was not happy. 'No way, you're not having that in my house!'

- 'Please! Please! Let me keep it!'

I had always wanted a pet, back then, but wasn't allowed one. I really wanted a dog, that was my thing. I *really* wanted a dog, but a kitten ran it close. I brought a cat home on a few occasions, but was told to let it go. So, I came home with this kitten and really turned on the charm. 'You're always coming home with these animals!' I was told. 'Get it out of the house! No more!'

I held this kitten up to Mum and gave her the puppy-dog eyes. She thought about it for a bit and finally caved in. 'OK. OK. But you will be responsible for it.' I loved this cat although it ran away soon after. I guess I wasn't looking after it properly.

I have always loved animals. My cousin Michael had a budgie and when that bird died, I cried my eyes out. That budgie dying really got to me. I would rather see people suffer than an animal. People getting hurt, can often leave me cold, but if you hurt an animal I will fucking kill you!

Big, Bad & Heavy

I really started to toughen up at school. I remember someone nicking my Mickey Mouse watch while my mate Vivian and I kicked a ball about in the playground. I went home, very upset. Frank Delano Thompson was a man who fought fire with fire. 'You need to go back tomorrow and do whatever you have to do, to get that watch back!' Dad barked. My dad was a bit of a, how can I put this, mischief maker. A rogue. 'Don't you come back to this house until you have that watch back, you hear?!' I went back to school the next day absolutely fuming. I found the kid who had my watch and marched right up to him. I got right up in his face. I had this big bit of tree branch in my hand and I swung it at this kid, whacking him over the head. 'Aaaarrrggghhh!!!!' He fell to the floor nursing his wounds, while I took that fucking watch off his wrist. *Rah!* That was the first time I ever hurt someone, I guess.

I was really quite small for my age, but I was learning to look after myself. Dad was not one to let these things slide so I needed to fight my battles. He was not going to have me getting picked on. I was so proud to have that watch back on my wrist when I walked into class.

I used to love making go-karts with my cousin Michael once I'd got home from school. We were brothers, man. We would make go-karts out of wood, which we nailed together, complete with pram wheels. We'd race them at Hillside Gardens Park. They had no brakes, these things, but we loved tearing down the streets in them. We never really watched TV much as I recall. We came home from school, did our chores and went straight back out to play.

Michael Thornhill

"My earliest memory of Nigel is of him falling down the stairs at Palace Road. We shared this massive house, that had four families in there and I remember him crashing down the stairs – bump, bump, bump – having suffered a lick or something. Nigel was always getting into arguments with his parents and it would get quite involved, innit. Nigel rolled down those steps until he got to the bottom. Thud! Then he just got up and walked back up the stairs like nothing had happened, to continue the row. He was four or five, something like that.

Nigel was bright, do you know what I mean? He was competitive, too. I remember beating him in a running race and man didn't take too *kindly to me winning and so man busted my head open! Ha ha. I had blood pouring out of my head.*

We would build go-karts and race them down the road. This white brother who lived nearby was a mechanic and he would do some work on our karts when they needed it. He was always helping us.

Without blowing smoke up his arse, Nigel was more outgoing than I was. He was wily too. We would both do things that only I would get into trouble for. Nigel would often escape the punishment. We climbed up into a roof one time and got covered in dust. I came down all filthy and got lashes for it and was told to stand out in the garden. Nigel got no lashes. I don't know why.

Evel Knievel was Nigel's shout, not mine. But I got jumped by the bike, though. Sometimes there were six of us, shoulder to shoulder, waiting for the bike to clear us. I once felt the tread of the tyre on man's nose and thought, 'This ain't the one!'"

We had a big garden with these massive rhubarb plants and stuff and so we were always having crumble for dessert. These plants and stinging nettles were cut down one summer and while trying to retrieve a football or something, Michael and I found this black leather bag. Excited, we opened this holdall to see what was inside. 'Woooaaahhh!!!' I looked at Michael open-mouthed, as I pulled out this gun. The bag contained two rather realistic-looking pistols and so naturally we started running around playing cops and robbers. It was great fun. Eventually, Dad came out when he saw what we were up to. I'm not sure if we were aware that they were flare guns, but that was what they were. We were alerted to this fact when my dad walked over, picked up one of the pistols and loaded it with a cartridge before firing it into the sky. Whoosh! I knew, there and then, that perhaps Dad wasn't the most responsible of parents. This was confirmed when he handed the guns back to us so we could continue with our games. These were real guns. Crazy! Why he gave them back to us I will never know.

Dad was a bit of a scamp. I wasn't aware of all the things he was up to back then, but even I knew that kids shouldn't be playing with flare guns.

Dad was always causing trouble and was in and out of prison all through my childhood. He was a loveable rogue, though, and used to hang out with Michael's dad, my uncle Barry. Our families got on really well, considering.

Ingrid Thompson

"I have four siblings from a very close-knit family. When Nigel was about two we decided to share a house with my sister Barbara on Palace Road, Tulse Hill, Brixton. Barbara had a son called Michael, who was two years younger than Nigel and those two formed a very close friendship and played together a lot. My mother lived in Battersea and even at a very young age, Nigel and Michael would venture up to the top of Palace Road to turn left, where the bus stop was. They didn't have to cross a road and Nigel was very good at remembering things, but that was still a young age for the pair of them to be taking the bus on their own to go and visit my mother. They even had to change buses at Herne Hill where they then took the 37 to Clapham Junction. There's no way you would let kids do that now.

Nigel and Michael once got the coach to Manchester to stay with my aunt who met them at the other end. On the return journey, my sister and I went to Victoria Coach Station to meet them, but they were nowhere to be seen. The coach came in, but no Nigel or Michael. I started to panic and went to a phone box to ring my aunt. 'I put them on the coach,' she said. 'Maybe they didn't get back on the coach after the stop-off!' We had no landline back then and so we couldn't ring home, either, to see if they'd made it back. So, we eventually got home and thank the lord, there was Nigel and Michael on the front lawn with their suitcases. 'There is more than one exit at Victoria,' they told us. They'd come home on their own.

Nigel really fancied himself as Evel Knievel back then. I remember him racing up this ramp and straight into a tree one time! He was also into Bruce Lee when Enter The Dragon came out. I think Nigel thought he was Bruce Lee and would make these gestures and noises. I remember telling him how important it was that he came home at a certain time, just to be safe. 'Nobody will do anything to me,' he told me.

- *'What do you mean, no one will do anything to you? What would you do if a grown man came after you?'*

Nigel then started making all these Bruce Lee noises. He was jumping up and howling. Ha ha!

Saturday mornings, Nigel and my nephew Michael, would go to watch movies at Tufty Club, which was held at Streatham ABC. Nigel was very close to all my sister Barbara's children. My sisters Barbara and Lorraine and my brothers Butch (Samuel) and Stan all lived in south London apart from Stan who ended up in Forest Gate. Nigel really looked up to his uncles and had a very close relationship with my mother. Nigel loved his 'Ganga' to bits.

I arrived in the UK from Guyana, South America in 1961. My mother Sybil Thornhill was already in the UK and sent for her children in two lots. We lived in Battersea for many years where we were raised as Catholics. My father Everard worked for British Rail and he was a very intelligent man who used to write short stories in his spare time. My father once wrote a piece on Clapham Junction, which he spoke about on BBC Radio and we were all very proud of him. Later on, my father wanted to get into PR and he wrote to British Rail, where he worked as a ticket collector. Imagine a black ticket collector wanting to get into PR, back then in the sixties. Needless to say, he never got a response. He then got involved with the church. I think he was the first black bishop in the UK. My father was a Doctor of Divinity and a Bachelor of Science and that was a great source of inspiration to us.

I learned the mechanics of English back in Guyana as a young child. When I came to the UK in June, 1961, I ended up finishing first in every subject at school except geography; I knew all about South America, but not much about Europe. But I knew more about English than some of the teachers; certainly, the mechanics of it. I was class monitor too.

I forgot to wear my school tie one day and the teacher decided to make an example of me. 'As class rep, you should be wearing your tie!'

- 'But Miss Casey, I forgot it!'

'I want you to write an essay on carelessness!'

'If that's what you want, then that's what I'll do...' I started this essay by defining carelessness and forgetfulness and then outlined the differences between the two. That didn't go down well. Ha ha!

I married young and had Nigel soon after. There were times when things were very difficult, but Nigel was a tough little soul. He would look after himself and his cousin Michael."

As well as Yolanda, I had an older half-sister Samantha who was Dad's daughter from a previous relationship (Rose was her mum) and half-brother Alva who grew up in care; his mum died when he was young. My mum Ingrid was an inspiration. Mum was a really hard worker who held down two jobs: not only was she a cleaner, but she also worked at the Peek Freans biscuit factory in nearby Bermondsey (nicknamed Biscuit Town). Mum would often come home with boxes of broken biscuits.

We had always been tight with Michael and his family as Mum and Auntie Barbara were very close sisters (still are). We both moved from Palace Road to temporary accommodation on Wandsworth Road in 1975, before going to a bed and breakfast in Clapham Common. From there, our family moved to Mudie House just off New Park Road, Brixton Hill, where we stayed for many years. Michael's family moved to Tulse Hill.

I met most of my life-long friends while at Mudie House. The estate was an exciting place to hang out. We would meet up and muck about on the street corners just like that pack of wild dogs. The wild dogs of Brixton.

CH. 3

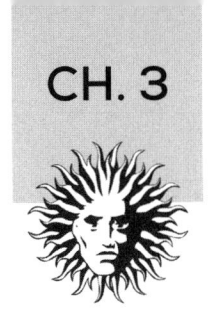

Don't Upset Toby!

The head of our family was Ganga. Ganga was my grandmother Sybil and so-called as I couldn't pronounce 'grandma' when I was younger. When Michael and I were very young (5 or 6) we would catch the bus to Ganga's (in Battersea) on our own. I can't quite believe it, but we did. I remember her waving at us through the window after we left hers in the evening. Little kids just walking around London on their own. Mad.

My grandmother was a massive influence on the family. Ganga came over to the UK from Guyana in 1961 with her five children: Ingrid, Barbara, Lorraine, Butch and Stan. We loved Ganga, but boy was she strict, man. We were very close to her, though and Michael and I often stayed at her house during the school holidays and at the weekends. We spent lots of time there with Ganga.

Michael Thornhill

"We were both very close to our grandma. Nigel named her Ganga and that title stuck, man. That name had reverence.

We would walk down Brixton Water Lane and jump on the '2'. We were young them times, yeah? We would then get the '37' to Clapham Junction. You wouldn't do those things now. Those were the times.

We would hang out at Ganga's flat, riding the lifts. We were told to go no further than the playground, but then we'd meet up with some other kids and would want to go exploring. Nigel's like my bigger brother really and our mums have always been tight. I can't remember a time when my aunt wasn't close by.

We would stay at Ganga's sometimes, sleeping in Uncle Butch and Uncle Stanley's old room. We had a bunk bed that had been split into two. So, there we would lie, giggling about farts and bogies. Our grandmother would warn us to be quiet when she tucked us in and it would be silence until we heard her walk off; the adjoining room was hers. Then we'd start laughing our heads off about stupid kids' stuff. Ganga would come back, of course. 'I told you lot, no noise! Go to sleep!' If she opened the door of her room, I often knew, as I was nearer the door and so I would shut up, real quick. We had started laughing this one time, when I spotted Ganga and closed my mouth real quickly. Boy did Nigel get it. She peeled back the bed clothes and peppered him with licks from head to toe with her belt. Pa! Pa! Pa! I started to laugh then and Ganga did a 180-degree pirouette, man! I was now on the same shout. I got licked! Suddenly it was silent in that room.

Ganga's belt was called Toby and it would hang over the kitchen door. We were the ones who named it Toby, us nine grandchildren. Toby was a symbolic thing. She would take Toby off the door and ask you to come over and sniff it. You respected Toby, do you know what I'm sayin'? Toby was the master in that house."

My grandfather Everard was a bishop, but sadly, he died a month after christening me. I wish I could have gotten to know him. Granddad was a policeman back in South America and somehow he made the transition to bishop over here. Other than his career as a law enforcer, life back in Guyana was never really discussed.

Because Ganga was head of the family we would always be at her house on the weekends eating pepperpot, the Guyanese national dish. A spicy meat stew, Ganga's pepperpot was the best. I can still smell that food, man!

My uncles Butch and Stan were a big influence on me. They were young men who had knowledge and wisdom. Butch and Stan would be listening to James Brown, Parliament and jazz at Ganga's. I was bewitched by the album sleeves and would read all the credits on the back. My uncles would have been quite young back then, in the mid-seventies, but to me, they were men of the world. I loved hearing their new records, sitting in the spare room at Ganga's.

Stan was really into electronics and would always be fixing amplifiers and other bits of equipment. I would watch him playing around with all these wires and circuits, totally transfixed. Stan always had a soldering iron in his hand as he tackled a broken amplifier or whatever. I would also get to have a go on his Linn Sondek turntable. I remember Stan buying a reel-to-reel machine too, which was like something from a spy film. I lapped all that up. He would set those tapes whirring with these big clunky buttons.

Owen (or Blackie) was one of the older boys from Ganga's estate and he would often look after Michael and me over in Clapham Junction. Other times, my uncle Barry (Lorraine's husband) would sneak us out of Ganga's for a day out in his grey Transit van. I loved going over to Ganga's, whether we were out playing with Blackie, out in Barry's van, or indoors getting a crash course in electronics with Uncle Stan.

***

'Hey Nigel, do you want to play some music?' My cousin Denise was so cool. Whereas the adults didn't want me anywhere near the fucking stereo, Denise was always encouraging me to play some tunes at family get-togethers. Denise was my favourite older cousin. 'You can play the records, man,' she'd say. I was just eight years old and yet here I was, getting the whole family dancing. Mum was really strict and Ganga was even fiercer, but Denise was so cool and relaxed and would always give me the encouragement I needed to play the tunes at family parties.

There was this calypso tune by Lord Kitchener called *Sugar Bum Bum* and everyone would leave the kitchen to dance in the living room when that came on. Everyone! Now, the kitchen was where all the food was and so I would deliberately play that track and then Michael and I would sneak into the empty kitchen to get at the patties, while my family danced away. I would put that tune on and strike! I was devious, man, and that song was my cue. This period right here was my first association with playing music, I guess. I would watch people's faces as they danced to the tunes I played and I loved it. It felt so good, watching them. This vibe was real!

A lot of locals would go to Brockwell Park in the summer for the annual reggae festival. They were big affairs and there was often a bit of trouble to be honest; stabbings and that. We never really went on family holidays and so big events like this were important. The reggae festivals were great at getting the whole community together and the music was great. Looking back, my love for music was definitely starting to establish itself.

My dad listened to Miles Davis and all the jazz greats at home. We even had a saxophone on the wall, but Dad couldn't actually play it. That sax just sat on the wall, man.

When I wasn't listening to music, I'd be outside with the kids from New Park Road. Our estate was formed by two squares. The 'top square' was by the New Park Road entrance and that was where the climbing frame was. We lived in the 'bottom square' on Forster Road. Our end had these work sheds to one side and you could see markings on the ground where the war shelters were once located. I loved living on that estate. We would spray-paint cricket wickets and goalposts onto the wall for our games, which would go on for hours.

We would always be round our friends' flats, having our tea and whatnot. It was a tight community and all our parents knew each other. 'Hey Ingrid, Nigel is up here having his dinner!' would be shouted down from a balcony.

The Knights Youth Centre was just across the road and it was there that we learned to play football. There were often day trips too, organised by the people at Knights. I also attended cub scouts at Brockwell High School with a young lad called Jonathan Sutter and our paths would well and truly cross, later in life.

Michael Thornhill

"As we got older, we would hang out at the adventure playground or we would go out knocking for friends and ride our bikes about, never venturing too far from home. Childhood was cool, man. We were always running around playing games or doing some sprinting and athleticism in the park. We were often sent to the shop by our mums with a shopping list, even though we were only seven or eight.

Our older cousin David would sometimes cajole us into things. 'See those two boys over there? If you don't beat them up, I will smack you up!' he'd tell us. I think he was toughening us up. David definitely pushed Nigel a bit, in terms of getting that street mentality.

Sometimes Nigel could be a bit of a snide and there were often little riffs at that time. Then Nigel started getting into fights. He hit me in the mouth once with a solid hit, but I didn't budge. He saw something different in me from that day on. I was a man now or some shit.

We now had that impish attitude and would blank the bus conductor and that. Those were the ills of the time.

Nigel was a mischievous kid, man. If his mum said, 'Come in at 6:30; he'd come in at 7 until 7 was the new curfew time and then he'd come in at 7:30pm. Nigel learned how to work his parents and knew how to push the boundaries. He was a cheeky boy. He would give you something in the morning as a gift and then take it back in the evening. 'Remember that thing I gave you? Well, I want it back!' Ha ha!"

New Park Road was a cosmopolitan community of black and white. Prince and his brother Errol, Paul Jerome and Joey Coleman all lived in the top square and together with Pat O'Driscoll, Mikey Bullforce, Robert Nicholls, Xani and me from the bottom square, plus Devon from the flats on Kingswood Road, we formed quite a little firm.

Our gang would stay out until late although I was still only eight years old. I would get some serious beatings off Mum when I finally got home, though. Our flat had a landing at the top of the stairs and you had to pass Mum in the evening in order to get into your room, so you knew you were going to get a few snaps of the belt. We all went through that shit for being out late. We never got up to any real trouble, we just used to play games and go off on adventures.

Barbara Thornhill

"My nephew Nigel was always a daring kid, you know? He was always getting into scrapes. He broke his teeth, scraped his knees; there was always something. I remember him standing on my new rug in his football boots watching the 1976 FA Cup Final. I was furious! But he wouldn't budge. I loved that rug! Ha ha.

Nigel was a colourful character with a strong mind and he spent a lot of time with my son Michael. They were inseparable.

Sometimes in the summer we would go to the Brockwell Park reggae festival. I can still see Nigel and his cousin whining. Whining is like twerking, yeah? Ha ha. That said, whenever you see photos of Nigel as a child, he looks so moody! A man of mystery, that one! But he had a very interesting personality."

Big, Bad & Heavy

I was an adventurous kid. My dad gave me a pound note one day and I remember taking all my friends to Buckingham Palace on the bus. My shout. 5p a ticket! I don't know why I chose Buckingham Palace or how I knew how to get there. So, off we all went. I paid for the bus and bought a couple of cans of Coke for the journey. Prince, Errol, Devon, Mikey Bullforce and I, all on our way to see the Queen. We had a quick look around and came straight back. I can't quite remember why I wanted to do this, but it definitely happened.

We were in awe of the older boys at New Park Road. Many of them would hang around the pub, The Hand In Hand, just outside the estate. Paul Jerome and Joey Coleman lived in the top square and they stole cars; Stags and Minis. Fucking hell, they were so cool. Prince's brother Lloyd was a don, too. Lloyd was like a pimp, man. A player. So was Clive Thompson. We all wanted to be like Clive and Lloyd. We all wanted to be like Clive Thompson.

Clive Thompson

"I know Nigel from way back as a child during the New Park Road days. I was an 'older' and used to knock around with his cousins and uncle.

Nigel was a good kid; rough, but principled. He was wise for a 'younger'. Staunch and always on the ball.

Nigel was a very forward-thinking kid back then and had an answer for everything. He was a very ballsy kid. I loved him to death.

These times right here were the last days of the teddy boys; the O'Driscolls and the Conroys. They were the Brixton gangs back then along with people like Razor Smith.

Brixton Hill was quite a mixture of whites, Indians and Africans all getting on. We were all grafters, you know what I mean? We were young boys doing criminal stuff like burglaries and whatnot, but we never robbed old ladies. We were called the New Park Dreads; a name I came up with.

Because New Park Road was inbetween Brixton and Streatham, we could go out to either neighbourhood, whereas the Brixton lot didn't like the Streatham boys and so forth. But we got on with loads of different types of people.

We would hang out to see sound systems like Stereograph and Frontline or we would go to Bali Hai or Cat Whiskers in Streatham."

I had become a challenging kid, you know? I was quite clever, but was always getting into trouble. There was no leader in our gang really, we would just hang around the estate with the older boys.

I never really got on with school. I got expelled from Richard Atkins for throwing a milk bottle at the teacher. Mum was devastated. School would prove to be an ongoing issue.

After the milk bottle trouble at Richard Atkins, I was eventually moved to Streatham Wells; a new school that had just opened on Palace Road. I got into constant trouble at Streatham Wells too, resulting in another expulsion. I was just one of those kids, always involved in some kind of argument or other. I would do crazy things, like throwing a compass at the teacher. This compass flew through the air and landed in her foot. Dad came to school to get me and I remember thinking, 'God I'm going to get into so much trouble here.' However, Dad didn't say anything to me. 'Go up to your room and wait for your mum,' he said rather casually when we got home. Dad was not a disciplinarian. Mum was very upset. My mum was so hard-working and very bright and it hit her hard to see me getting into trouble at school.

Dad went to prison around this time here and so the timing was pretty bad. I was an angry kid by now. I never thought to ask why my father was inside. Maybe I didn't want to know. Possibly no one wanted me to know. As I've said, Dad wasn't exactly a role model.

Dad was in Wormwood Scrubs and that first visit really shook me up. 'Why aren't you coming home with us?' I asked him when it was time to go.

- 'I've got to stay here for a while, do you know what I mean?'

It was a daunting experience going up to Wormwood Scrubs with my mum. 'Oh my God, what is this?!' Seeing your dad like that? In prison. Well, what can you say?

Dad was eventually moved from Wormwood Scrubs to Albany Prison, on the Isle of Wight. This was a high-security place. I remember going over there and there was no familiar sound of the keys and locks like Wormwood Scrubs. They had a map in reception that had all these lights on it that would flash if any of the 'guests' tried to escape. It was all computerised there. This was a high-security gaff.

I was still unaware of what Dad had done as we never spoke about it. I guess he was stealing stuff and getting into fights. I mean, he let us play with flare guns when we were kids and so even I could put two and two together. A five-year-old playing with a flare gun? Mad! Can you believe that?

Dad was a character, though. He always dressed *sharp*. He liked nice shoes and smart suits. He had *spirit*. Maybe too much spirit.

***

There wasn't much money about back then. We used to have these locks on the telephone to keep the bill down. We worked out that you could still make calls, though, by pressing those little white buttons for the same amount of clicks as the number you wanted to ring. For a number six, you would click it six times, then pause. But you had to be careful not to abuse this, though. A hefty phone bill would see you get the belt! Mum worked really hard to put food on the table.

I remember one Easter, we got up on the Sunday morning only to find that all our eggs had been eaten by mice. I remember coins going into the electricity meter with a giant turn of the rusty key. Many landlords wouldn't rent to us of course. This was the time of 'No Irish, no blacks, no dogs!'

I first encountered racism when I was about six. Wog was a common word back then. I would hear that stuff all the time, but I would always fight back. 'I will punch you up in the face if you come at me with that racist shit!' I didn't mind a little fight. I was fearless!

I was about 10 when the TV show *Roots* came on. Now, none of us knew anything about slavery up until that point, although we'd been exposed to racism. However, we were shocked by *Roots*. I just couldn't believe what I was seeing. I asked Mum if all this slavery shit was for real. 'Oh yeah, this is what happened. Black people were taken from Africa in slave ships and forced to work, blah blah, blah.' I was so *angry*. *Roots* was so important, man and I urged everyone to see it. If nothing else, black people were on the TV, although they were being beaten, raped and murdered. Monumental.

Another cultural shockwave to affect me, in an albeit rather different way, was *Star Wars*! That shit messed with my mind. I went to see *Star Wars* with my Uncle Stan and I thought I was Darth Vader for about six weeks after, as I walked around waving an imaginary lightsaber. *Star Wars* changed everything!

I didn't care much for the goodies in *Star Wars*, I loved the dark side. I loved Darth Vader. Most kids thought Luke and Han were the heroes, but not me. I loved the big, black dude! That fucker was the man. Just that noise of his heavy breathing was enough to get people in line. I loved that film.

Michael Thornhill

"I can remember Nigel getting into trouble at school; he was always questioning the teacher about history. 'Why is history always about the white man?' He was once excluded from class for it. 'Why do we need to know about the white man?' I think Roots had a big effect on him."

After three episodes of *Roots*, my mates and I started going out into the street and just randomly beating people up. 'Look at what they fucking did to us, man!' I was boiling with rage. After a few episodes, my friends and I had all seen *Roots* and we were all very angry. We got together in the evening and just went knocking on doors to beat people up on their doorsteps, all because of this TV show and what it told us. I was just ten years of age. Prince was only 8! 'Fuck this fucking shit!' *Roots* spun my head out, man. We would meet on the climbing frame to discuss what we could do about this shit. 'Look at what they did to our ancestors! Fuck 'em!' We were stupid to do the stuff we did, but we were so young. We would sit in the top square climbing frame, ten of us, just fuming. I couldn't get over it at the time. *Roots* was a real shock to the system, although its influence did wear off after a while.

I made my first trip abroad while I was at primary school. We went to visit my cousin Monty in Sweden with Mum, Yolanda and our cousins Ingrid and Candi.

For some reason, I went to Sweden wearing a pair of Bay City Rollers shoes. Can you believe that? What the fuck?! I didn't even like the band. Why was I wearing those shitty shoes? These shoes had a high heel and a tartan band with Bay City Rollers written across it. I will never forget those shoes. For fuck's sake.

We travelled to Vasteras by boat with Tour Line and I was sick all the way there. Really sick. I remember Yolanda nicking some money from Mum's purse before hitting the jackpot on the slot machines. Yolanda bought me a Tour Line baseball cap with the winnings. Mum was so pissed with her although she soon calmed down when she saw the pile of coins she'd won.

Cousin Monty was a DJ and often played out in Gothenburg at weekends. Monty played records on the radio too. I was constantly asking Monty questions as he played me his records. Monty made a big impression on me and I have never forgotten those days spent with him in Sweden. Sadly, Monty is no longer with us.

There was this massive ski-slope in this Swedish town, and you could go right up to the top of this fucking thing, which of course I did; in those fucking Bay City Rollers shoes. I could have broken my legs, slipping around up there in those stupid shoes.

We couldn't visit Sweden without me doing something silly and so I stole some food from a pizza shop as I recall. My cousin Monty was very disappointed. The people who owned the shop were very nice to me, but I had definitely left a bad vibe behind.

That trip was my first experience of being abroad and Monty was a real inspiration to me back then. Meeting someone I knew, who was making money from doing something he loved, was massively inspiring. Monty was a massive influence. I miss you, man!

CH. 4

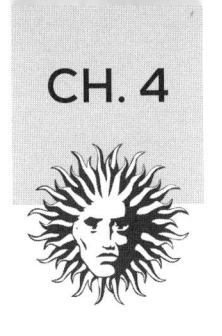

Street Tough

Cousins David and Barry used to take Michael and me out with them sometimes. David had a wicked sense of humour. The nickname he gave Michael stuck for years. Because Michael used to sip his tea, very loudly, David called him Sipatea. 'Oi! Sipatea!' David toughened us up, man. He would order you to rob a football off some kids and stuff like that. 'Take that thing off him or I will beat you!' he'd hiss. David was like a drill instructor in the army or something. I was fast becoming a pretty rough kid by then.

I was a fanatical Man United fan – my dad was a massive fan of Denis Law – and I loved playing football. I used to live in these moulded-stud football boots. One time, I was over at the adventure playground when someone on the swings boarded me in the head. I was fuming! So, I went over to this kid and kicked him in the head, face and teeth with my football boots. The studs were worn to shit, but they managed to kick his teeth out. I was about 10 years of age and becoming quite a handful. There were lots of incidents like that. Life was getting pretty rough, yeah?

By the time, I joined Tulse Hill Secondary School a year later, I was a bad boy. Tulse Hill was a big school and although it could have been a fresh start, I continued getting into trouble and had constant fights. Mum worked across the road from the school and every time the phone rang she feared it was the school informing her as to my latest spot of bother. Anything could spark the fights: rivalry, football, accidental altercations in the playground, anything. I wouldn't take any racist crap, either.

My love of music was a distraction, though and by 1979, I was totally immersed in the Jamaican sound system culture. Shepherds

Youth Centre in Brixton had sound systems playing there and we all loved dub. They had Nasty Rockers, Dread Diamonds, Frontline International and Small Axe playing there at Shepherds. We went there a lot, man. They would have dance competitions to see who was the best skanker and I was properly into that.

Jah Shaka was the best dub sound around, yeah? If you saw Jah Shaka on the bill, you had to be there. I was fascinated by the sound system guys. I would spend hours watching them do their stuff. You had the box boys, who helped shift the amps and decks. The selector, who would choose the records and of course the man himself, dropping the needle. You might also have an MC chatting on the mic. The atmosphere at these dances could get really fiery. You would get Brixton boys and crews from Deptford and New Cross skanking against each other. It was competitive, yeah? Dick Sheppard School in Tulse Hill was where Stereograph and sound systems like that started up and we attended plenty of skanking competitions there. There would be a whole crew of us at these events: Prince, Sean, Richard, Go Go, Colin, Robert and Richard Blake. Other times we would visit Bali Hai in Streatham, right next to the ice rink or Jubilee Hall Community Centre in Tulse Hill (right opposite Michael's house) where we would meet up with Rodney Haynes aka Skipper. This was a time of Gabicci and Farah slacks. Mum and Dad couldn't afford such things, but I managed to get the hand-me-downs from my cousin David. I can still recall getting Dave's Gabicci. I was made up, man. Now I was looking *good*! I also had an afro by now, bruv!

Warrior Charge by Aswad was important. *Warrior Charge* was released in 1980 and was a track from a movie soundtrack. That was a tune! *Babylon* was a film about us, yeah? Black youth and sound system culture in a racially divided London. This time here, really was a time of black awakening, you know? There was a lot of oppression back then.

I first identified with the Rasta vibe of peace and love among all men, back then, aged 13. Jah Rastafari: King of Kings. Lord of Lords. The Conquering Lion. Many people from the sound system scene were influences in this regard. I was starting to identify myself as *black*. We were afro-centric, man and the sound system culture reinforced that. Jah Shaka was the man and we would skank hard to *Warrior Charge*. Skanking *hard*!

I had always spent a lot of time in Manchester at my Auntie Ella and Uncle Berry's, who were also massively important to my awakening.

Berry and Ella were black activists who ran the Carmoor Road Centre for black youths up there. My uncle and auntie were very strong and opinionated and got a lot of respect from the local community. My uncle ran the Carmoor Road Community Centre while my auntie looked after the Nia Centre. Berry and Ella worked so hard trying to instil a black consciousness into the local youths, so they could become more aware of their history. My uncle was a strong character and a total inspiration, who once took the police to court over charges of brutality. Uncle Berry (Beresford Edwards) was chairman of the PACM, the Pan African Congress Movement, an organisation dedicated to the promotion and understanding of African history. He was a total hero to me and many more like me.

I was a young man, sneaking out to places like Jah Shaka's Phebes in Dalston or Glengall Hall, Peckham on a Tuesday night to skank. We would take the 37 bus from Brixton to Peckham. However, Peckham boys didn't like us and there were often run-ins. The Deptford boys chased us out of the area one night. You had to be tough because there was trouble around every street corner and we knew if we were caught, we'd get a good beating. We would get back to Brixton to regroup and count the heads back to make sure we were all there, safe and sound.

I had been carrying weapons since I was 11, but there was a big difference between carrying a blade and using one. I'd always had a fascination with weapons. Sometimes you would see rival gangs pulling out blades and so you'd get one yourself. That was how it worked. A lot of people at those sound system nights would have been carrying a weapon, but there was very rarely any trouble inside.

Skanking was a true tribal dance. Everyone had their way of doing it. You had to be *slick*. Devon was the best skanker. Robert, Go Go and Prince were good too, though, as were Sean, Richard and Chicken. That lot there were wicked skankers. I would try my best too, but I knew I wasn't quite up to their standards. We would always look forward to skanking against kids from different areas. We went to this open-air competition in Deptford one time and Devon was pulling some moves. Then, as this song neared the end, Robert Blake pulled out a copy of The Bible as his finishing move! Everyone was like, 'Woooaah!' It was mad, like a breakdance battle. People would make a circle and two people would skank in the middle. They were great days. Crazy, man. That was how life was going into the eighties.

Big, Bad & Heavy

I was still getting into trouble at school. I'm not sure why, but it had been a constant problem ever since I lost that Mickey Mouse watch. I was becoming more and more disruptive.

We were playing cricket one day in PE and I really wasn't happy. I hated cricket, but because I could bowl I was always expected to take part. I wasn't happy. I was at the crease and I think I'd just been bowled out or missed the ball or something when the teacher came over. 'C'mon, it's someone else's go,' he said, going for the bat. I wasn't having any of it and we started this tug of war. I hated that teacher and once I'd wrestled the cricket bat free I swung at him. Clock! I got him square on the head. 'Right, Thompson! To the Head!'

That particular incident got me expelled. I was kicked out of Tulse Hill, man. I hated cricket, though. I hated cricket with a passion; it was like watching paint dry. But I certainly hit the sweet spot with that PE teacher. Howzat?!

I'm not sure I was that bothered about getting expelled to be honest. I didn't rate school at all and was always in trouble. I was a bit of a liability. My dad didn't seem bothered, but Mum was really upset. Mum was a really smart, intelligent woman and she knew how important school was. I had now been expelled from three schools and I wonder, looking back, if I was trying to get to the point where someone would just take me out of the education system. Dad – who had been in and out of prison – had 'officially' left home by this stage and I'm not sure if that was fuelling my rage or not, but I take full responsibility for it.

I had private tuition for a while with Mr Wilkinson who was a really nice guy. Very tall and Scottish, I got on well with Mr Wilkinson. We would go to this education centre in Clapham Junction where I met my first girlfriend, Diane. Relationships were weird when you were young; we didn't even kiss, as things weren't at that stage yet. I was a bit of a late starter with girls to be honest.

Four months later, the next episode in my education kicked off when I was sent packing to boarding school. Me! In fucking boarding school!

Ingrid Thompson

"When Nigel started bullying other children we just couldn't manage his behaviour any more. Then he got expelled from Tulse Hill. I had met

another man and we had a son called Gary. Nigel hated Gary's father with a passion and this coincided with him going to boarding school. Nigel thought we'd sent him away to get him out of the picture, but it wasn't like that at all. Nigel sometimes remembers things differently.

We used to go over to Berkshire to visit Nigel. They provided transportation from County Hall. We would also see him at weekends and during the holidays. There wasn't any alternative to be honest. It was boarding school or home school."

CH. 5

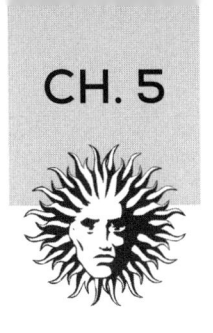

Boarding School

The tower blocks of west London whizzed past the window of the train before eventually disappearing, giving way to trees and parks. Berkshire wasn't that far out of London, but it seemed like a world away from Brixton.

Mum and I were on our way to Enborne Lodge in Newbury, to have a look around this boarding school. Mrs Lagden, the school social worker was also on the train with us.

I don't remember being nervous at all, as we pulled into the station. A cab then picked us up and took us to this grand old building sat within acres of green land. The Brixton boy was going to boarding school.

It seemed very nice, very cool, but fucking strange. I liked it, though and so once the papers were signed, I was duly shipped off to Berkshire, aged 13. I was well up for it, although I was leaving everyone behind in Brixton. I just took it in my stride and got on with it.

This Enborne gaff was major. Four acres of land, the building itself consisted of a new wing that was linked to an old listed building. I was a fish out of water, man.

There were stables (but no horses), beehives, workshops and beautiful gardens and tennis courts. Enborne had some great football pitches, trees and pebbled walkways. It was stunning, man. A stream ran through this pile that sat proudly against the beautiful countryside. It was something completely different.

Enborne was a total culture shock. I was from Brixton, yet now I was in the countryside, hearing bats and owls for the first time. 'What the fuck!? There are bats out there?!'

Big, Bad & Heavy

I was lying in bed that first night, unable to sleep. The dorms were quite daunting as all these boys, some much older, were all complete strangers to me. There were a lot of rules there too, which wasn't surprising when you had a shit-load of naughty boys living together. There were 40 boys at Enborne Lodge and they were mostly just like me; problem kids. They called us 'maladjusted boys'.

Every one of us had problems, but the staff were specially trained and pretty good to be honest. It was a difficult job, but they managed to settle most of us down.

I guess being away from home allowed me to grow up a bit, smoothing out my rough edges a little. You could *think* there, do you know what I mean? You had time to really mull things over.

I had an AM radio and would hang it outside of the bedroom window. I would then turn the volume down. Bang! Bang! Bang! Bats would come and hit against the window. Radar innit? I loved crazy things like that. We were in Berkshire, 70 miles out of London and Brixton this was *not*. This was bat country!

There weren't a lot of black kids there; just five or six of us. There were skinheads and mods from all over London, though. I hadn't seen skinheads before, only on TV. Roger Charles (RIP) and Glenn Walters stood out. This was a time of Madness, Bad Manners and all that. There were racists there as well. It was funny because I had never met anyone from east London before. I didn't even know black people lived in east London. I had no idea. I knew very little of life outside south London.

Kevin West was a skinhead and he was brilliant at cross country; he won every single race. We would jog around those four acres every week, and I hated it. 'Fuck this shit, I'm cold!' We would go cross-country every fucking week. Kevin had tattoos on his knuckles that said, 'Skins'. I was only 13 and all this was weird and scary shit.

The racism there was borne more from ignorance than hate. You would hear 'black bastard' and 'nigger' quite often. 'What the fuck is this?' I'd think to myself. It took a while to get used to it, to be honest. Some of the other black boys were listening to skinhead music too and I soon put them right. 'You need to get into dub, bruv!' I soon had those boys skanking.

Tuesday nights would see us go into Newbury where there was this club called The Waterfront. The locals would greet us black kids with that 'Okkkaaaayyyy!' from Lenny Henry on *Tiswas*. God, we fucking hated

Boarding School

that. I would get called 'Chalky' and would hear that 'Okkkaaaayyyy!' all night, man. I hated Lenny Henry for that. Talking like an idiot while dressed as a Rastaman. People like me paid the price, mate!

So, a typical day at boarding school... The bell would ring in the morning and we would go down to the common room for breakfast. Everything about boarding school was a culture shock. Even the full English breakfast was something I wasn't used to. What the bloody hell is this? What the fuck is that? Toad in the hole? What the fuck? Never seen that shit in my life. Toad in the hole? What the fuck? What's all this Yorkshire puddings bullshit? After breakfast, we would get ready for school.

I remember being really interested in this one particular lesson: semiotics. Semiotics was the practice of using the familiar, in order to market products or ideas. Make someone think they've seen something before and they would warm to it, instinctively. I kept thinking about this semiotics stuff a lot. I loved that shit!

Breaks were spent in the clubhouse that had table tennis, pool and record players. After school, you could do what you liked; play five-a-side and that.

I made some really good friends at Enborne and we all changed through our time there. We grew as people. The teachers were very hands-on and specially-trained to deal with difficult boys. Mr Reid-Brown was the sports teacher and he was a James Hewitt-type and all-round good chap. He took us for basketball, table tennis and football. Then there were the bees.

I was a bee keeper. That's right. They put me in charge of the fucking bee hives. My only experience with these creatures prior to this was getting stung by a wasp in Manchester. My face went red and swollen like a boxer's. I was terrified of bees and wasps as a result. But now I was in charge. I was a bee-keeper, bruv.

I had to wear the white suit and net mask, which went right over your head. I then had a can of smoke, which I would release into the bottom of the hive. The smoke would cause all the bees to come out of the hive and swarm, thinking a fire was under way. They would then take up residence in a nearby tree. Once the hive was empty, I would take out all the trays to extract the sticky honey. Then, once the smoke had died away, the bees would have a look about and decide to go home. It was a routine thing and I remember the process so well. Here I was, a Brixton boy, playing at being a beekeeper. I did a spot of gardening, too. I also loved carpentry and made a pretty sweet Betsy table or plant pot stand. It was crazy, man. We also learned canoeing. You had to perfect an Eskimo roll in the swimming pool, before they would let you go downstream for real. You would have to turn all the way over, under water, before flipping up again. We would then take the canoes down to the stream in Newbury. We would sometimes go fishing, too, but I played football every single day. I was a good footballer. I loved football.

Ingrid Thompson

"Nigel had always loved football and he played at boarding school to a very good level and later became a mentor to the younger children. I think it helped him to relax."

The teachers could be quite heavy-handed with the boys at times, but they never did anything like that to me. They left me alone, for some reason.
    One of the things I couldn't accept at boarding school, though, were the Christmas carols. I was raised a Catholic and I wasn't singing no songs from a religion set up by a man who killed his wives. I refused to sing that Henry VIII shit. I was christened by my grandfather who was a very clever, witty and smart man. 'You're not putting your fucked-up shit on me, bruv. I'm from Brixton, bred. I'm not doing it! No fucking way!'
-   'Get out of class!'
-   'Sweet!'

This was some radical shit.
    My reggae conversion therapy was working a dream on the black kids at Enborne. They were always asking to borrow my Jah Shaka tapes and I got their fashion game well and truly upped. 'You need some Farah slacks and some Gabicci. Ditch that Fred Perry, now!' Stanley Richards, Paul Becker, Nelson and Hamish were really liking my vibe and so I started taking my records to school when I came back from Brixton on a Sunday night. I played them David Rodigan, Dennis Brown, The Lone Ranger, Yellowman, Jah Shaka and various other sound system tapes we'd recorded at dances with a hidden tape recorder. They lapped it up.

We became regulars at the Waterfront in Newbury on a Tuesday night and danced the night away to northern soul. It was a funny dance, really. We started getting on with the locals, too as we slowly began to understand each other's cultures. We were not so different, really, we just came from varying environments, circumstances and families.

Globally, these were scary times, yeah? Just down the road from us was the Greenham Common US Air Base where the female protestors were trying to stop American cruise missiles from being deployed there. I was genuinely terrified by the prospect of a nuclear war and yet five miles from school was where these cruise missiles were due to be housed. I didn't want to be living near these fucking things! Protestors were chained to the fences just like the female Suffragettes as things got real deep down at Greenham Common, yeah?

Then, when the school complained to the air base about the jets constantly flying over, we were all invited to go over to the air base to have a look around. It was a really interesting trip. We got to sit in a helicopter and the cockpit of a jet as we walked around Greenham Common. I didn't see any nukes however.

Three weeks later, everything had disappeared. Gone underground. That's 100% true. It was as if Greenham Common had got up and disappeared in the middle of the night.

My parents had split of course and Mum had found this new guy. I didn't get on with this new man at all. It was not a great vibe at home.

My Mum and sister went on holiday to Canada to see relatives around this time and instead of taking me, I got a stereo system instead. I was told that I could have gone to Canada, but Mum made it clear that she would rather I went for the cheaper option. So, I now had my own stereo system! I loved that thing and was always up in my room spinning tunes at the weekend. I would play loads of funk, soul, reggae and dub on that deck. I would try and get hold of any tunes I heard Jah Shaka playing.

I was awoken late one night at home by loads of voices and music from downstairs. My mum had fallen in with a new group of friends after the split with my dad and clearly a few of them had come over for a drink and a dance. I turned my lamp on and blew a fuse. She'd taken my stereo! I was fuming! What the fuck?! I really resented this new guy, who was clearly downstairs listening to *my* stereo! Fuck him! I really resented him. 'Who the fuck do you think you are, listening to my fucking stereo?!'

Big, Bad & Heavy

Michael Thornhill

"Nigel got expelled when he was 12 or 13. He was in the second year at Tulse Hill. He then went off to boarding school, but we kept in touch. He would come down at weekends and summer holidays. Nigel used to tell me stories of what went on there. This new school had this military sound to it.

Nigel told me about this guy Colin who often got up without brushing his teeth and so, as a result, he got the nickname Shit Breath. Salem's Lot was a big TV show at the time and there was a famous scene of a vampire boy floating outside a window, tapping on the glass. They did this to Shit Breath by tapping on man's window. 'Colin! Colin!' They were waving their hands in front of their mouths.

Sound system culture gave identity to black kids at the time and Nigel started chatting on the mic, you know? Nigel had the diamond jumper, baseball cap, cords and Stan Smiths. Nigel was a gymnast on the dancefloor and could bust full splits when he was skanking. He was very good and rated among his peers. Nigel was getting well known, yeah?"

CH. 6

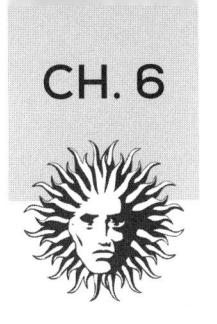

Bad Boys In The Fog

There was real fog back then. Sometimes you couldn't see more than a few feet in front of your face. When the fog came down in Brixton, you were fair game, do you know what I mean? Bad things could happen when the fog appeared. Bad boys ran riot in the fog…

I was at boarding school, but this wasn't Hogwarts and I was no Harry fucking Potter. As much as being at boarding school in Berkshire chilled me out a little, back in London, I was a different person.

I started shoplifting on my returns to London at the weekends and in the holidays. I would go on the rob in the West End, as soon as I got off the coach. There was quite a gang of us from Brixton and we would go out stealing these cassette tapes that we sold on to the sound system guys in Brixton. We would hit stores in the West End and get as many tapes as we could. None of us came from money and so we would do anything to get some decent clothes in order to avoid the dreaded hand-me-downs.

You couldn't nick stuff from your own manor and so we'd get the Tube into the West End to swipe tapes from Boots and places like that. We wanted C-90s and the Metal cassettes that were more expensive. We'd sell these tapes at the cab office on Coldharbour Lane. I was 14 and willing to do whatever it took to make sure I had enough money to finance nice new clothes and nights out skanking.

Slowly, this little posse of Brixton bad boys started to grow and we would all hang out together. We looked out for each other and had a growing reputation in the borough. Was it a gang? Possibly.

Our thing was Samsonite. We would steal these expensive Samsonite bags and used them to store the tapes we nicked. We had Samonsite cases, manbags and bumbags. I would take the bag into Boots and with a sweep of my arm take 30 tapes in one go, straight into my Samsonite. Sweet! To see 20 or 30 of us all hanging around in town, dressed in these fish-tail parkas mods wore, you'd have probably walked the other way. I guess every kid has a different reason for hanging out in a gang – protection, brotherhood, entertainment – but there was always one common theme: money.

Back in Brixton was this café called Stassi's. Stassi's was a Turkish café/amusement arcade with a pool room. Stassi's was our safe house and this place had a real reputation. Some of the older gangs used to hang out there in times gone by. The owners didn't mind us 'youngers' meeting there, though and they even bought some of our stuff. They would buy scrap gold and jewellery off us, once we'd progressed to 'stings'.

A sting was a mugging. You'd spot a nice chain on someone's neck and you'd pop it off and run. There was more money in popping chains than cassette tapes. This increase in revenue also meant we could go to all the sound system nights in our finest gear, which we bought from Baron's in Brixton. We were bad boys.

Back in Berkshire, the older, racist lot had left the school by now. I mean, some of the guys were as cool as fuck, you get me? There was Glen Walters and Martin Webb who was a mod. Martin was a cool guy, just like Bob Dylan. My two biggest mates at Enborne were Stanley Richards and Paul Becker. Paul and Stanley were on my vibe by now, as they were a bit lost before that. 'What the fuck are you doing, listening to all this *Baggy Trousers* nonsense and The Specials?! You need to get into reggae and the best place for reggae is Brixton, bruv.'

Stanley came from Kensington and Paul was from Finsbury Park. I often took them to Brixton at the weekends and they loved it. Sometimes I'd go to their boroughs too. Janika Burke was at Enborne too and he started hanging around with us at weekends. Janika's dad had a hi-tech recording studio on Great Portland Street and we would often go up there. I was really into buying records at this point and we would visit all the record stores.

You could buy weed or a draw for £1 in Brixton and so we often headed for the Frontline – the area within Coldharbour Lane, Railton Lane and Atlantic Road. There was good food to buy and always some wicked music playing on the Frontline. I had started smoking by now and Lambsbread and Colombian Gold were the ones. Frontline in Brixton was a legendary place for buying and selling weed, right there in the road. Your weed was wrapped up in a betting slip and it was £1 a draw down the Frontline. If you were flush you could get a £3 draw, which was an eighth. Big times there with an eighth of Lambsbread. Colombian Gold and Sensi were the big ones in Brixton, though. Hash was more east London. Brixton was weed.

The first time I ever smoked weed was at Tulse Hill. I was with Vivian, my school friend from the Mickey Mouse episode at primary school all those years back. We were 12 I think, when we started smoking. By 14, I was hooked and never really stopped from that moment on.

We tried to get to sound system parties every Friday and Saturday night and week nights too during the school holidays. I had my Farah slacks and waffles, Gabicci or Pringle jumpers and Adidas Stan Smith or Gazelles. Maybe some nice shoes. Baron's and Temples in Brixton had the Farah gear. We would wear berets too. We would put coat hanger wire into the lining of the beret to flatten it out into a circle like a crazy, flying saucer. That was the fucking shit! Although I was looking *fine,* this era coincided with me having six teeth out in hospital and so I had to wear braces as well as glasses. I have always hated going to the dentist and even now I have to be sedated. So, I now had the clothes and the attitude, but I also had these braces and specs. Teenage strife.

With our money from selling tapes we'd go to Shepherds Youth Centre to see Frontline, Sir Coxone, Blacker Dread, Screechy, Bikey Dread, Gappy and Levi Roots of Reggae Reggae Sauce fame, who was part of Sir Coxone back then. Sir Coxone, Frontline, Dread Diamonds, Small Axe and Jah Shaka Main Sound were the ones.

Brixton Town Hall would hold skanking competitions back then, knowing that sound system culture was so important to the black community. Lots of our culture wasn't getting played on the radio and night clubs were often aimed at white audiences. So, Jamaican sound systems allowed black people to reconnect with their culture and of course there was a whole new generation of youths who were discovering it for the very first time.

I was living two lives, really. I was living the country life at boarding school in Berkshire, eating English roast dinners and keeping bees. In Brixton, I was tapping into the dark side. I was becoming a real bad boy.

Being at boarding school allowed me to learn so much and I loved interacting with people out of my comfort zone. My communication skills improved too although I never got to appreciate toad in the hole, however a full English (without the bacon) came to be a favourite. I got quite good at table tennis too although not as good as some of those there. I was often given a 15-point handicap and still lost.

I looked forward to working at Lambourne Stud Farm, caring for the horses. A lot of the Country Code is still ingrained in my head. 'Always close the gate!' You didn't get many horses roaming around south London.

This disease myxomatosis was infecting rabbits at the time and I remember this one assembly when the teachers asked us to watch out for these rabbits with myxi. 'If you see one, pick them up by their ears and with one stroke to the neck, break it!' We were warned that their eyes were all swollen and red. But there was no way we were going to do that. We used a golf club instead. THWACK! The eyes sometimes popped straight out of their sockets. We went out looking for rabbits and never once picked one up and broke its neck. How savage was that?

It wasn't all violence, though. I remember planting a seed in gardening club and was truly shocked when it grew into this wonderful sunflower. I couldn't believe how big it was. It was amazing!

Back in Brixton, I was this bad boy. When my mum met Gary's dad, it had a big effect on me. I just didn't like him. I never disrespected him, but I never got on with him. We were civil to each other for years, but there were a couple of things I didn't like about him. I was always polite and respectful and never rude to that man, though. I just stayed out all the time.

Brixton Hill was a real mix of black and white kids sandwiched as it was between black Brixton and white Streatham. My little gang was a mixture, too. There was me, Prince, Errol, Devon, Richard Lewis, Sean Lewis, Robert Nicholls, Patrick O'Driscoll and Bullforce. From this point on, we really started acting up. We were out all the time, up to no good.

The police had their 'sus' laws in place and were constantly hassling innocent black people that they *suspected* of being up to no good. It didn't seem to matter if you were a bad boy or not, you would still get pulled. The situation was getting out of control and people were angry. There was a real tension in the air and then... boom! Brixton went right up in flames, bruv.

Bad Boys In The Fog

Robert Blake

"Shepherds was a local community centre on Railton Road, Brixton. We would meet at Shepherds every Wednesday to listen to the local sound systems. We were still at school at the time, but would follow the sound systems around every night of the week at numerous community centres. We went there to be entertained in what were safe havens for us. We could hang out with friends at these dances and get to know and understand each other. It was important to us to have sound systems in our community centre and gym. They also had events at the local high school. We didn't need to travel on those nights at Dick Sheppard's as it was right on our doorstep. Everyone would be at these events.

Our parents would never have let us out until 4am, where there were drugs, drink and adults and so we would sneak out at night and meet up. It was meant to be for sixth-formers and above, but some of us had older brothers who let us in. We enjoyed those nights dancing to Jah Shaka and loved the dub with its minimal vocals or 'voxes'. They were instrumentals, really.

It was great being allowed to congregate and communicate at these events. This was our culture. As we had no phones back then, it was unspoken that we would meet up every Wednesday at Sheppard's. Every Wednesday we'd be there in our Farah or waffle trousers, maybe drainpipes by Lois, Adidas Bamba or Stan Smiths. Oh and Nike Wimbledons. They knew you were somebody, then. You weren't one of these kids who did what they were told.

Those events, especially the all-dayers (10am 'til 1am), were brilliant. All of us, all in the same place. But we needed currency to finance all of this, whether it was clothes, transport or weed.

There was a big demand for cassette tapes from the sound systems at the time and so we started lifting TDKs from department stores. Little shits we were. We were ruthless and would hit the West End in our droves. We had all these routes marked out that allowed us to hit the shops in little groups of five and six, split from the original 30 or so.

We couldn't do it in south London of course and so we hit the underground map and chose stations to target. Every borough had a shopping centre with a Boots or a WH Smith that had the stuff we wanted. We saw it as a job, 5-6 days a week. We set off at 8am, just to go out and get these tapes. 100 tapes meant 100 sales. We started to meet others like us in Tulse Hill, Herne Hill and Stockwell and our little gang got bigger. The money then allowed us to hear the beloved music of the sound systems.

The West End wasn't policed as it is now. There was no CCTV back then. Sometimes, we would go out on our own, other times in a little group.

When Sir Coxone and Saxon played out in other boroughs, that gave us a reason to go there and steal. We would use the sound systems as cover.

Notting Hill Carnival was also an opportunity. We would go there from Friday night to Monday morning. There would be plenty of people willing to put you up for the evening and give you somewhere to change your clothes or have a sleep. The spirit of the Notting Hill Carnival was strong. People would open their doors to strangers. 'You're from south London? Come on in.' There was a mutual trust. They looked at us as adults. We were in love with the music so much we went all the way from Brixton to stay there all weekend. That was a real safe haven.

There would be 20-30 of us going to Carnival. The ambience was amazing. Sound systems playing all day and night. Some were in people's houses, others were in community centres. Carnival was also an opportunity for making money, do you know what I'm sayin'? As we started to look more respectable and presentable off the back of our tapes and increasingly back then, video tapes too – which made us even more money – we found that thieving got easier. We didn't look like little thieves any more. We didn't look desperate.

At Carnival, we would mix in with the crowds and rob individuals. We would grab chains off necks. There was no mad struggle or violence really, just a quick swipe. The bravest would take the chain while the rest of us formed a human wall behind the victim. We never really discussed these things, we just acted. Our associates would bunch up shoulder to shoulder to create this human wall behind the person we stole from, then if they turned and got angry they would see all these people and back down. No one would kick off over a necklace, not with so many of us there. They would see a group of guys and decide to move on, without making a noise. It was intimidating, yeah, with 8-15 people in front of you and behind. That's how we got away with it. Often, they wouldn't even acknowledge what you'd done. We used Carnival as a major source of finance, but it was never about being a criminal. It was just something that happened. We never discussed it, but we worked as a team. We were kids, but we had each other. Our parents couldn't afford to buy us new clothes and I had seven brothers and a sister. My mum worked two jobs and Dad had three. We had nothing, but together as a little firm, we had something and we stayed together in that sense. We had a bond and understood each other. I didn't want my brothers' hand-me-downs. You would watch that jumper travel all the way down from your older brother, through the ranks until it was yours. Everyone else knew this too and so we had to devise our own fashion. I didn't want to wear that jumper that my brother wore for two years straight.

Our thing was Samsonite. That was our thing. Samsonite did these £200-£500 bags and satchels and we had those items. We had shoulder bags, carrier bags, bum bags and man bags. We looked a certain way and for six months or so we were always sporting Samsonite. The bags helped us thieving too. We would have one bag on the shoulder and another one in hand. The security guards would see the expensive bags and look away. 'He must have some money.' We were the Samsonite-wearing team and to wear a label that cost that much, proved your worth. Only the rich bought Samsonite. It was a respect thing.

I eventually got banned from the West End after getting caught. I got collared twice on Oxford Circus. The judge asked me for my postcode, right off. 'Why are you asking me that?'

- 'So, you left south London to commit crimes in the West End...'

They took our pictures and passed them on to plain clothes police, so we couldn't go to the West End any more. So, we went to King's Road and Camden instead. We were 14 and 15 and very advanced in our operations. This was a time of sus laws and the way we had to live was sometimes horrible. No one took time out to understand us. What were our joys? We were all put into one big basket to be stigmatised. Our parents worked their butts off, but what did they have to show for it? The media at the time didn't show crime in every borough, it just broke it down into black people and other non-whites and this forced us to stick much closer to each other. They made us the people we became. When I was a little kid I wanted to be white. I thought that white boys had everything. No one teased them because of their colour. I used to wonder what life would be like if I was white. 'How cool would that be?'

Our little team was a bunch of kids from Brixton, Tulse Hill, Herne Hill and Stockwell. No one could infiltrate us. We had a base at Stassi's on Coldharbour Lane, which was our HQ. We felt safe there without anyone intimidating us. No one questioned us there. You could play pool and there were fruit machines. We would always meet at Stassi's after 6pm, when we'd done our chores. Once our parents were knackered and thinking about getting to bed, we'd be out of the house and off to Stassi's. The old guys there would play backgammon and even if we weren't spending money, they didn't seem to mind us being there. We sold stuff to them as well. No one could just walk into Stassi's. If you could walk in, then you were known. You entered at your own peril. We were renowned and that was our HQ. Even our peers wouldn't enter Stassi's. The owners were vicious gangsters and no one messed with them. Anything we stole, they would buy. If Stassi's didn't buy it, it wasn't worth stealing. We sold jewellery, electrical stuff and gold. We would get a good price for it too. We stayed good friends with them. They never took advantage of us and our lack of knowledge. Sometimes they even showed us how to evaluate jewellery and whether it was 9 carat or 14, 18, 22... They showed us how to spot platinum and diamonds. Stassi's was an asset to us. It was a win-win for everybody concerned.

Back then, Nigel was the navigator. Nigel knew the underground map and the train timetables from travelling to and from boarding school. Nigel knew how to get home, no matter where we were. We could be out in Watford, having fun and Nigel would always get us home, safe and sound. We would often be on the overground trains far out of London where we would see the countryside; a completely different lifestyle. I remember that vividly.

As we didn't want to be spotted we would take all the back routes to places and took our time; 15 or 20 young boys in a pack didn't look promising and so we weren't loud. We travelled quietly and took our time.

The fog brought opportunity too. There was a lot of smog back then from coal fires and whatnot and when the fog came down you couldn't see more than a few feet in front of your face. We could then go out and rob people as no one could see us coming. If someone got caught you would never grass. One member of the team would always go to the family home and tell them that their son had been pulled by the police so they knew what was happening. Somebody else would hide all the evidence. There was no leader of the team etc.; we were all on the same level and survived on solidarity and mutual respect. We only had each other for security and entertainment.

By sticking together, we had strength in numbers. The National Front was still active back then remember. But we were a family.

We would also go to the late-night pictures to see kung fu movies from 10pm 'til 4am. Those cinemas were frequented by people like ourselves. We would get the smallest guy to sneak in through the toilet window and then he'd open the exit, so we could all get in. It stank of weed in there.

There were three cultures essentially. There were the Irish and Scots, Indians and Pakistanis and Jamaicans and Africans. That was it and we had to learn to stick together to nurture our ways of life. In the early eighties, we had an understanding of each other that doesn't exist now. That sense of community has gone."

CH. 7

Brixton Is Burning

I turned left and looked down the street towards Brixton and all I could see was smoke and police cars. There were sirens going off and people walking or running towards me, all along Brixton Hill. Brixton was burning and I was heading straight into the fire…

There was a real tension between the police and the local black community at these times and over three days in April, 1981, Brixton exploded into flames.

January that year had seen severe criticism of Lambeth police after they failed to entertain the possibility that a house fire that killed 13 black youths in New Cross, could have been a racially-motivated attack. Tensions between black youths and the police were already high after the introduction of the controversial sus laws. The police were taking the piss and stopping, searching and planting evidence. They would just make shit up to frame you. They're still doing it now, only they're more sneaky. There had been a few marches into central London to highlight the growing unrest until the situation turned violent that spring. Operation Swamp was launched by the police that April during which time they stopped and searched 950 people during a five-day period. What the fuck?! 150 were arrested, man. The tension in Brixton was getting *intense*.

Black youth Michael Bailey was fleeing a gang of young men on the evening of Friday, April 10th when he ran into police. Bailey was bleeding, having been stabbed. Police then detained Bailey in a squad car while the locals pleaded with officers to take him to hospital. Eventually, Bailey was pulled from the police car by the locals who took him to hospital themselves, although the police tried to stop the car from leaving the scene. Bailey survived although he almost bled to death, according to a nurse who treated him. This incident caused the police to up their game and hundreds of black locals were stopped and searched, prompting angry blacks and a few local white folk to take to the streets. This was the spark.

Things got far worse the following day when a local painter was arrested after waving to a friend across the street. Within an hour or so, you had a thousand police taking on an angry Brixton Town. Looting and fighting ensued and Brixton was at war.

Windows were smashed and cars set ablaze. It took 7,000 police to take control on the Sunday, after three days of rioting.

The news travelled fast on that Saturday as Brixton burned. I had to go in and have a look for myself, didn't I? There was a good chance I could get some decent stuff from the shops. I was home for the weekend from boarding school and there was no way I was going to sit at home while all this was kicking off.

I quietly shut the front door and headed out. You heard the sirens first and then you saw the smoke, right at the end of Brixton Hill. I peered around the corner of our road and saw the flashing lights everywhere. Most people were fleeing the scene, coming up Brixton Hill towards me. I called for a few mates from the New Park flats along the way before heading straight into the fire.

There was me, Prince, Devon, Sean and Richard. It was chaos down there and we were running right into the centre of it to see what we could get our hands on. Cars and shops were on fire and people were throwing stuff at the thick line of police who held up shields against the bricks and bottles.

We were looking for stuff to nick and so headed straight for the jewellery shop. The windows had already been smashed in by the older boys and so we scrambled around on the floor, which was covered in broken glass, looking for scraps that had been dropped. I picked up necklaces, rings and bracelets and stuffed it all into my sports socks. I guessed I had about two or three grands-worth of shit.

Now, the police would do you if you got caught and so you had to be careful. You had to avoid the backstreets because that was where they collared you. We needed to get to the main road now, so we were in full view. My socks were stuffed with gold and I had sovereign rings rubbing against my ankles. I had my hoard and now it was time to head home.

Police were searching for looters and we certainly saw people walking around with TV sets and video recorders. We knew of some who took vans down there to make off with washing machines and fridges. We had to be very careful as we made our way up towards Brixton Hill. Suddenly, one of us shouted, and we started sprinting, realising that the police were behind us. This happened two or three times along Brixton Hill and on each occasion, the group got smaller as people peeled off to hide in the flats along the way. I don't know how I made it home, it was like navigating a maze with burning cars and police everywhere. It was as if I was inside a computer game or something. My heart was fucking *racing*, bruv.

Finally, I got back to New Park Road. I shut the bedroom door and sat down in my room to examine my haul. My heart sank. Most of my gear had fallen out of my socks. Fuck! I had just three chains left. I risked all that for just three silly necklaces. That was all I got out of the Brixton riots. It was fucking rubbish. I had been loaded when I left that shop and now I was down to three gold chains. Still, I got about £100 for them, which paid for my weekend, but I was so pissed, man.

Brixton was a war zone that weekend and the police just didn't have the manpower to stop it. Brixton was on fire. Everything was looted.

Brixton was always seen as the black capital of London. The National Front had threatened to march to Brixton on a number of occasions. The NF would always march to Lewisham, but just stopped short of Brixton. I don't think they fancied it.

People were properly fighting with police that weekend. That March, a demonstration in anger at the police's investigation into the New Cross fire, saw 20,000 people marching to Hyde Park and so by the time April arrived, a massive bonfire had built up, just waiting for a match. It took many years for things to calm down and there was to be lots more trouble to come. I remember hearing that some people tried to burn down Brixton Police Station. They were mad times, then. Mad.

Although I got through the riots unscathed I got arrested for the first time in 1982.

I was in Boots on Piccadilly Circus with Stan when I was nicked. 'Excuse me, can I have a word with you two?' I was home from boarding school and had headed straight to Boots after getting off the coach at Waterloo. I wanted to get some money together for our weekend as pocket money wouldn't be enough for records and weed. So, I hadn't even made it home after school, before I was up to my old tricks. I had just swiped a load of tapes into my Samsonite when a security guard clocked me. I shat myself.

The police were called and they took us to the nearest station. 'We're going to have to call your mums,' they told us, as we sat down in the interview room. Fuck!

I can still recall the look Mum gave me when she turned up at the police station. 'You're dead, mate!' For fuck's sake. Stanley's mum was well angry with me as well. Stan's mum blamed *me* for leading him astray. She was quite right, really, as he'd never been in trouble before that (or since). There was silence all the way home after we left Piccadilly Circus. I didn't get any beatings or anything, but she was pissed, you know what I mean? *Pissed!* The only time Mum had got that angry with me, was when she blamed me for eating a cake that Yolanda had scoffed. She got the belt out that time there, and the buckle made a real mess of my eye. She later found out that I was innocent, at least where cakes were concerned. I don't remember Mum being that angry when I got expelled! Mum couldn't wait to kick me back to school after that weekend. She was MAD!

I was just 15 at the time and was ordered to attend the Juvenile Court at Seymour Place just off Oxford Street. I was shitting it.

We were given a caution or a fine or something and Stanley really learned from this and never offended again after that. Sorry, Stan. Me? Well, let's just say that I wasn't going straight. Not just yet…

***

I had one foot on the ladder of the sound system world by now, which was good. I was now a 'box boy'. There would be three or four 'youngers' or box boys travelling around with the sound systems and it was our job to pick this bloody great system up – numerous boxes, hence the name 'box boy' – and move it from the van to the venue and back again after. This was a great introduction into how sound systems and dub culture worked. Our system was Frontline International, but there were loads of others operating in and around London, such as Sir Coxone, Stereograph, Dread Diamonds, Small Axe and King Tubby's. There would always be these soundclashes going on, where two systems took turns to play the hottest dubplates of the time. Dubplates were vital back then as there was very little dub on the radio. Dubplates were a great way of hearing the latest sounds before they were officially released; *if* they were officially released. Jah Shaka was king back then with Sir Coxone just behind. Jah Shaka played himself in the movie *Babylon* and appeared at the end in a wicked soundclash. Jah Shaka not only inspired young black musicians, but also white punks, such as Public Image Limited, The Clash, The Pop Group and The Slits. Shaka also had his own record label Jah Shaka Music. That guy was a don, mate. I was now hanging around with Frontline International from Brixton and was proud to be a box boy.

Now, these sound systems weighed a ton and it was the box boys who had to get them into the vans that moved them about London and beyond. You started off by lifting the speakers, which were either 'four faces' or 'double boxes'. They could be 6ft tall and 3ft wide and we would have to lift these bloody big boxes into the dances. The older lot took care of the pre-amps and power amps. It was a real privilege to be a box boy, though, and to travel in the back of the van, which had those shutters at the back. Great days, mate, travelling around with Frontline International and all the boys. I was still just a kid from boarding school, really, but I was there during school holidays and at weekends, lifting those boxes.

All of this was part of a positive cultural revolution, just after the riots. We went to so many different places with Frontline. We went to north London a lot. There were early MCs there like Baby Welly and Flux who were chatting on the mic. There was also Werton Irie and Younger Welly. Frontline was the Brixton sound and we had Ricky Rankin who would come and chat on the mic, as well as Horseman. 'I want to chat on the mic,' I thought, during one particular night out with Frontline. So, when I got back to boarding school I started toasting and chatting on this little mic I had. I didn't want to stay a box boy forever. I wanted to be a name that people would remember.

I was listening to the David Rodigan Show on Capital one day, when I heard something that stopped me in my tracks. 'What the fuck?!' This guy was changing the game! This reggae MC was chatting non-stop with flowing lyrics rather than repeating lines two or three times like the others. I was blown away. Burro Banton was an original Jamaican DJ who played with the Gemini sound. Burro had a released a number of singles and was a massive inspiration to me and many others. If I hear Burro now, I am instantly transported back to my room that evening, listening to him for the very first time. That was important, man.

The school clubhouse had a mini hi-fi system with a mic and I would practise there every break time, with Becker, Stanley and Paul. I had the confidence, but it was tricky. Chatting on the mic was a lot harder than it first appeared. Burro made it sound so easy.

I loved dub, but it wasn't to everyone's liking. My cousin Eric lived in London – he was Monty from Sweden's brother – and I really looked up to him. He loved Miles Davis and Issac Hayes and he was the coolest guy ever. I remember Eric telling me to stop listening to that 'stupid dub music'. Ha ha 'Get into funk, George Clinton and jazz. Forget the dub stuff!' he'd say.

When I wasn't out with the sound systems, we would try and chat up girls in nearby Streatham. The club to go to for girls was Cat's Whiskers, which was a soul club. Girls went to Cat's Whiskers and although we were rough boys from Brixton, we would walk around whistling at girls, who weren't really having any of it, to be honest. Streatham boys had that wet-look perm; they dressed like soul boys. We were reggae boys from Brixton and so it was difficult for us to even talk to Streatham girls. We would go there on a Tuesday and I would pay close attention to the DJs. Tony Blackburn and Steve Walsh would play Cat's Whiskers and I studied how they worked the crowd. And believe me, they *worked* the crowd. For me, Tony Blackburn was the 'King of DJs'; pure entertainment and so magical. Tony was very funny and had that club in the palm of his hand. There was such a rapport between Tony and the crowd. Steve Walsh was famous for recording a version of *I Found Lovin'* and, sadly, died in a car crash a few years later. Tony Blackburn and Steve Walsh were the dons, though. Prince, Devon, Sean, Richard Lewis and myself would go down to Cat's Whiskers a lot. There were often fights there and sometimes we were thrown out, but it was a different vibe to the sound system nights. Cat's Whiskers mostly played soul: Direct Drive, David Grant and Cheryl Lynn, stuff like that, although we heard the early hip-hop releases there too, such as Grandmaster's *The Message*. Tim Westwood started out at Cat's Whiskers, carrying Steve Walsh and Tony Blackburn's bags and shit. That was where Tim did his apprenticeship. So, all hail Tony Blackburn!

We also went to Streatham to go ice skating. Now, I hated skating, but I desperately wanted to talk to girls and so if that was what it took, so be it. Those skates were on! I was just getting interested in the opposite sex and the more I went skating, the better I got, and the better I got, the more girls I seemed to meet.

We left the rink early one evening and were chased off by a group of skinheads who were loitering outside. There was a quite a lot of racial tension back then and the racists were much more upfront. There was a constant unease in the air.

The skinheads gave chase for over a mile, but because I had been doing cross country twice a week at boarding school, they didn't stand a chance. I was on my toes, mate. Flying!

These were interesting times, here. We would go to open-air all-dayers at Herne Hill and Brockwell Park, where there would be thousands of people smoking weed and enjoying good food as the bands and sound systems played. A favourite tune of mine back then was *Watch Out* by Brandi Wells. I always played that track at family get-togethers. Everybody danced to that.

Then there were the late-night kung fu films at the Brixton Ace (the Ace would later turn into a club called The Fridge) on a Friday night. We would get there for 11pm to see three movies in a row. People would bang the seats and let off foghorns during those films. I would fire my starter pistol in the air when they busted a cool move. Pah! Pah! Pah! I bought this starter pistol from a shop in Streatham that sold knives and shit. It was mad thinking about it now, but a starter pistol was quite easy to get back then.

I would do all the kung fu moves in the street on the way home from the Ace. When the Ace stopped showing films in 1981 we went to the Streatham Odeon instead. They were good times, then. You could still smoke in cinemas and those kung fu nights stank of weed. My favourite martial arts films were *Warriors Two*, *The Prodigal Son*, *Snake In The Monkey's Shadow* and *Five Deadly Venoms*. Bruce Lee was a big part of my childhood. I even had the yellow tracksuit with the black stripe (from *Game Of Death)* when I was younger. I had all the Bruce Lee shit. These first few years of the eighties were carefree, I guess, as we skated after girls, moved some amps with the sound systems and sat back in awe at the mighty Bruce Lee.

CH. 8

Let's Play Hangman

I left Ganga's house and made my way to the bus stop. I was more than a little wary, as I bowled on down the street. First off, this wasn't my patch. Secondly, a group of boys had fronted me out on my way to my grandmother's that day. Then I saw them again on the way home.

I had a feeling that these boys were not actually from Clapham Junction as I knew a lot of the locals and sometimes chatted on the mic for the local Hustler sound system there, but it seemed as if they'd been hanging around, waiting for me to show. Now, I'd had a run-in with these boys before, at a party or something and we'd had a tussle. They definitely recognised me when they started on me earlier that day. Because I was on my own they must have thought I was easy pickings and these two boys started moving towards me.

One of them was mouthing off. 'What are you fucking doing here?' My heart was beating like crazy as my hand went down to the front pocket of my jeans and just touched the outline of the ratchet. These boys were about to start something and being outnumbered, I produced the knife. I popped the blade out and went for the mouthy one.

'Aaaaaarrrgghhh!!!!' I cut him on the left-hand side of the back of his neck. It was a cut rather than a stab or slice. He put his hand up to his neck as his friend rushed over. Cue my escape. I just ran and ran and ran. I looked back just before I turned the corner and these boys were nowhere to be seen. I popped the blade back in and stuck the knife inside my pocket.

I caught the 37 bus and sat at the back, trying to calm down. I was nervous as fuck, yeah? I grew up in that area a little bit and so there was a chance that my name was known. There was also a chance that this guy was dead. I was pretty sure he wasn't, but these are the things whirring through your head when you've just stabbed someone.

Because the police tended to come to your home very early in the morning, people who lived the road life always woke up extra early when something had gone down the night before. I was worried as hell about this boy I cut. Then, a week or two later, a friend of mine told me that he'd seen this kid and that he was fine. I was so relieved. I was shitting it, man. I stayed away from Clapham Junction for a few months after that, yeah?

Everybody in my world at that time carried a knife. I'm not saying it was the right thing to do, but it was what we did. What we all did. That was how it played out back then.

Adjusting to life after boarding school was hard, man. I was now back in Brixton all week and couldn't just nip off back to Berkshire when I fancied it. I started a YTS (Youth Training Scheme) in 1983. That's right. I worked on a building site, doing painting and plastering. I fucking hated it.

I would get £25 a week and my mum got the lot. She wanted to teach me the value of money and although I disagreed with her at the time, I can see now that she was right. I wish I'd kept a fiver to myself, though.

I hated life on the building site. I would get handed a spirit level and would just stare at it. 'What the fuck is this for?!' I didn't mind the actual work so much – I had been quite good at woodwork at school – but sitting around at break reading a shitty old copy of *The Sun* was not my idea of a good time. I would just sit on an upturned paint tin in the portacabin and have a roll-up. The building site was a dusty culture shock of decorating and heavy boots. Out in all weathers we were. Fuck, it got cold. 'Fuck this!' I often imagined jumping into a barrel of cement just to escape it all. It was demoralising. I lasted about a month. YTS. Fuck that shit.

Away from the YTS, I was still popping chains and selling nicked tapes to the drivers at Granada Cab Station on Coldharbour Lane. I had to dodge my uncle Glenroy, though, who worked at the cab office. Glenroy would have kicked my arse if he'd known. But I *needed* this money to pay for the clothes, parties and weed, so I just carried on with all the dodgy activities. Prince, Robert, Devon, Richard, Sean, Go Go,

Let's Play Hangman

Colin aka 'Rippa' and I were still hanging out in Stassi's, but we'd also started meeting at the Pool Parlour on Water Lane.

I'm not sure when it first appeared, but now our firm had a name. Hangman. Lots of gangs were named after cowboy films back then with many different posses ruling the postcodes. You certainly didn't mess with Hangman.

I was popping four to five chains a day now that I'd left school and had fucked off the YTS. I would just pop that chain and run for it. I would then sell the gold for scrap at Stassi's. I had also started hanging out in north London, where my face wasn't so known. My sister Samantha lived up north and Hangman would pop chains up there, while checking out the girls at Wood Green shopping centre. I would visit various colleges too and pop chains there. I spent so much time at North London College I should have enrolled on a course.

We did many stings. Stings were my thing. I wouldn't discriminate: black, white, male or female, I would pop your chain. I was 16 years old and earning £200 a day. I would then buy some weed and hang out at the People's Club in Paddington where sound systems such as Saxon and Sir Coxone would play out. We had stopped going to youth centres like Shepherds by this stage. Some of us were doing burglaries too. I wasn't so much into 'creeping'. A few of the boys would creep into people's homes while they slept, to take their jewellery, but it wasn't my thing.

As I've said, I'm not sure exactly when the name came about, but Hangman was quite notorious. The Hangman Posse would turn up to parties and cause trouble. We would stick people up at knife-point and rob them. We still had these fish-tail parkas that mods wore, but now we had the mopeds or scooters to go with them. We were bad boys.

The Notting Hill Carnival on the August bank holiday weekend had always represented an opportunity to make some money. If you were at Carnival, with jewellery on, you were fair game. Pop, pop, pop. The chains were coming off. We would roam around the crowds popping chains.

The best place at Carnival was under the flyover of the Westway in the 'caged area' listening to the Mastermind Roadshow; a legendary north London sound. There would be 20-30 of us down there and we would rob *everyone*.

We had a secret weapon: Jif lemon juice. We bought loads of those little yellow bottles of Jif and emptied all the juice. We then filled the

Big, Bad & Heavy

bottle with ammonia. If we came face to face with a west London gang, we would 'Jif 'em'. There would be this cloud of the stuff. It was toxic! People wouldn't know what was going on, there would be that much smoke. That's when we went in with the knives.

We had these ratchet knives; a nasty little blade from Jamaica. A fish knife. It was a mechanical piece you opened up with your thumb. The ratchet made a clicking sound. Click, click, click. We were all very fast with the ratchet in our hands. I had been playing around with knives for years and it was not long after getting my ratchet, that I had that run-in over Clapham way.

We had that flyover under siege during Carnival. There would be massive wars down there, so much so they stopped people from playing there a few years later. We stabbed a lot of people. We would slice the knife to wound, rather than to stab and kill. It was a slicing motion. I'm not sure if that was much comfort to the people on the other end of the blade, but there you have it. Sometimes we would use the Jif to soak the blades, which meant that the wounds would sting like fuck and would take longer to heal. We were bad boys, I can't dress that up. But the weird thing is that I always considered myself to be a good person. Inside. I can't quite understand it myself. I take responsibility for what I did, but this culture was just there. People around me were doing it, quite often our parents had been involved in things and it didn't seem that strange to us. You had to do these things to get the money.

I used to chat on the mic at Carnival too and so one minute I was robbing and Jif-ing people, the next I was chatting on the mic with Frontline and the other sound systems. My MC name was Boga.

I really wanted to chat on the mic at the Ace during one of their notorious MC competitions. Then, one Sunday afternoon, the opportunity presented itself. There would often be me, Maddix and Robert Blake there at the Ace listening to Hustler, Dread Diamonds and Frontline. I also spent a lot of time with Ricky Rankin and Horseman, back then, during those Sundays at the Ace. The competitions were fierce, but I desperately wanted to take the mic. I wanted to take that step to the next level. If you were shit, the crowd just booed you off, but I still wanted to do it. 'I'm gonna do it one week,' I told myself. I really thought I was good enough. A guy we knew called Daddy IP (RIP) was wicked and he won this contest with the mic three weeks in a row. Then one week, I just got hold of the mic, got up on stage and started chatting my lyrics. It wasn't good! I got booed so badly! 'Boo! Boo! Get off!' I walked off stage and just dropped the mic. I had fucked it up.

I didn't live that down for a month. 'Boga got booed on the mic! What the fuck, man!' I just wanted the ground to swallow me up. Everyone was looking at me. I got cussed by all my friends. 'Boga! Boga! Boga got booed off the mic, man!' People recognised me in the street as the guy who got booed off at the Ace. That really was the worst thing and it totally knocked my confidence. At least, when I was up in north London, not so many people knew about my disaster with the mic. Fucking hell, mate. That was *rough*!

Rock

"Brixton was crazy, growing up. We were 16 in 1983, and part of this Hangman Posse. Hangman was notorious. We were robbing people of their chains and all that.

A lot of us were from one-parent families and back then you needed the latest trainers. We would rob people at knifepoint. We didn't discriminate either: black, white, women, men.

Rival gangs got stabbed, of course, but you didn't stab to kill. You wouldn't stab them in the chest. We would 'wet' people and use the knife with a slicing motion. You would slice with the knife at the arm or leg. We never killed anyone.

There were lots of gangs back then: Brixton Posse, Wackod Posse and Stockwell Posse. We all knew each other a bit. But it all got a bit hectic for such a small area and so we would sometimes go to north London where no one knew us. You couldn't do those same things in our own borough where we were known.

Nigel wanted to be a rapper and he was called Boga on the mic. He was right into the sound system thing, but he didn't get very far. He wasn't all that, ha ha, but he was alright. We grew up with Tippa Irie and I think Boga wanted to be like him."

When we were north of the river, we would go to Ozzie's in Clapton to play pool and hang out. We started to make a few friends over there. I would also hang at North London College with Ranger, Roger Sylvester (RIP), Charlie Benjamin, Jennifer and Sarah, Tony Brown, Matt Sterling,

Cass Manhattan, Doreen, Annette, Maxine, Judith Rook Wood, Darren, Natalie and many more.

Ranger

"I know Nigel from college days. 1984, North London College. Nigel was from south London, we were from north. People generally stayed in their own area, back then. Nigel was from Brixton, though. Wow! A Brixton boy. We clicked straight away. We would hang out in the canteen and get up to all sorts of trouble, aggravating people and nicking things. Nothing too terrible, just general stupidity. We were drinking and smoking too and girls were there.

Nigel was an MC, Sugar Ranks or Boga. His posse Hangman was notorious!

I remember we went to this party in King's Cross once and there were 10-15 of us; a real mixture of boys and girls. We were being a little rowdy and went into an off-licence and nicked a crate of beer. We took this crate to a nearby estate and got pissed. By the time we got to this party, we were drunk on Special Brew and they wouldn't let us in! We were rascals really, but we have the best memories.

We lost a few friends along the way; Roger RIP. Some aren't here, some are addicted to drugs, some of have been stabbed and many more have been inside. But we're still going strong. After college, we all went our own ways, but our paths did cross again, later in life."

North London had some wicked sound systems. Unity had Flinty and Deman Rockers (who would go on to form Ragga Twins) chatting on the mic. Unity was our favourite in north London; we would also see Deman, Flinty and Chargan playing at the Africa Arts Centre in Finsbury Park. There was also the Eastman Sound, run by the guy who would go on to start Kool FM. We always behaved ourselves at their parties, as we liked the Eastman Sound. The other parties? We would be on the rob. Hangman had a proper reputation; we even took the gate money and cash from the tills at some dances. We would take the lot.

Andy Bartman

"I used to hang with Nigel in Covent Garden. There was a collective of us, from all over London and we'd all meet up in the West End.

We were the original hip hop crew and we'd hustle a bit, selling tickets to Empire and Hippodrome at Leicester Square. We were wheelers and dealers from inner city boroughs who all met up through a love of hip hop and rare groove. We would sometimes go clubbing too.

Nigel came from Brixton and he had a different mentality to some of us. I came from Hackney, the other side of the coin, but I grew up with Frontline and all that. But Brixton boys were revered a lot back then.

It was great being in the West End hanging with so many different types of people. It was easy to stay in your own area, but you got a broader perspective by hooking up with new people.

There were so many stories, but we had a definite moral code in how we operated. We weren't as reckless as other groups. We had breakers and graffiti artists; Robbo was one of us, the guy who went on to have a beef with Banksy. We just hooked up to hang out.

I distinctly remember the Tube parties. We would all meet up at Burger King, Leicester Square and we'd take a boombox and some drinks into the train carriage. Then we'd take out the light bulbs and hijack that carriage for a party. There were boys and girls, you see. It was never harmful, although once or twice someone got punched or robbed. We were mischievous I guess, but it was all done in good spirit."

Hangman was making money and as a result, our taste in clothes went up a notch, too. We started buying Stone Island jeans and headed out to the King's Road to places like Reiss. We sometimes wore the chains we popped, too. I used to zip about on this little 50CC Honda moped, as you only needed a provisional licence to ride one. We were out *every* night.

People's Club in Paddington was our favourite spot for a little dance. You could check out Sir Coxone, Frontline and Saxon there. Hip-hop was getting big as well.

Saxon was from Lewisham and that was a no-go area for us Brixton boys. The Saxon and Coxone rivalry was massive. But we were Brixton boys so we weren't meant to like Saxon. Then Tippa Irie – a Brixton boy – joined Saxon and that was major news. Controversial. 'Have you heard? Tippa's joined Saxon, bruv!'

We heard Saxon in Shepherds one time and they had this MC called Maxi Priest and fucking hell could this guy sing! Papa Levi was good on the mic too and he had his own way of chatting on the mic and was way ahead of his time.

We ventured into Lewisham one evening, just the three of us. We went to Lewisham Boys Club to see Papa Levi clash with Leslie Lyrics on the mic. Papa Levi won that one. Saxon Sound was amazing. We also saw Saxon at Upton House, Homerton as they were our favourite sound at the time. Watching Tippa and Saxon at the People's Club was the perfect night out in the West End.

Tippa Irie

"I grew up in Brixton during the seventies, just as the 'no cats, no dogs, no Irish, no blacks' was coming to an end. The racist vibe was still present, though, but black culture was becoming more confident and angry. The police had the sus laws in place and that for me was just a normal thing back then. I wasn't a bad kid, you know, but I still got stopped and searched even though I was into the normal kid things, like playing football and sports and that. I still got stopped by the police. My dad was a disciplinarian and so I didn't get up to no good. I was playing 'penny up the wall' and games like that. Then I would go to work at Brixton Market with my dad, who was a greengrocer. I would come home from school, work in the shop, then go to the Marcus Lipton Youth Centre at Loughborough Junction. They would sometimes have sound systems there.

My dad had a sound system and that took over my life for a while. My parents would host dances in our house. I would sit on the stairs, out of sight and watch them all dancing and having a good time.

Music was my get-out clause from the road life. Hangman was the crew back then and I remember Nigel and his friends. But I was fully focussed on music at the time. I committed the odd little wrong, but not as much as Nigel! Ha ha. I was too busy being idle or playing table tennis.

Dad's sound system wasn't mobile, it stayed in the basement of our house. People would come to ours to party on a Friday and

Saturday night. I learned so much about Jamaican culture by watching them party. I then started to chat on the mic a bit as I got older. Family members would encourage me to pick up the mic. They said I had talent. 'Go on boy, let them hear your stuff!' I then started working for King Tubby's sound system and that got my name out there. It wasn't long before I eventually moved to Saxon Sound, which was based in Lewisham. It was easy leaving Tubby as he was, how can I put this, a little careful with his money. Ha ha! My wages went up working with Saxon and it was around this time that my reputation grew. I was 15/16 years old and I was going up and down the country with Saxon.

I got on OK with the gangs because they knew me through my music and I wasn't around them much, but the bad boys respected me because I was a good MC. There was no conflict, there. I showed them that there was an alternative to crime.

Then I hit the Top 40 with Hello Darling in 1986. I made some money with that and it was great to see the fridge full. Although Dad was a greengrocer the fridge always seemed empty. Ha ha! I bought Mum a house and we didn't have to worry about money and bills for a while. I was only 19 and it totally changed my life. I got to travel the world: the Caribbean, America, Africa and Australia. It was amazing and really opened my eyes. I also bought my first proper car. There were not that many black people on TV back then, and so to be on Top Of The Pops was amazing. I have been told that I made black people feel proud and I was so happy to hear that. I still am."

CH. 9

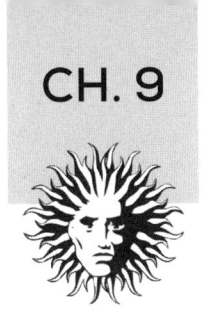

You're Nicked!

Although the robbing was still going strong into 1984, I was finally pulled by the police for something I didn't actually do. Maddix and I were on the platform at Oxford Circus Tube, off on a trip to buy some jeans, when a plainclothes policeman grabbed me. 'I saw you slip your hand into that woman's handbag, to steal her purse!' he said.
- 'What?! No I never! What are you on about? Where is she? Where's the purse?'
- 'She got on that train. I'm arresting you for attempted theft of an unknown person.'

And he did. It was a total fabrication. So, the police got their man, for a crime that never happened.

Maddix and I went to Knightsbridge Crown Court where I was certain we'd get off. We didn't. Instead, we got four months at a youth detention centre. Fuck! Not only that, but at 17, I had only just missed adult prison by just four months.

Hollesley Bay (Suffolk) was known as Holiday Bay, but this was no Butlins, believe me. This was a fucking brutal place. You were not allowed to walk anywhere. You had to *march*. You had to ask permission to speak, smoke or take a piss. Fuck!

I admit that I was a bad boy, but it was weird to be banged up inside an institution like this when you hadn't actually done anything wrong. I'd been framed. Maybe it was karma? I don't know.

Big, Bad & Heavy

Ingrid Thompson

"Whenever Nigel got into trouble, he'd say he had nothing to do with it. Sus laws were coming in back then so black people were getting unfair treatment. That did happen. However, I never really got to the truth."

Every morning, every guy in the dorm had to pack their clothes up into a tiny square-shaped bundle that would have to fit perfectly inside this box. It had to be *just right*. If one guy let the side down, you all paid, which meant that the guy who fucked up inspection would get a beating from the other lads. We were responsible for each other, you see. If we failed inspection, we would be given the hardest circuit route in PE. There were blue, yellow and red circuits; red being a bitch. Hence the guy who let the side down was always given a good kicking. Consequently, I made sure my clothes were folded up with *precision*.

The gym was a fibreglass dome, which meant that on hot days in there, it was a fair few degrees warmer than outside. It was sweltering in there, man! We were doing this red circuit one day when one of the boys fell over. And died. Right in front of me. Dead.

They ushered us off into the changing rooms and put everyone on lockdown so they could clean up their mess. This guy had just keeled over and died. Maybe he was asthmatic or something. Fuck! That had a real effect on me. These people had the power to kill us and I was in there for something I hadn't even done. That poor bastard.

There was also a drill when showering and changing back into your clothes after PE. You had two minutes to shower, get dressed into your jeans and boots and be ready 'on the line' for inspection. One boy failed that and man, did he get a kicking. It was brutal in there.

There was another time when someone got caught talking after 'lights out'. So, the guards burst in and made us get our boots on before marching us all out into the courtyard outside. They then handed each of us a pair of scissors and ordered us to cut the grass. At 2am. In our pyjamas.

Luckily, I got a job in the kitchens, which meant I could smoke a little weed at break times. The kitchen was a good place to be and you had more freedom there. I made a few life-long friends in Holiday Bay like Bertie Brown and Buddah. However, there were also some people from east London that I didn't get on with and I knew an altercation was coming. I just didn't know when.

Let's Play Hangman

Inside these places, you soon realised that you couldn't just wait for something bad to happen. You had to get in first or face the shit that was coming. I knew these east London guys were cooking something up and so I decided to leave them a message. It sounds odd, but I don't regret what I did, as I knew I had to do it. You had to send a message to people to prevent any future trouble; stress that could be well out of your hands. You had to take control of the situation and stand your ground. Failure to do that could be fatal.

I slipped into this dorm one morning when everyone was out and found this guy's bed. I rooted around in his bedside cabinet and there it was. A bar of soap. I checked that the coast was clear and I took that bar of soap apart. Once it was in two halves I placed three razor blades into the middle and sealed it all back up. I then had another check to see if anyone was about and legged it. It was now a case of sit and wait.

I hadn't heard any news of my plan working for about a week until I heard a scream from the showers one morning. 'Aaaaarrgghhhh!!!' This guy had sliced his chest open with the blades. He was fine and I know this might not convince everyone reading this, but I had to do it.

I got a letter from my dad while in Holiday Bay. It said, 'Dear Son, I had always hoped that you would be a racing car driver when you grew up.' That was it. That was all it said. What the fuck?!

The four months were soon up and I was out. I was loose again. Did it put a halt to my bad behaviour? Did it fuck.

I met my first girlfriend Olinka at Knights Youth Centre just before I got fitted up. Once my four months were up at Holiday Bay I was back with Olinka in our little flat. Olinka was a few months away from dropping. That's right. I was going to be a father. A dad. It was 1985 and I was just about to turn 18. Suddenly, my priorities had to shift a bit. Now I was robbing and wheeling and dealing for the three of us.

Around this time here, I got into a row with a bloke at a blues dance. At a blues dance, the place was often pitch black and I happened to be back in the kitchen area talking to this guy when a row erupted. I can't remember why, but we really started getting into it. It wasn't until the lights came on and these girls started screaming that I realised what this fucker had done. He'd sliced my face open. From my eye, right down to my mouth, my face was flapping open. Girls were running around screaming. I honestly hadn't realised until that point.

Luckily, the long snaking wound hit my laughter line and so it was masked a little, but this attack was not going to go unpunished. This fucker was going to get it one way or another. It was to be an act of revenge that I now deeply regret, but at the time I couldn't allow it to go unchallenged. You showed weakness, you got taken down again. And again. And again. I would look in the mirror just staring at this scar that joined my eye to my mouth. I was brewing, man. I was brewing. This fucking cunt was going to get it!

I don't know if it was my time in the detention centre that inspired me, but this mission was planned with military precision. I put out some feelers about this razor guy and found out his name and address. I then recruited a few friends.

We were to hit his house at 6am, before he had the chance to get up. This was, and still is, a police tactic. We pulled up on the side of the road and moved silently in the dark down the front path to his house. We then booted the front door open before bundling in down the hall.

This guy lived with his parents and before I knew it, his mum and dad were right up in our faces trying to fend us off. We pushed them to one side and the dad got a few blows to the head. The mum was going crazy and we kept her at arm's length too. We weren't interested in them, though. We wanted the son.

We found the guy we wanted and dragged him into the living room where his parents were. It was then that I took out my carpet knife.

I cut his head. I cut his face. I stabbed him in the arse in front of his parents. Then we dropped him to the floor and walked out. We drove off, hearts racing.

I got home and just lay on the bed, trying to calm down. I had been in and around trouble for a while now and incidents like this were serious. I was capable of doing some real harm.

I knew this guy we'd cut had a big brother and so for a while I was expecting some sort of backlash, but nothing ever happened. There you go. I wasn't proud of it, but it had happened. The only upside was that it forced me to stop and think about what I was doing. It was such a bad thing to do. To cut someone up like that? Well, it horrified me. But what the fuck was going to rescue me from this increasingly violent cycle of crime?

***

Tanya was born at 6.01am on Feb 4th 1986.

Ranger

"I can still remember when his first child, Tanya, was born. Nigel walked into college, looking so tired and knackered. We were only kids ourselves, but he was so proud. 'Wow! You're a dad!' Although he does get mad and lose his temper, I know Nigel's sensitive side. I have seen it first-hand and it's genuine."

CH. 10

Fresh Beats

I was 18 years old and a father. A dad. Although my life had changed, dramatically, and I loved Tanya more than anything, I continued playing up. I was hanging around north London, more and more. I would often go to these nights at the Electric Ballroom in Camden where they played funk, soul and hip-hop. I met this girl called Natasha there and we soon started seeing each other. When it comes to girls, I am weak. What can I say?

I was from Brixton and so I stood out as a reggae bad boy in north London, which often made it difficult getting into places, never mind chatting up women, but the Electric Ballroom was cool. Natasha was cool.

Natasha was a 'funky dread' and a really good dancer. She was different to a lot of the girls I knew back then. She had real attitude. I remember listening to mixing for the first time, back at her house. 'What the fuck is this?' I knew the two records playing, but couldn't quite work out why they sounded so different. The two tracks were *Dreaming* by B.B.&Q. Band and *All In All* by Joyce Sims. I didn't quite get it, although I loved the sound. 'It's called mixing, you fool,' she said, looking a bit confused. 'Haven't you heard of mixing?' I hadn't, but I wanted to find out more.

I went to see the Rapattack sound system at a warehouse party in Camden one night, where Alistair was *the man* at mixing the tunes. Wow! My fascination with mixing just grew and grew and it soon became an obsession. I had grown up around music of course, but it just didn't sound like this. My cousin Michael was a b-boy, but to us reggae boys, b-boys were just little punks.

I had been chatting on the mic for a while, but I knew I had to get involved with the mixing side of things and slowly this became my focus. Although I was still robbing people at dances, I now started to see the potential in working the parties in a different way. I wanted to be a DJ.

I was still robbing plenty of people at that time as I brought money home to my family. Asians wore the best jewellery and so I was taking their chains. In fact, I would just pull out a knife and they would hand them over. Stand and deliver, your money or your life. I would rob people on the way to North London College and on the way back.

Back down south, I was hanging around with Delroy from New Park Road and his friends from school: Wilfred and Steve. We were just listening to records and smoking weed. It was around this time that we started getting into that funkier vibe; James Brown and all that.

I was started hanging out at the Africa Centre at Covent Garden on Sunday nights. Sunday nights at the Africa Centre was Soul II Soul. There were some great nights there. Jazzie B was a total inspiration to me and these Soul II Soul bashes were a form of religion. It was like going to church, man. Trevor Nelson aka The Mad Hatter would sell records from a stall, knocking out rare groove, funk and soul. The Africa Centre was a great place to be. That said, my street side was still there.

I robbed someone's Rolex at a Soul II Soul night. I saw the geezer, and of course his watch, as he went into the toilets. So, I followed this guy in. I then kicked open the cubicle door, bent his arm back through the gap and stole his watch without him even seeing me. Later that night, Jazzie B came over and said, 'Someone's had their watch stolen; it wasn't you was it?'

- 'Nah, nah! Not me, bruv. C'mon! As if!'

I'm not sure Jazzie believed me, but he had no proof. The watch was nestled inside my underpants as I raved it up on the dancefloor.

Jazzie B

"Nigel was south London and I was north. There were a few faces from south London who would come to the Africa Centre on a Sunday night. In fact, people came from all over London.

Nigel was a boisterous figure, animated sometimes, but that's Frost you know? Frost was a funny geezer. But he behaved himself when he was inside.

There could be all sorts of dramas in there (Africa Centre); all types of nonsense going on during those sessions and events, but people behaved themselves, within reason. We were young men and women at the time, all looking to make names for ourselves and Nigel would make his presence felt. He was such a character.

East, west, north, south, the tribes all came together on a Sunday night. It was maybe a testament to Soul II Soul that we all came together in town on a Sunday afternoon. There were no drifters at the Africa Centre, just people who needed to be there. It was a mixture of cutting loose and networking. This was the place to be in terms of catching up with whatever was going on. You had such a great cross-section of people from all the boroughs, getting involved in fashion, music and style. Records were being sold and friendships forged. We had a solid relationship with the Japanese for example, all through the earlies, because of the fashion and the shop, so it was interesting there. They were memorable nights.

I remember one particular bank holiday or something and it was so packed there, we had a few hundred on the street who couldn't get in. I announced this half way through the night and, would you believe it, a few hundred people left the club to let the others in. That was nice. Another time, I stopped the party and got on the mic because someone had lost a Walkman or something and I asked whoever had it, to leave it at the control tower, and they did. It was a friendly vibe, even though some of the people there would be considered very 'dark'. But they were well behaved while inside.

Africa Centre was such a good place and this is bringing back all the memories. We had a barber chair there and the record shop, which sold more expensive and rare albums. You would also get people swapping singles and that. It seems very strange, seeing as how sterile clubs are now, because that place had everything.

As a sound man, what was very important to me was a wooden floor. Lots of people didn't understand that a wooden floor made the music sound ten times better. We made a real effort to make a genuine atmosphere and vibe there and it was probably important to kids like Frost to go walking into a place that already existed, rather than one you made your own. There was already a sense of camaraderie at this focal meeting point. You got no bad men standing in the corners because there were no corners. I flipped everything on its head. We wanted this to be a haven, a sanctuary for music and for people to express themselves. No stone was left unturned in establishing this vibe. If Frost had had a bad day on a Sunday, he could come over and feel at home, no matter how many dodgy geezers were there. It was something to behold. We were on our own musical tip, so you could hear every genre in that venue; not the shit tracks or commercial stuff; we were breaking new music. A lot of us were from a working class, West Indian perspective and from the school of electro, as well as reggae and that. Early house was played there too and we had Daryl Pandy, Bobby Byrd and Ziggy Anderson doing sets, as well as anyone else who was in town at the time, who wanted to would grace us with their presence.

It was like going to school or church. People would come along every Sunday, religiously, to get together. It must have been inspiring. We were in our early twenties, man! Mad!"

A revenue stream that was a little less stressful than popping chains was selling 'dud hash'. There was a house on Dorset Road, Brixton, that sold weed and hash all day and night. It was more like three houses. They were doing big business there and getting over a hundred customers an hour. This gave us an idea.

Delroy and I would go to the corner shop, buy a shit-load of Oxo cubes and wrap them up in cling film just like the hash. We would sell our 'dud hash' to all the customers that congregated around Dorset Road. Man, we were killing it! We were making £200 a day selling dud hash. A mate of ours called Dave Angel would join us too. Dave had just got out of prison.

Delroy and I got jobs as removal men at one point and you would sometimes get dibs on bits and pieces. We met this one guy who gave me over 3,000 records. It was an amazing haul. There was funk, soul and rare groove in this amazing collection. It must have been worth thousands. 'Have the lot,' he said. That free gift was much more than just an incredible collection of music. It was an opportunity.

I was mad busy buying records at that point and so all this vinyl was amazing. There were old albums by James Brown and Bobby Byrd bootlegs from the Wag (Whisky A-Go-Go) and vintage jazz. It was a major record collection and similar to the stuff I was hearing at Soul II Soul.

1987, was a transition period for me. I was starting to veer away from robbing people as we sold more and more dud hash. The dealers hated us selling that shit to their customers however. Olinka and my daughter didn't live that far from Dorset Road, so it was also very handy and I needed the money to look after them.

If you were going to pop a chain, which I still did from time to time, then you went for the Arabs in Knightsbridge and Sloane Square. These guys would wear these little leather pouches on their wrists, which would contain all their cash. There would be a minimum of a grand in there. One of my mates got £6,000 in one snatch. But high stakes were high risk. Police would be around and there was always the chance of a have-a-go hero that you might have to take care of. You just had to snatch and run, as fast as fuck. I once got two or three grand from one of these stings. Happy days.

On the music front, Delroy had just acquired some decks and it was round his flat in Kennington, Oval that I started to learn the art of mixing.

Delroy

"When Nigel came out, (youth detention centre) he was very driven. He really wanted to be a DJ. He was practising and learning all the time.

We were inspired by the music at the Africa Centre and it was by playing that same kind of music in my flat that Nigel learned to DJ.

The nights at the Africa Centre were lively and so diverse. Jazzie B seemed to like having us there. Maybe we gave it an urban feel. He knew we were troublemakers, but he liked us and always let us in because when it came to music, we knew our stuff. I have to give Jazzie credit for that.

I was only 16 and having my own place gave us the freedom we needed to do what we had to do. There were no parents there, telling us to do our chores. That was the start of it all. Nigel got into the mixing really quickly. He got his own decks after a while and mixed music with a tape recorder. Hit & Run Records started with Nigel, me, Wilfred and Steve."

My mate Wilf got some decks in '87, thanks to his rich girlfriend Amanda, and I loved playing on those decks. I was also encouraged to

Big, Bad & Heavy

play by Barry White from Touch Of Class sounds who was kind enough to let me play on his decks.

With all my freebie records at our disposal, we started making funky mix tapes. Delroy had decks too and a flat we could use. We called ourselves Hit & Run Sound, which was maybe not a great idea as it referred directly to our 'day jobs'.

We started playing out all these tunes I'd been given, at house parties, community centres and local clubs. I loved the party vibes at these nights. I got so much energy from playing out. I was buzzing. The connection between the DJ and the audience was just magical. I felt like I was at the centre of the fucking universe, man!

It was around this time that I started dabbling in a bit of coke now and again. Just a few lines here and there. Weed had always been my thing, but I did start having a few lines to keep me going during those late nights with Hit & Run.

The more I got into music, though, the more I realised that I had to be careful when it came to my street life. If I wanted to make it as a DJ, I had to try and keep those two worlds as separate as I could. Looking back, my life has always been a struggle between two versions of me. The Bad Boy Vs The DJ. I wanted the DJ to prevail, but often the bad boy got on top. It was a constant battle.

Back to the real hit and runs and it was around this time that we managed to get our hands on a load of top-end designer watches; Gucci and Rock etc. We threw the driver from this van and made off with the lot, as well as some cash he had. We went around for weeks selling these watches. It was a good little earner. There must have been 400 watches in there, plus we got £500 cash from the driver. I would drop by Brixton pubs to see if anyone wanted a cut-price Gucci.

I was walking past the Normandy pub on Brixton Road one night when I heard this amazing music coming out. It was the same sounds as all the tunes I'd been given on that removals job; rare groove, funk and soul. Intrigued, I went inside and tried to sell the DJ a watch (I had about 10 left). As this Rasta guy inspected the watches, I started raving about the music he was playing. 'I've got all these tunes, man! They're fucking great! Rah! Rah! Rah!'

I could tell that this guy was a bit wary of me as I had a scar right down the side of my face, but he said he wanted a watch. 'Come and see me after my set,' he told me.

So, after he'd finished, he picked a watch and we started chatting. Bryan Gee was his name and once he'd realised how into the music I was, he suggested that I give it a go myself. On the radio.

'I work for a pirate radio station called Quest in Balham. Why don't you do a demo and see if you can get a show?' Bryan and I got on really well, although we had very different personalities. Bryan was thoughtful and would take his time when talking. I was a nervous ball of energy and emotion.

I did a demo, as asked, but you know what? It wasn't all that. So, Bryan offered to help me do another one. He coached me through putting together a proper playlist for a radio show. He was a massive influence on me, back then. A proper mate too.

The radio station then went bust, but this guy called Howard Hill aka 'The Brixton Don', stepped in and took it over. Howard moved the station to Brixton and Passion Radio was born. Bryan put in a good word for me and I was in. It was 1987 and I was now a pirate DJ playing rare groove, jazz and funk.

Bryan Gee

"I was living with a mate who was selling puff and we were both from out of town and living on this Brixton estate, which was one of the roughest. You see, I am from Gloucester originally.

I'm positive Nigel and some of his boys came knocking at the door for some puff one day. Straight off, we didn't like the look of them because they looked like proper thugs. We were new in the area and we could have easily got turned over and so we were well suspicious of these rude boys.

Nigel came to the door with a big dirty scar on his face. That scar was fresh; he'd been recently cut. I took one look at them and said, 'Nah!' I didn't want to invite them in, in case anything went down. I can still remember the cut. It was right across his cheek. That was my first meeting with Nigel.

I was DJing at the Normandy pub in Brixton at the time on a Sunday night. I'd play funk and rare groove, stuff like that. Then one evening, Nigel walked in. He was selling watches or something and asked me if I was interested. I told him to wait until I'd finished my set.

> After, Nigel was asking me about the funk I'd been playing. 'I've got loads of this stuff, man!' he said. He seemed very enthusiastic about his music. 'Why don't you play some on the radio?' I suggested. He shrugged it off. 'I'm serious!'
> I was on Quest radio in Balham at the time and asked him to put together a demo. This guy wasn't a DJ yet, but he knew his shit. He reluctantly agreed. When Quest went down I suggested Nigel as a DJ to the owners of this new station Passion. He was in. Nigel did his first show and that was that.
> Nigel didn't have a name at first, although he'd been playing out as Hit & Run. Then the name Underworld came along.
> Nigel got the gist of DJing very quickly and soon he was venturing out to clubs where this funkier stuff was getting played. We forged a real friendship, which seemed very unlikely when I first set eyes on this man, you know what I mean? I was a bit scared of him actually!"

Passion Radio was based in some offices of an Afro Caribbean centre on Brixton Road. The owner Howard Hill was a reggae producer and there were loads of big names hanging around Passion. Michael Prophet, Tinga Stewart, Ashman and King Kong were often there at the studio. Michael Prophet was a legendary singer and so it was a real inspiration having these guys from Jamaica around. It was such a big thing. I remember Leroy Smart coming over to Passion and I was so nervous. He was the don. I was with King Kong a lot as well and he became my good, good friend.

I was so nervous during my first show, I was actually shivering. I had never felt so nervous. But after a few weeks I started to find my way. I was loving it! Oh, and I also had a name: the rather appropriate Underworld.

Ingrid Thompson

> "When Nigel started with the pirate radio, he was very humble about it. I used to hear about him through his friends and I was really proud. He had a nice voice and a real passion for radio."

I played a lot of the rare groove and funk I'd heard at the Africa Centre on a Sunday night, during my shows on Passion. I was also still attending Soul II Soul every Sunday without fail. The Africa Centre was so important to me and many more like me. I was introduced to so much music through those Soul II Soul nights.

Passion Radio was my apprenticeship and I would stay at the studio until late into the evening just to talk to King Kong and Tinga Stewart. I loved spending time with Kong. Bryan Gee was the station manager at Passion and he worked so hard, sorting out the schedules and all that. The studio was actually at Bryan's house at one point.

The roster at Passion was me, Bryan Gee, Pete Stewart, Ray Holiday, Mike Ruffcut Lloyd, Gary Chef, TC Fords and Jimmy 'Drive Time' Davies. Derek Irie and Patrick Isaacs were major inspirations at Passion too. I knew Patrick from hanging around the Pool Parlour back in the day; his big brother Yankee was an 'older head' and always had the youngers' backs. Jimmy Davies was a real professional and sounded like a proper Radio 1 DJ. I learned so much from Jimmy and his drive-time shows. Slowly, but surely, I started to get the hang of this DJing lark.

Underworld. What the fuck was I thinking? I really liked my name at the time, though and it meant that I could be a character. Someone else. It made me more confident, I guess. I brought baby Tanya into Passion one evening and there she sat on my lap, talking on the mic in between the tunes.

There was a shop near the Passion studio called Graffiti Printers and I started seeing a girl there called Dawn, who was a little older than me. I felt like a big man about this. Everyone was shocked. 'How the fuck did you get that nice woman?!'

Passion had a real family atmosphere and it certainly opened up a new world to me. When Passion's Pete Stewart found a venue called Le Vie En Rose in Earl's Court, we started putting on a regular night there. These Passion nights were not reggae, but all sorts of funkier stuff and rare groove. There was always a good turnout there.

We were always on the look-out for new tunes and one of our favourite shops was Red Records in Brixton. Phil could sell you anything! You would just walk in and he'd bombard you with stuff. 'You need this! You need that!' I went in one day, in 1987, and Phil clocked me. 'You need to listen to this!' he said. He dropped the needle and my jaw dropped. Wow! It was a track called *Land Of Confusion* by Armando. It was fucking crazy! I loved it. It was an acid house track and although I didn't fully understand it, I started playing this tune at Le Vie

En Rose. I was also bang into Public Enemy at the time, too. Chuck D and the boys just got me, you know what I mean? They spoke to me.

"Have you forgotten, that once we were brought here, we were robbed of our names, robbed of our language, we lost our religion, our culture, our God, and many of us by the way we act, even lost our minds!" – Dr. Khalid Muhammad on Public Enemy's *Night Of The Living Base Heads*.

The biggest thing to hit Brixton in 1987 was Public Enemy. The tabloid press had whipped up such a fury about this controversial political rap group complete with their own security team (the S1Ws) that by the time they came to play Brixton Academy, there were riot vans everywhere. That gig had such an effect on me. One of the best gigs I have ever seen. Brixton was on fire from the moment they took to the stage.

As music started to take over my life, I knew I couldn't make it in this game while still being a bad boy on the streets. I had made sure I behaved myself at the Africa Centre, after that incident with the Rolex, but I had to do all I could to stay on the right path. I could have blown all my hard work in a single moment of madness. But it was a proper battle. Even if I wasn't doing stings, I still had a temper and that was my Achilles heel. I needed to control that bad boy, because a major opportunity had just come a-knocking.

CH. 11

Aciiiiiiiiiiiiidddddd!!!

WHAT THE FUCK?! *I was stunned. I didn't know what to make of it. There was an atmosphere at this place like no other. There were geezers hugging each other and passing bottles of water around. Women were dancing away with the men, but it was different somehow. Everyone was wearing bright colours and seemed completely hypnotised by the music. This wasn't your typical club either. We were in some abandoned building in London Bridge. I couldn't quite get my head around it, but I LOVED IT!*

I had heard bits and pieces of acid house – *Land Of Confusion* being an example – before this night, but I will be honest, I didn't get it straightaway. However, you could tell that this scene was going to blow up. Everything had been turned on its head. You couldn't just go back to what you'd been doing before. This was the future.

So, thank you to Pete Stewart and Bryan Gee who decided to take me to this warehouse party in Borough. I had heard of this thing 'acid house', but this party at Clink Street was my first real taste of it. It was mental.

Unlike traditional nightclubs, there was no bright neon sign outside and dressed-up party-goers at this dance. It was just a door in the wall and a few bouncers milling about. The punters were wearing T-shirts and jeans, very dressed down. The real fireworks were inside.

Bryan, Pete and I walked into this warehouse and boom! The music was LOUD! What the fuck?! I was used to the reggae nights and everyone standing around in their corners. Reggae nights could be moody, man. You didn't want to cross the line with no one, yeah? But this warehouse party was different. There was no tension. You didn't have to keep your wits about you in the same way. Blokes were hugging you as you went through. 'Hiya, what's your name?' It was weird, man. Reggae nights were black, but this was a real mixture. OK, most people were white, but there were black faces in there, but none of that seemed to matter. This vibe saw no colour. A Brixton boy, I couldn't quite believe the love I felt as I looked around. It was wicked! I then heard *Land Of Confusion* and it suddenly made sense. This was its home.

I had heard of ecstasy of course, but didn't really know what it did. But I saw this first party without any pills inside me and it was still amazing. It was a night that opened up so many possibilities in my brain. I was *wired*.

We didn't stay long as we were a little shocked by it to be honest. I just hadn't seen anything like it before. I got home and just kept smiling. I was pumped! I had to get involved.

Bryan, Pete and I then went on a mission to get as much acid house as we could. Promotional companies put us on their mailing lists so we would play their tunes on Passion. Secret Promotions, run by Simon Goffe – a big soul DJ – sent us loads of good stuff. Lisa Loud was head of promotions at Virgin and she really looked after us. *Acid Man* by Jolly Roger (Evil Eddie Richards) came out around then and that was a BIG tune. It was a truly exciting time.

Passion were really not happy with this new direction, but we weren't really hearing it. We just followed our gut instinct and started playing acid house on a reggae/soul station. The bosses fucking hated it.

Working on a radio station meant that Bryan and I were plugged into the promotions companies, who were eager to get their records played. Then Bryan Gee started working for Rhythm King (a subsidiary of Mute) at the time, doing promotions himself and so he was getting very well connected. Things were coming together nicely and fair to say, that meeting Bryan that night at the Normandy, was the start of so much. By playing on Passion, I was learning my craft as a DJ. It was a massively positive experience.

Bryan Gee

"We went to our first rave together in 1987. It was an acid house thing in Borough. It was Ashley Beadle's sound system with Evil Eddie Richards. What the fuck was going on in this warehouse? There were colourful T-shirts and men hugging each other. I was from a reggae environment, where you could get stabbed for spilling a drink on someone. You could die, do you get me? This acid thing was different. We didn't get it at first as it seemed so crazy. But it started to make sense once we'd absorbed what had happened. From there, we got more and more into it. From there, it was one rave after another."

Our mate Tank had started up an acid house night at a car wash on Lambeth Road and he asked Bryan and me to play out there in '88. There was real momentum building in this acid house thing. So, Friday and Saturday nights, Bryan, Pete and I played sets at Car Wash with Fabio and Grooverider who also played at Brixton's legendary underground spot Mendoza's. Fabio and Groove were from rival Brixton radio station Phase 1. Phase 1 was more dance-orientated, whereas Passion was more traditionally black. But with us doing our stuff, Passion was beginning to change. Fabio was a Brixton lad and a good boy – not a wrong 'un – and although we moved in different circles I knew his name from way back when I was 11 or so. He also knew mine. 'You're a DJ?!' he said during that first night at the Car Wash. Fabio knew me as a bad boy, see. 'What the fuck?! You're playing music now?!' He clearly found my career change amusing.

Fabio

"There weren't that many black men playing acid house at the start. Certainly, in south London, myself, Grooverider, Frost and Bryan Gee were the only ones playing out at that time. We were rivals, really. We worked on rival stations.

Acid house didn't sound like black music. People would come up to us and say, 'What the fuck are you lot doing?'

I knew of Nigel and his reputation, so I was quite surprised, to say the least, to see him playing out at Car Wash during those early days of acid house. Nigel and his friends were bad guys from the ghetto and so

I was very shocked when I saw Boga playing a night devoted to peace, love and unity.

Rave started from the eighties warehouse scene in London that kicked off in response to the New York parties. The set lists then would include funk, rare groove and hip hop. It was properly underground and great fun with a dangerously illegal angle to it. I mean, Car Wash was actually a car wash. We just moved the cars out and turned it into an after-hours club, around 1988. It was rammed in there.

Frost and Bryan were DJs from Passion, and Groove and I were working for Phase 1 and the south London stations had a fierce rivalry. It was more of a friendly competition between us and the Passion guys, though. Then it went a bit edgy when the owner of Car Wash, Tank, took us to one side after a set. Now, Grooverider and I had the main slots at Car Wash, and Frost and Bryan had Tuesday nights and so we weren't expecting what happened next. 'Really sorry lads, but this is your last night here…' Tank informed us.

- *'Sorry?! What the fuck?!'*
- *'You know what? I'm going to give Frost and Bryan a go. They're going to play every night.'*

We were really pissed off. Our rivalry was never that flagrant, more of an unspoken one up until that point, but boy, were we pissed off now. We got bumped by our rivals. That was a sketchy time, but looking back, it was great. It gave Groove and me a really heightened sense of competition. We were well up for it, now! This was war and we improved as a direct result and thus a legacy formed.

We never really fell out with Frost and Bryan, although our pride had been dented. In fact, it forged a bond between the four of us that was to last for a very long time. There was a lot of mutual respect there. This episode brought me and Groove and together too."

I started seeing this German girl Regina who used to go to Car Wash. She was a little older than me, just like Dawn from the printers. Regina couldn't speak an awful lot of English, but we were inseparable for a while. Regina lived in Notting Hill and kept on at me to give up the bad-boy bits and bobs on the streets. 'Just concentrate on the music! You don't have to be a bad boy anymore!' she pleaded to me.

I had already questioned the things I'd been doing around this time and definitely veered away from any real trouble, especially now my daughter Tanya was growing up. Plus, the music was starting to make it very difficult for me to carry on with the madness anyway, but I was still dipping my toes into familiar waters. Regina's words stuck with me, though, and I vowed to retire from the road life, around this time here.

Crime was disappearing, but I still had this, sometimes uncontrollable, anger. My little brother Gary was going through a tough, tough time. My stepfather's son, so my half-brother, my mum gave birth to Gary while I was in boarding school. When Gary was five years old, both his kidneys collapsed. It was heart-breaking. My mum had already lost one child (Nicky) when I was two, and the thought of anything happening to Gary was too much for me to handle. I remember this rage built up inside me and it exploded when someone said something to me in the street one day. I couldn't hold back and just started on this bloke. It destroyed me. I'd lost the plot. I was terrified that my little brother was going to die.

I could see the strain that Gary's situation was having on my family. My mother was studying a degree course at the time so she could become a social worker and so it was my job to take Gary to Guy's Hospital three times a week to get his medication. We would get some food there and once we'd got his cyclosporine we'd come home and I'd drop him off at school. People would stare at Gary on the bus because he had this hair that had sprouted up all over his face. He looked like a yeti or something. They were hard times right there. But although we were all in bits, you know what? Gary never once complained.

We met this Iranian family at Guy's and their son had a similar problem to Gary, but they couldn't get the meds on the NHS. This father had sold his house and given up everything for his son. It broke my heart to see that. Really distressing. It changed my outlook no end.

Before this period of my life I would have stabbed you without thinking. I would have robbed you. I would have that chain off your neck. But seeing what Gary was going through affected me. I started to question what I'd been doing.

I don't know what happened to that Iranian kid, though. I hope he pulled through.

So, I started moving away from robbing people and although I still sold some dud hash to keep things going, I knew that this wasn't the life I wanted to lead. I wanted a life in music.

The bosses at Passion were still not happy with the acid house stuff. Passion was a black, reggae station and they saw this new dance music as the devil's work. Initially, it was seen as white music and we had to really stick to our guns. The listeners just didn't get it. 'What the fuck is this shit?! What happened to the nice soul music?' Even in the streets, people didn't quite understand what we were doing. Howard pulled us into the office one day and gave us both barrels. 'What the fuck are you two doing? Fuck this fucking shit! What is this acid rubbish?'

- 'That's what we're playing now. We can't go back to the other stuff. This is it!'

Bryan Gee

"The local community thought we'd lost our minds! They honestly believed we'd been possessed by the devil or something. 'Electronic music?! It sounds like a washing machine on the spin cycle.' It was initially considered a white thing, too. The name didn't help either. Acid. The black vibe was all about weed and Guinness, not programmed beats and amphetamines. But we just loved it and knew that this was where our future lay. We really had to fight through that shit, do you know what I mean? Passion did not want the mums and dads at home listening to Jesus Loves Acid! Ha ha! They wanted Whitney Houston and Bobby Brown. Reggae boys didn't want to scream: 'Accciiieeeeeeddd!!!' Hugging, kissing, getting loved-up? You didn't do that on weed and Guinness. Reggae boys were unsure about the benefits to standing in a field with a bottle of amyl nitrate.

We loved the fact that this music saw no colour. For the first time, racial barriers came down. Black, white, European, hip-hop, indie, rare groove... all these genres blurred into one movement and one culture. Peace, love and unity, man!

Car Wash was great. A lot of the first wave of rave DJs played there: Pete Tong, Nicky Holloway and Paul Oakenfold. I guess we were the second wave of rave, more from the underground. But we were so proud to be a part of this fresh new scene and slowly the black community started to discover it for themselves."

CH. 12

Jumpin Jack Frost

I was playing Car Wash every weekend now as well as The Mad Max on Walworth Road with Danny and Chrissy Brown and Kenny Charles. Mad Max was a rave held in a carpet shop, of all places. Well, I guess it was on a par with a car wash. I had stopped going to Soul II Soul by the time acid house kicked in, though. I was getting *busy*.

Pete and Tank – the promoters of Car Wash – were not making a lot of money out of these nights, but it was a great thing to be involved with. I never really got into E, but I was still taking a few lines of coke now and again. Nothing too serious, but when I was with mates I'd have the odd line or two. I was as happy as a pig in shit. I was spreading myself thin, but I was having fun. I was a pirate radio DJ and playing out at raves.

I was now able to get the house fixed up too. Things were sweet! No more robbing, no more fights. This infectious acid house vibe swept me right up.

Clayton

"I knew Nigel from the days of hanging out in the West End. I think he smashed a friend of mine over the head with a glass some years before when he was with Hangman. But nevertheless, we became friends and spent a long while hanging out, right up until rave hit.

I was lucky enough to witness that first summer of love in 1988. E brought blacks and whites together and that was great because it wasn't really like that before. Rave saw no colour.

My first rave was a magical mystery tour. We got on a bus at Trafalgar Square that took us to Santa Pod raceway.

My mates had some pills and so I took one, not knowing that it might take hours to work. I got bored dancing away, waiting for this thing to happen and so I did another. Bad move. Come 7am, I started coming up – on the bus home! It hit me like a fucking brick! That was my introduction to E. Brutal!"

The government started to give out legal licences to community radio stations in 1988 and the only way to apply for one, was to go off air. Passion did just that, but rather than let things go cold, we moved to east London for a bit while the application went through for the licence. To evade the authorities, we had to change the name of the station (to Lightning) as well as our DJ names. For some reason I came up with Jumpin Jack Frost. I think it was based around the 'semiotics' I learned at boarding school. Because Jumpin Jack Flash was a Rolling Stones song, people had an association with the meaning behind the words. People would often say that they'd heard me playing out, when it was an actual impossibility. Semiotics. I loved that shit!

I liked the name Underworld and didn't want to give it up to be honest, but something happened over there in east London that consigned Underworld to the dustbin.

As Jumpin Jack Frost on Lightning Radio, I went full-on Cockney geezer. My persona completely changed and the audience lapped it up! 'Who is this guy Jumpin Jack Frost?!' they'd ask, paging me and the other guys. My show went through the roof.

Lightning started doing a party called The Galleries in east London once a week over at Bromley-by-Bow and we had these massive masks of our heads made from plaster of Paris. The heads hung from the ceiling during this rave to fit in with the gallery vibe. Then, a week later, we heard that an east London promoter was using these heads for their party; called The Galleries! So, me, Bryan and Pete went over to the venue to see what they were up to, using our name as well as the heads. Apparently, these boys ran the legendary pirate Centreforce. Hot-headed as always, I went into full Brixton bloodclaart, giving it the large one. 'Rahh! What the fuck are you doing? The Galleries is our night! These heads are ours! Fuck all of you!' Andy Swallow was the main man there and he was having none of it. He was quite polite, actually. At first. I just kept mouthing and mouthing and mouthing and they did say sorry

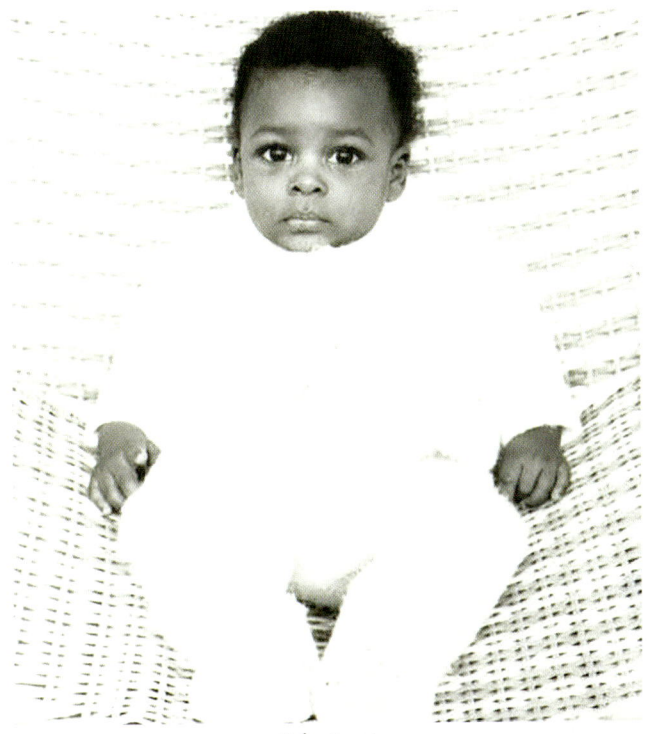

Baby Frost

Me and Mum when I was two years old

I was such a good kid

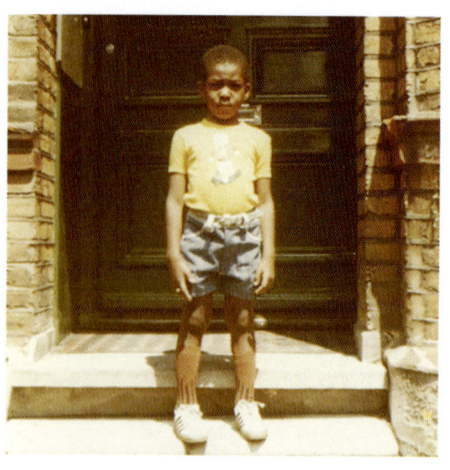

5 years old outside the house on Palace Road

Palace Road with my cousin Michael

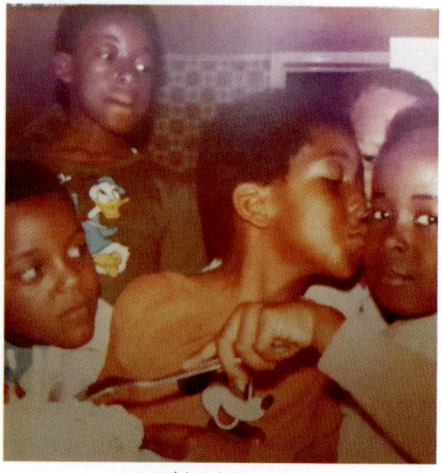

With my cousins Michael and Stephen

My 5th birthday party

Butch and Jackie's wedding. I'm far left with a miserable face

My Grandfather

My Grandmother (Ganga) Sybil Thornhill

My Grandfather. Everard Thornhill

Yeah mate

Scallywag

Young and innocent

Enborne Lodge table tennis team. Check the hair

Me and Mum

Inta Natty F.C

Back Row = Fluxie, Juicey Johns, Grooverider, Face, JJ Frost, Killer
Front Row = Dezzie, Pete Nice, Diesel, Danny B and Benny

Inta Natty FC. Good times

Me, Oliver, Goldie, Bryan Gee and Storm

Old skool Roast. Me and Grooverider

In LA. Rolling in the limo

Grooverider
(The Living Shock)

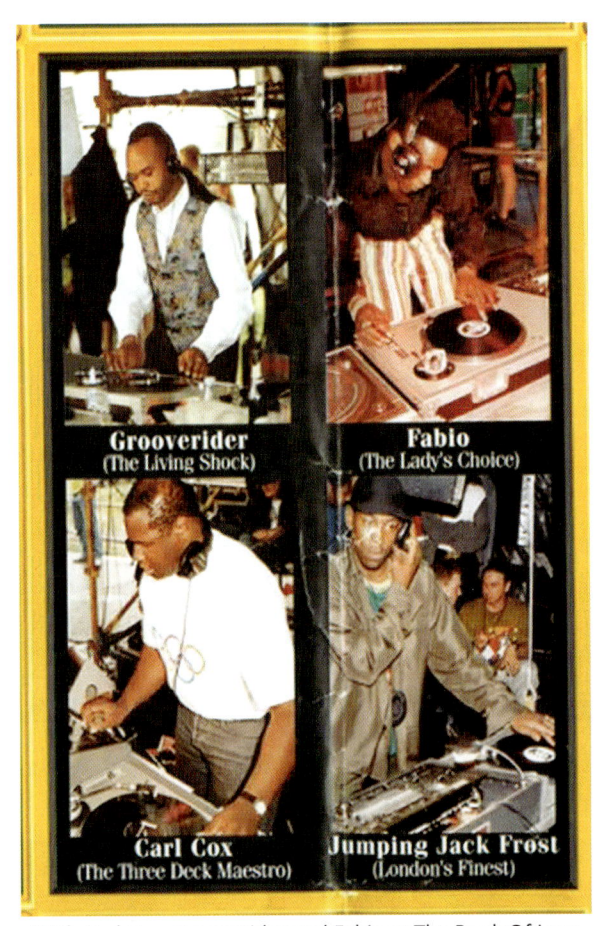

Fabio
(The Lady's Choice)

Carl Cox
(The Three Deck Maestro)

Jumping Jack Frost
(London's Finest)

With Carl Cox, Grooverider and Fabio at The Book Of Love

Old skool shot of the Brixton Boyz in the 80s. With Stevie Culture, Ripper and Prince

Old skool shot by Samantha Williams - Artypix.co.uk

Who you looking at?

a couple of times, but then they got bored of it all and gave us a proper kicking. They jumped us and administered a sound beating. 'You don't come over here from Brixton or wherever you're from and tell us what to do on our manor! Fuck you and your big fucking mouth!' Sorry to Bryan and Pete because we took a few, I can tell you. I deserved it, actually. Our egos were well and truly bruised, but sometimes you just had to take it on the chin. And the head. And up the arse. We were in the right, but perhaps we went about it in the wrong way.

Andy Swallow (Centreforce, Labello Blanco)

"I started off organising house parties in '88 and then the opportunity came up to do a pirate radio station with a load of kids from around our way, in the blocks of flats in east London. We ran with it.

Centreforce became the only 24 hr-a-day pirate playing house at that time and we stayed on for quite a while without any bother from the police. We later found out that their lack of hassle was due to a six-month police observation, which ended up with us in court. They threw the lot at us: drugs, illegal broadcasting etc. They claimed we took 25% of the door at certain parties, but we weren't. Then there was talk of 500,000 E tablets. The 'information' came from a grass amongst us and they wouldn't be identified and so the police dropped the charges. We walked. Because we were associated with West Ham's ICF (Inter City Firm), they thought we'd dropped the I, which left CF (Centreforce). But the station was actually set up by an Arsenal fan. But I guess it sounded so good it had to be true.

There was this venue we started to use, which was a warehouse stuck on a motorway going into the Blackwall Tunnel, which sounded good for the parties. We'd been using a warehouse for three weeks previously, situated at the back of an old bus depot. We met these two guys from a church who ran this venue and agreed to take it on as a legal until 6am. We asked for the postal address to put on the flyers and was told that the venue was called The Galleries. We advertised the party on the radio of course and got a good crowd there.

The following week, we were doing this night of ours when we heard a lot of shouting and shit. Some geezers from south London had come over and were claiming that we'd nicked their night. This one fella was saying he was going to do this and that and saying that he was south London. I said, 'I don't care where you're from, mate, you're in east London you mug!' He said he wanted half the takings at the door. I couldn't quite believe it. This guy was raging that I had stolen his idea. 'The Galleries is my name and they're my heads!' There were these funny-looking heads hanging from the ceiling and I tell you what, considering he was surrounded by the ICF, he was lucky to leave with his head intact. 'I'm from Brixton!' He went on and on. Anyway, we put up with it for so long until one of our lot knocks this gobby one's mate down the stairs. They took a kicking to be fair, but this one fella wouldn't shut up. As they left, he said, 'I'll be back and I'm going to shoot the place up!' We all laughed when they eventually left. 'He was game wasn't he?!'

Two weeks later, the venue bosses sent us a letter and at the top of it was the address of the club. The club was actually called The Library, and not The Galleries, and so this geezer was right. We had stolen his name, that he had spent quite a few weeks building up. Ha ha. He was lucky, though, as he was bang in our area and he wasn't going to get very far mouthing off like that. Funny really, because not long after that we started working together."

I actually saw Andy later on, at one of his nights and we had a drink and a laugh and shook hands. I played on Centreforce a few times after that. I was out of order that day. Still, a beating aside, Jumpin Jack Frost was booming!

We all went back to Brixton after losing out to Choice for a legal licence. This meant that we could all go back to our original names. Passion was back, although they actually kept the name Lightning. Bryan dropped 'De Niro', which he hated anyway, but I was not giving up on Frost. 'No more Underworld! I'm Jumpin Jack Frost, mate!'

***

I remember Bryan and Pete Stewart getting really taken by the Bristol club scene at the time – Bryan came from Gloucester – and so we planned a coach trip there to play this party for Dave Walker who was a big-name promoter.

We got to this club only to find that the decks had been wired the wrong way around. On purpose. The right deck was coming out of the left channel and vice versa. This DJ Dirty Den (now known as Easygroove) had done it, as he hated acid house and techno. I was fucking fuming. This guy was giving it the big 'un. 'Bristol will always be hip-hop!' he said. I went fucking ape shit when I realised that it was him who had played around with the decks. 'Bristol is hip-hop?!' I wasn't having this prick sabotaging my set, so I fronted him out, but stopped short of hitting him. What a prick! The weird thing is that this Easygroove later became TechnoDread; a fucking rave DJ! Cheeky fucker. 'Bristol will always be hip-hop, yeah?' Fucking dickhead.

***

Business was looking up. So much so, Bryan and I started walking around with a mobile phone attached to a briefcase, which was owned by Lightning. We'd carry this phone around with us as we went hunting for the latest tunes, three or four times a week. The battery on this thing only lasted about 20 minutes. For fuck's sake!

City Sounds and Blackmarket were good for new tunes. Now, Dave at City Sounds would sell you the shirt off your back, that cunt. Never seen anyone sell records like that. I got rinsed every time I went in through the door. Dave could sell records and Ray Keith was his apprentice. I got loads of good stuff from those guys, which we played out at raves and on the radio.

I was at Lightning one day, doing my show, when this guy rang in. 'Who's this?'

- 'My name is Tony Colston-Hayter and I put on a night called Sunrise. I want you to come and play it. I'm doing a night at Heaven with Evil Eddie Richards, Paul Anderson and Colin Hudd and I want you on that bill.'

Sunrise at Heaven was great. I was actually refused entry to Heaven when they hosted Babylon on Thursdays, but now I was going to be playing there. The bouncers at Babylon thought I looked like trouble back then. Well, I was trouble. So, it felt real sweet to be playing that club. People were really starting to get interested in this Frost fella. It was a great night.

I played a massive warehouse party for Patrick who hosted In Search Of Space and he was one dodgy fucker, I'm telling you. Then I got asked to play Energy, which was a massive rave.

We were driving round all night trying to find Energy. 'Where's the rave? Where's the rave?' You never knew where these raves were going to be until you got to the meeting point.

We left home at 10pm and arrived at Energy at 5am. Fuck me. We spent all night driving round and round the M25. We eventually found the rave and had to walk across these fields in the pitch black, carrying this big old record box. I didn't know where we were going.

I spotted the lorries first. There were these massive lorries that contained the giant speaker stacks. I remember peering through the gap between two of these lorries and saw all these people streaming down the hillsides and over the fences to get to this venue. I was terrified!

I was due on at 6am after Frankie Bones who had flown in from New York. The sun had just started to come up at 6am when I was due to start, and unlike a dark warehouse vibe, I could actually see the crowd. Thousands of them! I was shaking like a leaf, man. It was MENTAL! My hands could hardly position the needle. Terrifying!

I look back on those early raves with a good deal of fondness. They were special days before the real criminals got involved. There was a hippy vibe, you know? Everyone was just loved-up and having a great time. It was so new. Nothing was planned that much. I remember people like Chalkie White, just getting up on stage with a mic. 'Oi! Oi!' Up until now, clubs had been high-street affairs and people dressing up. This was a different world, mate. The game had changed.

Chalkie White

"I was the original rave MC. No one had done it before. It was a role I created and it was to take me on one hell of a journey.

I got into MCing at raves by accident really. I used to go to the raves from 1988 onwards and would hear all the DJs playing, but because no one was introducing them, you never really knew who you were listening to. So, I thought, 'Yeah... people will come to listen to a certain DJ, but are totally unaware of when they're on. So, I wonder if I could go on stage and introduce them?'

I started bringing a mic with me to raves and once or twice plugged it into the equipment and hopped up on stage. I would hype the crowd up a little and then let the DJs do their stuff. It was just a natural thing.

A couple of times I got thrown off stage by the promoters. 'We don't want it and don't need it!' I was told. Then in 1989, a rave called Genesis started and they asked me to host their party. 'Introduce the DJs and hype the crowd up, mate!' It was very successful and then the promoters who initially told me to clear off, now wanted to book me. The rest as they say, is history.

I mean, the dance community back then, was small. There weren't that many raves happening. There would often be just one big event at the weekend that everyone would go to and there weren't that many DJs either. I was certainly the first MC. I first met and worked with Frost from early on. Frost was there from day one, really.

I never planned what I was going to say on the mic, I just let rip and whatever came out, came out. I always got the crowd involved too; it was never about me. My job was to hype the crowd up and make them feel important. I played all the biggest parties: Energy, Biology, Raindance, World Dance and Dreamscape. All the major ones.

I was not into taking anything at raves initially. People would give me a little fella and I would take it and they'd later ask, 'You buzzin'?' The thing was, I'd already sold it on to someone else. 'Havin' a brilliant time!' I'd say. I wasn't lying. I was just enjoying the parties without pills.

Then a couple of years later, someone gave me half a pill on my birthday and I did it. I was buzzing, mate. And that was it. I started going out and getting on it every night of the week.

It was a magical time back then. The difference between then and now, is that it was all done for love. Of course, the promoters wanted to make money, but the money came from this passion for raving.

The people who came out were really friendly and you'd often meet the very same people at all these events. It had a real community vibe. One particularly magical moment was when someone lost a suitcase with £25,000 in it. Only at a rave, would a suitcase stuffed with a lot of money, be found and handed in. That was crazy. To witness that, was an amazing, magical thing."

***

I knew there were better DJs than me, but that wasn't the whole story. You needed something else to get to the next level. Charisma? Possibly. You definitely needed luck. Sometimes the luck was with you, other times it deserted you. I was lucky. Although, I was a wild kid who pulled out knives and had a raging temper, I had good people around me. Ultimate respect to Fabio and Grooverider. Being friends with Bryan Gee was such an asset. Bryan was a real calming influence on me and whenever I had problems I knew that Bryan would help.

I remember attending a DJ seminar around this time and started noticing this guy Dr K who went on to become DJ Hype. He was putting together some really progressive stuff at this Islington Music Workshop (IMW) mixing hip hop with house and stuff. Like hip house I guess. It was a young offenders course and served as a first step into production. I loved what he was doing on this scheme. DJ Ron was there as well, a guy whose mum used to look after my sister. Ron's family were from Guyana too and I really looked up to him as well as Dr K and Rebel MC, who were also at that workshop.

One of the nights that changed my life was seeing Cutmaster Swift win the DMC World Championships at the Royal Albert Hall in 1988. That night inspired me so much, as he battled against DJ Aladdin. That evening taught me that anything was possible. It was an amazing showcase of turntable skills.

I became good friends with these two DJs HMS (RIP) and Rob Elliot (RIP) in those early days. We played out together and would always call a real tune, a 'window smasher'. 'This tune could smash windows!' So, we called ourselves 'the window smashers'. It was a shame that neither of them kicked on. Just goes to show, that there were many DJs who had the talent, but lacked that certain something, but we had some enjoyable nights back then.

CH. 13

Frosty's Gone To Iceland

I can't remember how, but I ended up as a security guard at this shop Mash on Oxford Street. Mash sold acid house gear and once the boss found out I was a DJ, Bryan Gee, Pete Stewart and I started playing out in the shop's basement. We hired some equipment from this guy Chris Sweeney we knew, but we never actually paid the dude. Up until now he still hasn't had his money.

Mash was a busy shop on the busiest shopping street in the world and our tunes blasted out of these external speakers, straight into the West End. That place was heaving. People would come just to party. Many of them were off their nuts.

Mash sold smiley T-shirts, hoodies, records and tickets to raves and it was doing good business. It was then that I decided to knock crime on the head for good. No more dud hash and popping chains. I was going straight, mate.

Then, the owner of Mash, Abel, asked us if we wanted to set up a record stall inside the shop. Fuck me, we sold a shit-load of records in there, plus we could take home any clothes we wanted. 'If you want anything, just take it,' Abel told us. Abel owned the shop with his brothers Karim and Hamed. Abel was one of those guys who made things happen and he gave us free rein at Mash.

So, I now had a radio show, a record shop and loads of bookings. I was buzzing. Then Abel bounced into Mash one morning with a plan. 'Right, I have this girlfriend in Iceland, yeah…'

Big, Bad & Heavy

- 'Yeah...'
- 'Well, I want you two to come out to Iceland with me to play at her birthday party.'

Iceland was a great experience. It was the first time Bryan and I had ever played abroad. There were girls everywhere in Reykjavík. We went in the hot springs – where I fried an egg on a rock – and partied the nights away with these ravers. The trip was real fun. They said there was zero crime in Iceland yet someone nicked my fucking passport and so I needed a note to get home. That was the only downer.

We ended up on this local radio station with this DJ called Big Foot. We played all the latest tunes from the UK – including Adamski as I recall – to these Icelanders. They loved it. We were mobbed when we left the club, later that night. Then it was back to the hotel with the girls. Boom! Boom! Boom! It was gobsmacking. Here I was, a violent criminal, playing acid house music, in Iceland. What a turnaround!

***

Bryan and I were making a shitload of connections working in Mash. Then there was Guy Carlton and Dave Lee (Joey Negro) from Republic Records and through people like that and their friends Mark Ryder (aka Cheeky) and the producer Tony Thorpe, we just absorbed all this knowledge and know-how, as we saw first-hand how they promoted their records. Simon Goffe from Secret Promotions was a massive help too. Simon had this assistant Nick Halkes for a while and we hooked up with this Bristol boy a lot. Simon would go on to play a major role in our careers and we are always in his debt.

Nick Halkes (XL, Positiva)

"My first job after leaving university was a part time role at Secret Promotions working for Simon Goffe. I started off as an office assistant, stuffing envelopes and printing returns. I was aware of Frost back then as someone on the mailing list, being as he was, a prominent club DJ and a name in pirate radio.

When I was put in charge of club and radio promotions, I became more engaged with Frost and Bryan Gee and Nigel would pop by the office to pick up promos. I got to know Frost and Bryan Gee quite well. I would sometimes go to Lightning, in south London, just to hang out while they were broadcasting. I was interested in getting them to play our records. The pirate scene was crucial to us in breaking dance records and so we really needed to get key players on board; people like Frost and Gee.

Frost was so enthusiastic and passionate about the music. He was a ball of energy and keen to spread the word. I was promoting Double Trouble with the Rebel MC and tunes on Republic such as The Turntable Orchestra with You'll Miss Me When I'm Gone. Frost would have been playing those."

So… the network was becoming *solid* and Bryan and I were getting loads of advice and expertise as well as truck-loads of promos that we could play out on Lightning, or at raves. Failing that, we'd sell those tunes in Mash. There were so many people hanging out in that shop it was like a mini Las Vegas in there. People were properly buzzing from the night before. Others would come in to buy clothes to wear at the raves that night. That shop had such a vibe.

I was DJing all over. Car Wash, In Search Of Space and loads of the bigger raves. I played Ziggy's in Streatham every Sunday with Carl Cox. Britain was one big smiley face as it fell in love with this musical revolution. But of course, where there was money, there was always crime.

One of the biggest knocks in the rave world came from a party that never happened. I won't name names, but we were all booked on this line-up, but the promoter simply took the money and ran. It never happened. From then on, ticket agencies only released the funds once the event actually happened. Now, 25,000 tickets had been sold for that non-event. Tut tut. It was just a massive scam. It was a shame really, as it went against the vibe that kicked the scene off in the first place. It was meant to be about freedom not corruption.

There was this one open-air rave I was booked for, where we spent the usual four or five hours driving around the M25 trying to find the fucking thing and we eventually found it thanks to the heavy police presence outside. 'Go home!' the police ordered through their loud hailers. The police blocked off the whole area. I had just struggled across the motorway with my record box and I was fuming. Then this smart chap came forward and told us to ignore the police and carry on through. 'It's OK. I'm a lawyer working on behalf of the organisers.

Ignore the police and come on in!' So, I marched on past the feds and into the warehouse. It was a mad time back then. Seems like a lifetime ago to be honest. But you could see that the scene was expanding and the promoters were having to up their game to survive. The police wanted the raves to end and were under a lot of pressure from the tabloid press, who were really banging on about the E generation. Headlines like 'Ecstasy Airport' and 'Spaced Out' were putting the fear of god into the public regarding this 'evil drug'. It was fast becoming 'us' against 'them' as the government started preparing legislation to curb the rave explosion.

***

There was quite a little crew of rave DJs in south London by then. There was me, Bryan Gee, Fabio and Grooverider. The initial hostility we faced down south had started to fade. Now, we were seen as innovators. We seemed to meet up with the east London DJs a lot at parties like Raindance at Jenkins Lane, which were always classics. East London had Ratpack, Frankie Valentine and Ellis Dee and we always had a laugh and shared stories when playing out. Not only was acid house taking off, but it really felt like I was taking off with it. They were exciting times, yeah?

CH. 14

Murder

Bang! Bang! Bang! I got up and rubbed the sleep out of my eyes. It was 6am. Fuckinell. There was someone banging on the front door. I put my jeans on and stumbled towards the door.

There were two policemen there. 'Nigel Thompson?'
- 'Yeah?'
- 'We're arresting you as part of a murder investigation.'

Sat in the squad car on the way to the station, I was trying to get to grips with what they'd just said. Murder? What the fuck?!

'This has nothing to do with me! I ain't fucking murdered no one, yeah?! Fucking murder?! You kidding me, bruv?! What the fuck?!'
- 'Do you know a Mr Mark Jones…?'
- 'Yeah. He's a mate.'
- 'Mark says he was with you on the day of…'
- 'I made him a mix tape, yeah? But that's it.'

I was terrified. I mean, just the word 'murder'; this was serious shit. What the fuck had Mark done?

I had a friend called Mark Jones. Now, I'd seen Mark just a day or two before my arrest and he'd asked me to do him an acid house compilation. So, I mixed a few tracks for him on this tape and dropped it off through his letterbox one day. That exact same day, Mark decided to burn a house down, killing 2-3 people inside. Now, the cunt was using me as an alibi, saying that he was with me on that day. Fuck me, talk about landing you in the shit.

They kept on and on at me. 'What do you know of his whereabouts? What kind of mood was he in? Did he mention anything to you that now seems suspicious?'

I couldn't think of anything that could help them and all the time I was thinking about what had happened. People had died.

Eventually, they bought my side of things and let me go, but I was severely rattled. Sometimes, there were these odd reminders of the street life I'd led, making it a hard world to truly escape from; talk about unwanted hassle. Mark got 20 years or something for that.

My love life has been very complicated and looking back, I was playing around like a headless chicken. People got hurt in the process and because of that, certain aspects of my home life and love life are going to be left unsaid. I never meant to cause any grief, but I accept that I could have acted with a little more care. What can I say? Sorry? I *am* sorry.

I was still seeing Regina in Notting Hill, on and off. I would see her for a little bit and then she'd go missing. I was a late starter with girls, so maybe I was making up for lost time. I don't know.

It was a difficult time all round. Gary was in and out of hospital and so I was taking time out to be with him, too. Gary had a couple of transplants, but the new kidneys were rejected and so his future was constant dialysis.

Gary Richards

"I was in hospital all the time and Nigel took good care of me. It was a difficult time. I would often ask Nigel about the raves etc. because it was fun knowing what he was doing out there. Being stuck at home or in hospital a lot of the time made Nigel's world seem so exciting.

I remember Nigel coming home from a rave once and it had been raining heavily. Nigel had been carrying his record box when he slipped in the mud and he was covered in this stuff when he got home. That always makes me smile."

I was so worried about my little brother. It made me so angry and frustrated. I have always had problems with my temper. If something made me angry, I was like a boiling saucepan of water, with the lid clattering away. Sooner or later, the lid would fly off. I felt very protective of Gary and this in turn, could make me very angry.

I still had my show on Lightning, but I decided to ditch it around 1990, so I could concentrate on playing as many clubs and parties as I could. Tin Tin, who ran Energy, had started up a new club night on Shaftesbury Avenue called Fun City and we would play out there on a Friday night, which was cool. Fun City and Enter The Dragon were some of the first regular spots in the West End and loads of big names played there.

Quentin 'Tin Tin' Chambers (Energy and Fun City)

"I started clubbing at an early age; 15 I think. It was 1986 and I'd just been thrown out of school. I would go to places in London, like The Embassy, Mud Club, Camden Palace and The Wag, where we'd dance to northern soul, hip hop, go go, electro and early house. Around 1987, I started going to acid house warehouse parties every single night, where I met up with so many different people involved in this emerging scene.

Jeremy Taylor organised the socialite 'Gatecrasher Balls' and I helped him out with his promotions for a bit. Then, when he got ripped off by a business associate, he shut the company down. I remember him asking me, 'What should I do next?'

- 'Well, I'm into acid house. Why don't we put on some parties? You have the organisational skills and I know what works and what doesn't...'

- 'OK, let's do it!'

Our first rave was a magical mystery tour in 1988, which got busted by the police. Then we put on Hypnosis at the Brixton Academy with a little help from Wayne Anthony. 2,500 turned up to Hypnosis, but it wasn't brilliant. Hypnosis got busted too, which was disheartening. But we kept on trying.

In 1989, we started the Fun City club night on Shaftesbury Avenue. Anton Le Pirate helped us with the promotion for that and Fabio was resident DJ. Frost played there too and this started us off as serious promoters.

Fun City was a good club and one of the first all-nighters in the West End with a licence. We did a lot of work with the decoration and invested heavily in this idea. It was a mixed crowd, with west London kids partying with football hooligans and freaks. It was a good scene there.

We did a big Energy party at Westway Studios on the May bank holiday in 1989 and it was considered the best acid house party ever, by many who went. The production guy was Marc Holmes, who is now Ridley Scott's art director and stage designer. We got Marc straight out of art school to build the props and design the lighting; it was an amazing production. No one had gone to these lengths at that point. It was sold out and there were 5,000 outside this film studio who couldn't get in. It was a great line-up.

That Energy party set us up alongside Sunrise really. The police would shut the parties down, but we kept going forward and getting smarter as the parties got bigger.

I was still young then, which seems mad. I was 18/19 and organising these massive parties that attracted criminals, gangsters, drug dealers and police. Plus, it could get pretty hairy. It was a lot of fun, though; a high-octane game of cat and mouse every night of the week. I would always sleep until after lunch every single day. I really lived the life back then.

Frost was always a real character; integral to the south London scene. Promoters Paul and Dave had a house in Brixton and they were the biggest ticket sellers for Energy. Fabio, Grooverider, Bryan Gee and Frost would hang out at Paul and Dave's too. We would sometimes go to Mendoza's and places like that. It's all a bit blurry to be honest. There was quite a little scene down south though, and Frost was a major part of it. He had a real history in Brixton, which was very, very lively.

Someone tried to stab Frost inside one of my clubs once after having a ruck with him. It was late '89 and he came bounding over to me. 'Someone just tried to stab me. He pulled a knife on me!' He was quite good-humoured about it, though. Ha ha.

Frost had this brilliant cheeky grin and was always easy to get on with; one of the sweetest guys. I worked with him on Energy and Fun City from '88 onwards. It was always a joy."

As well as the warehouse parties and illegal raves I was also starting to play nights like Club Labrynth and Dungeons in east London as I ventured out more. I would hire drivers to take Bryan and me to gigs. Labrynth hadn't yet moved to Four Aces at this point, but it was a great night with a real character of its own. It felt really good to get out of south London for a bit.

Sarah Sandy (Groove Connection)

"I started raving in 1988/89 after finishing a degree at Goldsmiths University. I was initially going to apply for the producers course at the BBC, for TV production, but once the rave scene really kicked off, I decided to delay applying for the course, as I was enjoying partying too much.

I needed a job, though and ended up doing some clerical work in the same offices as Simon Fuller, the music agent. I was running around helping with tax and VAT returns for this management company. A few years later Simon actually asked me to be in a girl band as a ginger singer. Ha ha! But I loved the underground too much for that.

Simon Fuller had been doing some stuff with Danny D and D-Mob back then and you could tell that dance music was starting to become big business.

Caroline Robertson was a music publisher at Westbury Music and had offices in Brixton, but she also did publishing work for artists at CMO and 19 Management. When I met her, I was living in Brixton and told her about my idea to work with DJs and she encouraged me to go for it, and do what I believed in. She said that if I ever needed an office space in Brixton, she could help out. Initially I helped set up a company called DJs United with DJ Frankie Valentine based in Kensal Rise at the end of 1989, but there were too many people and DJs involved and when some of the agency wages got absorbed into an overdraft due to an unscrupulous investor, DJs United fell apart. However, I had this unwavering belief that DJs were going to be massive, even though people were laughing at me. But undaunted, in September 1990, I decided to launch Groove Connection Management/Agency for DJs who were getting paid peanuts at the time. We were based on Brixton High Road, above the Abbey National and Red Records. I knew Fabio, Grooverider, Frost and Bryan Gee from living in Brixton and hearing them DJ on the pirate radio stations and at raves, and I found out that they really weren't getting paid what they were worth. Most of them were just chuffed to be playing and never believed it was going to be anything more.

It all kicked off with six DJs. We had Fabio, Grooverider, Frost, Bryan Gee, Micky Finn and Frankie Valentine. I knew Fabio and Groove from Phase 1 radio and Frost and Bryan from Lightning.

Nigel was full of energy. A real whirlwind. We hit it off straight away. I knew Nigel was a real bad boy, but we got on. I treated people as they treated me and he respected that.

The agency took people by surprise, especially the promoters who had been getting away with murder up until this point because the scene was so raw at this stage. Groove Connection brought us all together as a family, though, in what was a rather crazy, structure-less scene back then.

We started off with two phone lines and within a month we had eight. It went ballistic. We had no mobile phones of course and so many calls were made to phone boxes. Nigel had a phone, though. Nigel's phone was a real 'basher', the size of a brick. The battery would last for about 15 minutes. Ha ha.

Once the big events like Sunrise and Energy gave way to clubs, we had so many more bookings. There was Steppers in Brixton, Coventry Eclipse and Starlight in Birmingham. These clubs would often book five DJs at a time and I could provide all of them. The agency's business started to grow out of control with numerous bookings further afield. We would all travel together to Belgium, Italy and Germany, places like that. Some of these DJs hadn't been abroad before. Others had criminal pasts, which meant loads of paper work for me. But it was hilarious and we had so many laughs. The agency Dynamix came along within a few months, and they looked after Evil Eddie Richards and those guys. It seemed as if my timing had been just right.

So, the DJs on Groove Connection were now getting five times what they had been getting. Some of the promoters really weren't happy, ha ha. 'Who's this fucking middle-class girl telling us what to do?'"

I joined two agencies in 1990: Groove Connection and Dynamix. I first met Sarah Sandy from Groove Connection at Steppers in 1990. I really believed in Sarah and she became a really good friend and colleague. Sarah was full of good advice and was able to calm me down a little. I was known for being a bit of a hot head.

Sarah Sandy was just one of those people so bubbly and enthusiastic that you couldn't help getting caught up in it all. We got a lot of work through Sarah and it meant that we could just concentrate on playing out, doing as many as three gigs at night.

Evil Eddie Richards was a rave legend – he released *Acid Man* as Jolly Roger – and I remember him telling me how he was going to start up a DJ agency too and did I want to be involved. Dynamix had some big names on their books, including Sasha and Mr C and so I signed up. Through Dynamix and Groove Connection I started getting gigs up north for the first time. Suddenly, this rave thing opened right up; parties in Birmingham, Leeds and Manchester.

A fine club at that time was Zen in Slough. Run by father-and-son team Chris and Ed, Zen put on some massive parties at this warehouse in Slough. It was a real family affair, with the mum taking the cash on the door. They were wicked nights, I'm telling you. Massive parties. You could get a few thousand in there. I became firm friends with the Zen lot and played the Slough Centre a lot. By this time, Car Wash had run its course at Lambeth Road and I was playing out all over the place.

Duffus

"I was 18 in 1989, when I started driving for Frost. They were crazy, exciting times. I had a rep for being one of the best drivers going. If you needed to get somewhere fast, I was the man. It was to be 12 years of continuous madness. It scares me to think of what we got up to. Ha ha!

I drove Nigel and Bryan from party to party, sometimes three or four in a single evening. I would drive like a maniac to get Frost and Bryan to their gigs on time. I was playing games with juggernauts, the lot. I remember this one truck trying to stop me getting past him and so I got in front of him and slowed right down, thus really pissing this geezer off. I remember Frost shouting at me, 'What the fuck are you doing?! You're going to get us fucking killed!'

We had loads of fun. Girls, drugs, drink, they were naughty times. The Holiday Inn at King's Cross was always a favourite 'rest-stop' when we eventually got back to London. We had some mad parties there that went on for days.

I remember getting pulled over by the feds one time along Embankment after swerving in and out of traffic. They put the blue light on and had a word. Then they spotted Frost. 'I've got a gig in town, so sorry if we were speeding, officer.' The police seemed to calm right down after that. In fact, instead of getting points they enrolled me on an advanced driving course."

I remember getting this gig in Plymouth through Dynamix with Mr C from The Shamen. We travelled down there with his missus and when we got to Plymouth, we bumped into the Ragga Twins. I first met Deman and Flinty when I was in Hangman. I would chat on the mic and I was nowhere near as good as them, but they obviously remembered me. I will never forget their faces when they saw me on the decks. 'What the fuck are you doing here?' They knew me as a bad boy who robbed people. I remember Deman laughing, 'Well, if he can get involved in this game, then so can anyone, because he's fucking terrible! Ha ha!'

Back in Brixton, a friend of mine called Raymond started a night at The Fridge (the old Ace where I got booed off the stage) and he wanted me as a resident DJ there. The night was called Hell and it was held on a Thursday night with me, Ellis Dee, Paul Trouble Anderson and Evil Eddie Richards forming the spine of the line-up. That night absolutely took off! It was certainly the place to be, south of the river. It was like Brixton's answer to Rage at Heaven in the West End. There was this local legend called Dudley (RIP) and he really supported us through those early days and really looked out for Fabio and Groove, demanding that they were put on bills all over London. 'We want Fabio and Groove!' Dudley – nicknamed 'Megatron' – really helped us south London boys. And so, Hell at The Fridge was born. South London's answer to the legendary Rage at Heaven on Charing Cross Road.

Rage was the mecca at that time. You had Colin Favor and Trevor Fung in the main room and Fabio and Grooverider in the upstairs bar. It was such an iconic club night. South London DJs were booming, mate.

Dave Angel was another face emerging from south of the river. Dave was well known around Brixton and when he was released from prison in 1990, he decided to turn his life around. Not long after his release, Dave did a mix of Eurythmics' *Sweet Dreams (Are Made Of This)* as a bootleg and soon word got out that the band wanted to find him. Scared that the band would sue, Dave lay low for a bit until we finally heard that the Eurythmics actually wanted to release it. They loved it.

Dave had some amazing studio equipment and made great techno at the time. He had come out of jail and was really turning his life around. It's not just a lazy cliché; music really did help to save people from a life of crime and punishment.

***

1990, I was booked to play Germany for the first time. Frankfurt blew my mind. We got to the hotel – I was with Bryan Gee and Fabio – and decided to take a walk once we'd dropped our bags off. I knew Fabio from the adventure playground when we were kids and later, through Mendoza's and Car Wash. We would often meet at Mendoza's in Brixton with Dudley, Tank and that lot, so it was great to be out in Frankfurt together. As a first taste of Germany, Frankfurt proved a rather shocking experience and not what we were expecting.

Frankfurt had loads of demonstrations going on when we arrived. I mean loads, including several rival groups of Neo Nazis. We were walking through the town when one of these groups of Nazis clocked us. 'Are they marching towards us?' I asked Bryan.

- 'Looks like it.'
- 'What the fuck?!'

These demonstrators were definitely on to us. Within seconds they were trotting over before running full pelt. I didn't know what to do. Then, just as they were within punching distance, they moved away, shouting, 'Wooooooooooooh!!!' What the fuck! Then they turned and came back at us. They did the same thing again. They didn't touch us, they just shouted, 'Wooooooooooooh!!!' We went down this tunnel under a flyover and somehow got trapped between two sets of Nazis. We just stood there, not knowing what to do. After a while, they departed the scene, but we were more than a little anxious.

Slowly, we made our way into town, not knowing who was who. There were all sorts of different factions and we didn't know who, if any, to trust. It was a weird one.

The gig was at a club called Dorian Gray, which was part of the airport complex. Sven Väth was playing with us that night, although he was known as OFF back then. I remember getting a promo copy of Snap's *I've Got The Power* on that trip and *Radio Babylon* by Meat Beat Manifesto from the people at Logic Records who took us over there.

The party was wicked, but that run-in with the Nazis really put me off Germany for a bit. It was such a crazy day. We just weren't expecting that sort of reception to be honest. Were the Nazis trying to provoke us into reacting? I really don't know.

***

I would often bump into this DJ, Alex Hazzard at various gigs and it wasn't long before he suggested driving me to the gigs rather than us taking separate cars. As we often shared a bill, it made a lot of sense. I remember Alex driving me to this one gig in Stoke when a few of my friends managed to cause a shitload of grief before we'd even got there. Steven Sonny and Simon Wilson were cheeky chappies and always up to no good. They were lunatics, actually. I had known Steven Sonny since I was a kid and he was only five ft. 1, but this guy would fight *anyone*. He was a popular guy, but as I've said, he was a lunatic and would never back down from a fight. We got to the club in Stoke and there were police everywhere. 'It's shut, lads!'
- 'What do you mean it's shut? We've just driven from fucking Brixton to get here.'
- 'What's your name, mate?'
- 'Frost. Jumpin Jack Frost?'
- 'Frost?! It's your mates who started the trouble.'

It turned out that Steven and Simon had taken on the bouncers. It was my mates who got the night shut down. As starts go, my journey up north hadn't started well. I think Alex was wondering what he'd gotten himself into by becoming my driver. Apparently, a bouncer got jiffed in the eye during the fracas. Fuckinell. Trouble was never far away.

Groove and Dynamix were getting me loads of gigs, plus I had the residency at The Fridge (I had quit Mash at this point), but I was desperate for a calmer life outside of work. I came from a good home and had a caring mum and loads of aunts and uncles around. I really wanted didn't want my name getting wrapped around this kind of trouble for ever.

The work I got through Dynamix allowed me to get my own flat in Oval, south London. It was a nice little pad on the edge of the posher bit of Brixton. I was young, on top of the world and wanting to move forward. I also wanted to break from the past.

That Christmas I volunteered at a homeless shelter at Centrepoint on Oxford Street. I wore a Santa hat and gave out breakfasts to the homeless. It felt really good. I felt a need to do it. I didn't tell anyone I was going there and then when I'd finished I went home for Christmas dinner. That morning opened my eyes to a lot of things. I saw the value of life, right there. I will never forget that feeling of helping others on the one day of the year that everyone was with their families. I felt so blessed. My sins were piled high and in some small way I felt that I was eradicating a few of them.

CH. 15

Hardcore

The early days of rave were experimental. A DJ could have played acid house, house and techno all within the same set. There was a freedom there, and many DJs loved that period. Then, as the nineties kicked off, there was a split. Some carried on following the housier, uplifting sounds while others went towards the harder, darker sounds of hardcore. Unlike the early days, you could no longer play a selection of tunes, as club nights were now targeting certain types of ravers for the first time. Telepathy was a much harder, darker night, often plagued with shady characters; the sort of rave I would have played up at, had I not drifted into music.

Hardcore was less worried about image. Hardcore was all about getting on one and it was often ridiculed by the supposedly more sophisticated house community. Most of the younger ravers were drawn to hardcore however as it still had that ravey spirit. Indie kids loved hardcore too, as it crossed genres and boundaries. I guess Prodigy and Altern 8 were great examples of a music that appealed to both the underground and the overground. Hardcore had a lot going for it and when the breakbeats started to appear, many in the community could sense that something very exciting was just around the corner. Producers like Shut Up And Dance, 4hero, Johnny L and our old mucker Tony Thorpe were making music that signalled something much more exciting than pianos and chipmunk vocals. Tony's *Funky Zulu* as The Moody Boys (XL Recordings) was an incredible piece of music which mixed 303s and a funky beat with a dirty sub-bass. I loved Ragga Twins who put a really interesting twist on things too with their reggae/hip-hop injections. Lennie De Ice's *We Are E*, was often played out at early Roasts at Turnmills. Suddenly the rhythm, rather than the melody, was being taken to the fore.

Bryan Gee had been working at Rhythm King (helping out with Outer Rhythm) since 1989; both labels were subsidiaries of Mute. 1991, Outer Rhythm was more strongly associated with Belgium's R&S Records and Warp from Sheffield with their early LFO stuff, than it was straight-up acid or house. LFO's *LFO* was a gamechanger, man. That sub bass changed EVERYTHING.

Bryan got a call one day from this guy Mark Ital who had come up with an act that was inspired by this bass and bleep sound from Leeds and Sheffield. Mark's influences went back to Jah Shaka days and he and his partner Russell came over for a drink with us once, with this young dancer called Mel B. Mark Ital and the Ital Rockers were such an influence and we hooked up with them a lot when Bryan and I played The Voyage in Leeds.

Bryan signed a former punk rocker from New York around this time, called Moby, who was relaunching himself as an electronic artist. Bryan was learning so much about the industry and making so many contacts. He had his ear to the ground and was always putting great new music my way. Bryan released his own track too. *The Magus Project* was a good little tune for his first effort. Bryan was a perfectionist and had a lot of patience when working with other artists. Patience was something I had precious little of. 'Where are the fucking tunes?!'

I was playing on the same bill as bands like The Prodigy at this time. Liam Howlett was such a talent and you could see it even more back then when Maxim, Keith and Leroy were just dancers. Liam would sit behind this bank of technology, driving the entire show. This guy was so young back then, but a real wizard. The dancers added something truly dynamic to their shows and they were very polished and organised. I played alongside Adamski back then too, just as he was making it big. People forget how big he was back then. Number one in the charts, mate. Adamski's vocalist was a complete nobody called Seal, although I hear he went on to do so some stuff as a solo artist.

I was playing a lot of Joey Beltram and R&S techno because once you spotted that horse on a label, you knew you were getting a *tune*. We were at the centre of all that with fresh white labels and acetates popping into my record box every single day. Because of my family connections up in Manchester, I was up at Eastern Bloc all the time getting new tunes. Mike E-Bloc always looked after me and would sort me out with all the white labels and promos from all over Europe including R&S and Amsterdam's Lower East Side Records. Euro techno was starting to take over around this time here. I would often spend the entire day in Eastern Bloc talking to Mike while bagging new tunes to play that night. The dance scene was so different up north and it allowed me access to the cutting edge through armfuls of imports. I was totally committed to this world by now and Eastern Bloc, as well as City Sounds and Blackmarket in London, were my family. I lived and breathed this world.

Having Bryan Gee inside the industry was very useful. I remember him saying that a top award was given to a famous female singer simply as a favour to someone. It was well dodgy and at times a cut-throat world, according to Bryan.

The people at Mute really valued Bryan's opinion, which was great news. People were not only taking notice of Bryan, but me as well. I remember playing T-99's *Anasthasia* – a big banger from Belgium – at some outdoor rave and XL's Nick Halkes came over and demanded to know what it was. 'It's fucking amazing!' he said. Two weeks later he'd signed them to XL Recordings. Nick could sniff out a good tune, as seen when he signed The Prodigy. I remember him frothing at the mouth when he first heard me play T-99 at that rave.

Nick Halkes (XL, Positiva)

"I went to work at City Beat as an A&R and signed Numero Uno by Starlight as my second record and that hit the top ten in the UK, which enabled me to have more juice within the organisation. Then it was suggested that we set up XL Recordings to focus more on the burgeoning underground scene. My role then, was looking for records to sign. So, my relationship with Frost changed as I went from wanting him to play my records, to seeing him as a source of future signings.

The early days of XL I had a blank piece of paper with no signings to my name and so I was always on the hunt for the good stuff. If there was anything Frost supported heavily, then I would be interested in it. My radar was up right across the pirates and club DJs to get to the records they were playing that I thought had potential to get bigger. That was my focus. So, I would pop up on stage or in the DJ booth

Big, Bad & Heavy

demanding to know what it was Frost had just played. I was out and about on the scene during those buoyant and exciting times, when there were interesting events kicking off left, right and centre, every night of the week.

Frost was at the front end of XL, as we were carving out our niche and was one of the key guys we'd look to when finding new records. We would be hearing what he was playing as he was leading the scene culturally and we wanted to reflect that by identifying records that could help shape the label. Records that could stand the test of time, rather than merely DJ tracks. I wanted stuff that went beyond being a 'banger' and The Prodigy were the biggest act to come out of that rave culture. They had killer tracks that turned into something truly phenomenal and I still manage Liam Howlett to this day. A lot of those acts and records were built on the back of DJ support; DJs like Frost."

***

Sterns at Worthing on the south coast was a party and a half. They called Sterns 'the house on the hill'. A lovely old mansion sat on top of this hill, run by a guy called Mensa, you would go down the stairs and into the basement. Everyone wanted to be down there. It was euphoric, man. Sterns was one of my favourite places ever, which had over 25,000 members at its peak. Mensa was a cool guy. I remember he invited us over to Canada with him in '91. Canada? Yes! This was next-level shit.

So, I joined Mikee B from Top Buzz, Ellis Dee and a few others on that trip to Toronto. Mikee B had just come out of jail and this was one of his first gigs since his release. Mikee had real history in this scene going back to Funky Express and rare groove. Mikee had reinvented himself as part of the DJ/MC outfit Top Buzz with Jason K and Mad P. Top Buzz were massive at the time.

This party in Canada was financed by a kid who had just won the Lottery and he didn't have a clue, mate. It was meant to be Canada's first big rave, but no fucker turned up. I remember this dude kept giving us presents. 'You want a CD Walkman? There you go, have one!'

We played this party and it was shit, then, when it was time to go and get paid, he started coming out with all this bullshit. Because the party had been a disaster, we weren't going to get paid. Can you believe that? Suddenly, the bad boy returned...

Hardcore

We were in his hotel room and I just saw red. I went fucking insane. 'What do you mean, we're not getting paid?! You're a fucking lottery winner! I'm getting fucking paid, mate!'

- 'But we didn't make any money!' he pleaded.

I hit him over the head with a chair. I totally lost it, I have to say. I kicked him, whacked him and eventually he agreed to pay us. I marched him down to the ATM and he paid us all. Cheeky fucker. I wasn't having that. It was only after that, while sitting in the departure lounge that I really considered what could have happened as a result of my behaviour. I could have been arrested for that. I could have been FUCKED! I could have caused some serious damage.

The trip to Toronto wasn't a complete disaster, though, as I got to see my aunt Angela and cousins Brenda, Gloria and Peter while we were there. So, thanks to Mensa for that. Sadly, Mensa died in a car accident not long after that trip. I miss you fella.

Rimini, Italy was a great trip. I flew to Rimini with Frankie Valentine, who had been around for quite a few years already. Rimini was amazing. A beautiful, shimmering holiday destination with gorgeous beaches and people; I was hooked. The architecture was breath-taking and I spent hours walking around with Frankie, staring up at the old buildings. Frankie had been loads of times before and was happy to show me around. Frankie was a really forward-thinking, futuristic DJ and I learned so much from him. I was in my element.

The Cocorico Club was built into the side of a mountain and the whole club was made from crystal. Then, when the sun came up behind you, the wall dazzled like a waterfall. It was the most beautiful club I had ever played in.

We went to an after-party at a different club after and it was interesting to see the police getting paid a backhander when they called at the club at about 9am to 'shut it down'. Italy, eh?

That trip saw me changing my image a bit too. I bought a pair of Police sunglasses while I was out there as I started to dress up a little. I started to enjoy having jewellery, dark glasses and looking *good*. I had started mixing with different people now and wanted to be treated with respect. I started shopping at Browns on Bond Street and places like that, which seemed to fit in well with trips to Italy and the like.

We went to Pisa to fly home and I had to go and see the leaning tower. I was gobsmacked. I nearly fell over when I saw that fucker. I will never forget that moment, when I turned a corner to see that wonky tower. This was something I had only ever seen in a book, and yet here I was being paid to play music *and* go sightseeing in Italy. It was such a memorable trip.

Although foreign trips were picking up, it was the UK that paid my way. Weekends were spent driving up and down the country, playing multiple gigs virtually every night.

Alex Hazzard

"A school friend of mine was putting on these fantastic nights called Zen at the Slough Centre and Chris introduced me to Frost one New Year's Eve. We stayed in touch from that day forward as we played many of the same gigs. I was a resident DJ at Reincarnation for 691 in Herne Bay, Kent. 691 was a basic set up: two decks and a mixer on a table.

Frost was with this Groove Connection agency set up by Sarah Sandy and he started to get me involved. I was more of an independent really, but as we were playing similar parties and travelling separately, I suggested I pick him up. Within no time, I was Frost's driver.

I had this old-school VW Beetle and we were hammering around the country in this thing. Frost was squeezed into the passenger seat with Bryan in the back and he was not a small bloke. Sometimes there were others. I would leave Egham in Surrey and then pick the boys up in Brixton and off we went.

We would often hit three venues in one evening, before heading back down south. It was hard work. For me. They just sat back and enjoyed the ride.

I remember stopping at a service station one morning to get some pop. We had run out of weed and the boys wanted more. I was queuing up to pay for the petrol when I started talking to this big bald guy, in a green bomber jacket and DM boots. I was totally buzzed. I leant across and said, 'Excuse me, but have you got any puff?'

- *'Yeah mate, no problem.'*

I followed him round to this coach and that was when I realised who he was. It was Buster Bloodvessel from Bad Manners. His Winnebago was full of his band and roadies and so he broke us off a big lump of dope and gave it to us. Nice one!

I went back to the car and told the lads. 'No fucking way! I know him,' said Frost. 'I met him in Iceland.' So, we all went back to their coach and had a catch up. Big hugs and laughs in the middle of nowhere.

There were so many parties it was ridiculous: Sheffield, Leeds, Manchester, often all in one night. Lots of mileage and stress put upon me and this Beetle, but I could stay up all night back then. We used to stop at this rave in Sheffield if we were up north called CJs. Now, that place was an after-party and it always got really messy there.

We were often only at these gigs for an hour or so. Then you'd find the promoter, get paid and you were off again. 8-10 hours in a car on a Friday and Saturday night. This is what we did, but it soon became a chore after a while. Well, for me it did."

CH. 16

Black Man In The Royal Ulster Hall

Glen Molloy

"When Nigel came to Belfast, it was probably the first time that many people here had seen a black guy, aside from those serving in the Army. Nigel was not the norm, do you know what I'm sayin'? Forget the Clash's White Man In Hammersmith Palais and think of Black Man In The Royal Ulster Hall.

Belfast was a very closed-in society; not many outsiders. If anyone was out of the norm they were probably a soldier. I knew that Frost came from Brixton, but this was still a culture shock even for him on that first visit.

I was putting on nights at the Royal Ulster Hall at a time when many DJs wouldn't come to Belfast. It was a scary time and so Frost went down in folklore as one of the few who was actually prepared to play out here.

This was the time of the Army, armed police and paramilitaries. We had army checkpoints, helicopters and tanks. We had executions and bombs. A man tends to be quite brave until he has a gun pointed at him. Nigel was right in the thick of it and must have been shitting himself that first time.

Belfast wasn't really the same as a mainland city; we didn't have things like McDonalds or the latest toys or football kits when we were kids. It was a bit backward. But when it came to violence, we excelled. So, getting a rave DJ from London to play there was a big thing for us.

The atmosphere at these raves was immense. Frost came out with Moby who did a one-off appearance. Moby didn't do too many live things after that, but that night was a big, big, big night!

The rave scene in Belfast saw the everyday tensions transferred into positive energy inside the raves. Outside there could be a bomb scare or a shooting, but inside it was peace, love and unity. I played a conference room in a hotel one time and the very next day it blew up!

The atmosphere at these raves was ridiculous; frenzied. E came along and everyone was hugging each other from both sides of town. Blokes were meeting girls in secret who lived on the opposite sides of the tracks. I would shit myself if I was seeing a girl in a nationalist area. You could get executed for that.

The days before the paramilitaries got involved in raves were electric. You could ask the police where the raves were in the early days as they didn't know what they were. Ha ha! Later on, police would always search you at these nights, looking for drugs and guns. There would have been guns at all these raves. Also, people would be monitoring what their enemies were up to and reprisals could be taken. One of my friends got murdered by the IRA. They took him away and subjected him to two days of torture. He was found on derelict land in a half-moon lake with bullet holes in his head. It was intense.

The raves were an escape for us. We had raves up in the mountains during the summer although sometimes you got pulled out of your car by maniac soldiers, many of whom were paranoid. There was a joyriding epidemic around the time of rave and half the cars outside these parties in the mountains, were stolen. When you came out at the end they were often on fire.

Belfast was an oppressive city for everybody whether you were republican or loyalist. People escaped from the Troubles for a short period of time at the weekend and then back to work on Monday. Back to the same old shite again.

There was a dangerous contradiction at raves. It was hands in the air on a Saturday night and yet 3-4 days later, you could get your door kicked in by a man in a balaclava. It was a war zone. Belfast is a rough town anyway. You soon get a punch in the head if you speak out of turn here. Things were heavy, but you just got on with it. I lost 11 friends and family."

I have a bit of a love affair with Belfast. This was Belfast *back then*. The Troubles and all that. I don't know whether growing up on the streets of Brixton had toughened me up to a point where I felt at home there or not, but I have been back so many times since that first trip.

Hell at The Fridge was going from strength to strength. They got people like Frankie Bones in from New York and the club was building up a real reputation. Dynamix and Groove Connection were really working for me too. I remember getting that call asking me to play Belfast for the first time. 'Belfast?! Fuckinell!'

We flew into Belfast airport, which was quite a distance away from the city. This was a city where the security started up once you'd *left* the airport. Seeing those armed soldiers for the first time, threw me a little. This was a war zone.

We drove through these lovely open green spaces and golf courses until we hit the city itself. Checkpoint after checkpoint and tanks and armoured personnel carriers were everywhere. Seeing those giant murals that you see on the news, with paramilitaries wearing balaclavas and holding machine guns, was quite chilling. I don't mind admitting that. It was a shock to the system. That first trip had me shitting it a bit, but I just puffed out my chest and once I'd checked into the hotel, I went for a stroll. I didn't really attract too much attention, which was surprising, considering that I must have been one of the few black men over there, aside from those serving with the British Army. Everywhere you looked were soldiers guarding street corners with machine guns and checkpoints were stationed at the end of all the city centre streets.

The venue was The Royal Ulster Hall; a massive Victorian theatre. It was very impressive. It was Moby and me, at that first party. I was booked by this guy Gareth from Belfast whose family ran a chain of bookies over there. He was chuffed to get Moby and me. Moby had just released *Go* I think. I spoke to him a little, but we were very different people. He was quite shy. I don't know what he made of Belfast, do you know what I mean?

The vibe at the party was amazing, it was like the whole city – Protestant and Catholic – was letting off steam in there. They said I was one of the first English DJs to play the Ulster Hall. It was an honour, either way and that night was apparently considered a legendary party in the history of Belfast rave. The vibe and love I got from the people there was wonderful and it holds a special place in my heart.

Big, Bad & Heavy

Steve Lopresti

"I first bumped into Nigel in the early nineties. I was working in the Italian rave scene. My mum's English and so I was the guy who would deal with the British DJs who came to play. I was also busy doing promotional work for labels over there. I would often be the one to pick Nigel up at the airport in Rome.

Frost was invited because he was on the flyers of all the big raves in England. He was a very positive person and nothing ever troubled him, even though he was in another country and didn't speak the language. He was not fazed by that at all and was very accommodating, when many were demanding.

When he played in Rome he had these acetates; something we just hadn't seen before. One of them had someone saying his name, over and over and he started scratching it. Our mouths were wide open. We'd never seen anything like it. He had this unique way of reacting to the crowd who truly loved him.

In Rome, we liked the Detroit techno and so you'd get a bit of Richie Hawtin and Plus 8. We would also invite British acts like Nightmares On Wax and Adamski. Frost was popular over there too.

I got to know Frost quite well over the years and he eventually hooked me up with Dan in Belfast, who owned Underground Records on Queen Street. Dan needed someone to take the shop to the next level with imports etc. as well as speaking to booking agents for raves. I went over, having been introduced by Frost and stayed for a couple of years.

Belfast was quite a hairy place to live with the entire centre of town cordoned off with checkpoints everywhere.

I remember Frost coming to play the Ulster Hall, which was a fantastic venue. We had to be out of there by 4am on a Saturday morning as they had these big Protestant gatherings there on the Sabbath and so you couldn't have a party going on into Sunday, 'the day of rest'. So, Friday was the night.

The Royal Ulster Hall had the more bouncy, bouncy stuff, while David Holmes hosted the Sugar Shack nights at the Art College, playing more arty/housey stuff. They had the better girls. Ha ha. We had men in hi-vis jackets waving glow-sticks.

Ulster Hall loved the emerging German and Belgian sounds of people like Frank De Wulf and the Mentasm stuff of New York's Joey

Beltram. Frost played what the ravers wanted and they lapped it up. This was quite a hard crowd to please, believe me. To be honest, it was getting a bit silly by the end, with this bouncy, high-bpm stuff and speeded-up lyrics, but the initial wave of hardcore was immense."

Belfast was a tough town, though, yeah? There was something in the air. I came from Brixton, which could be a bad place, but Belfast could be scary. You could cut the tension with a knife.

There was one party I did in Ireland where a rumour was circling around that I'd been arrested. I hadn't, but that didn't stop 30 people going down to the police station to try and bail me out. I will never forget that kindness.

I remember playing Circus Circus one time and, I'm not naming names, but they said they had to move me from my hotel that night. I didn't want to move and wondered why they were fucking me about. 'You have to move out of the hotel!' they demanded. The next day, the hotel was blown up. Prince from Brixton was with me and we were both like, 'Fuuuuuuuuck!!!' Make of that what you will.

MC Magika

"I used to see Frost playing the M25 events and nights in and around Birmingham, my home town. He played the Midlands a lot: Quest (Birmingham) and Amnesia at The Eclipse (Coventry) etc. Although, I'd seen him around, I had never actually spoken to him. Then I got asked to be his MC on a trip to Belfast.

I was bloody terrified to be honest. You just associated Belfast with bombs, terrorists and tanks. I grew up in Birmingham, which could be rough, but it wasn't bloody Belfast. Ha ha. I was counting down the days if I'm being honest. I was very, very nervous.

I flew out of Birmingham on my own; I was to meet Nigel at the hotel. I was struck by all the security outside of the airport. That did nothing to calm my nerves I can tell you. I didn't feel good about this at all.

We drove past the murals of the men in balaclavas with machine guns and it was dawning on me again. Why the fuck had I agreed to this?

I checked into the hotel and was scared of leaving my room. I kept walking up to the window and would look out, quickly, before walking away again. It was a challenge to see what I could spot during the few seconds I was brave enough to peep out. Every time I looked out, I saw soldiers and tanks. I was so nervous I ran up a £144 telephone phone bill, because I kept ringing home.

Then, later that evening, there was a bang at the door and in walked Nigel. Nigel didn't seem fazed at all. 'Don't worry, man' he said, 'I know people here. It's cool, yeah?' I don't know if it was his upbringing or not, but Nigel just marched around that town. I couldn't believe it. I felt safe with him there. We walked to the nearest shop and on the doorstep was a soldier with a gun pointing up in the air. Fucking hell, mate. We bought some drinks and went back to the hotel. 'You OK, pal? You seemed a bit nervous there...'

- 'I am a little bit nervous, yeah.'
- 'Don't worry, next door is the British Opera House; the most bombed building in Belfast.'
- 'What?! You need to move me! What the fuck?!'

Frost was a lifesaver actually. If I'd been on a sinking boat and Frost had said he would walk on water to save us, I would have believed him.

We then went on another walk up to the Shankhill Road. I started bricking it again. Nigel walked up there like it was Brixton, you know. Then we saw this mob of young men and I thought we were done for. Fucked. The next minute, they're hugging him. Thank fuck!

I remember soldiers asking him where he was going and Frost would say, 'Why?'

- 'You're out of your jurisdiction?'
- 'Rah, going for a walk innit? We can go where we like.'

I asked Nigel why they were so bothered by us and he said, 'Well, it's a bad neighbourhood.'

'Well, why didn't you tell me?!' I was following him around like he was the Piped Piper. You see, he was very comfortable in himself and I think the locals respected him for it.

This gig was in the middle of nowhere. The car journey there was like a scene from a gangster film. We were driven far, far out of town and I thought, 'This ain't no rave. Where are we going?' It was so desolate and I couldn't see any street lights. We were in the middle of no man's land. I thought we were being taken off to be executed.

Nigel could see I was shitting it and so he nudged me. 'You gotta have some Lucozade, mate.'

- 'Lucozade? That's not going to help right now, Nigel!'

It turned out that this party was organised by some paramilitaries. One guy said to me, 'You're safe here.' I thought, 'Well if I'm not safe here, where am I safe?' Once the rave started I finally calmed down.

On the drive back we were stopped so many times at checkpoints. 'What are you doing here, lads?'

I missed my flight home the next day and thought, 'Fucking great!' Here I was, 18 and on my own in a conflict zone. I have never been happier than when I realised Nigel had missed his flight too. 'You're happy, aren't you?' he laughed.

Nigel was telling me about some guy he was speaking to at the rave who had done some 'missions'; one of which, was knee-capping a drug dealer or something. I really didn't want to be hearing these stories to be honest. That said, playing Belfast with Frost was something I would never, ever forget!"

CH. 17

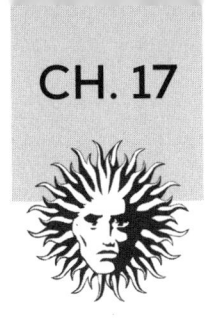

The Ghosts Of Athens

I knocked out another line while sitting on this ancient stone. The sun had disappeared hours ago, but it was still warm. It must have been about 3am. I could hear the city murmuring below. I wiped my nose and went back inside the Acropolis. I was looking for ghosts. I think I'd lost a piece of my mind amongst those ancient ruins. I can't really explain it.

It was the summer of 1992, and I had been in Greece for a long weekend, playing Athens as well as some parties on Mykonos and Paros. I had really enjoyed the vibes out there, but by the time I got back to Athens I was feeling tired and had started on the coke.

The cocaine in Greece was good; so clean and pure. I'd been on a right session when I grabbed my moped and rode to the top of the hill. The city was noisy and smelly. Sitting high up, overlooking the town, I could see the smog above the streetlamps. Athens got so congested by traffic that depending on your licence plate, you were restricted to going into town on your moped or in your car on certain days of the week.

I was buzzing. I got it into my head that I wanted to look for ghosts. What the fuck?! This seemed perfectly normal to me that evening. Yeah, let's go to the Acropolis and look for ghosts. They don't warn you about this in drug prevention programs. 'Don't do cocaine, you'll end up hunting for dead souls!'

I think I had just seen *Clash Of The Titans* or something because I had this idea that I would find some spooky shit up there. So, I hopped over this little fence and started exploring this ancient temple, whilst puffing away on my spliff.

I'm normally scared of ghosts and spooky stuff like that, but on this particular evening I was determined to find something. I walked around, staring at the ancient columns. This place had history! I racked up another line. My head was buzzing like a pinball machine. Every time I looked up at the sky I stumbled forward and back. I was off my fucking nut, mate. What the fuck?!

I didn't find any ghosts, but my head was full of bats or something and realising that I had better get some sleep, I left the crumbling stones and pillars and went back to the hotel. There were many moments like that back then. It was while sitting in the Acropolis that it occurred to me just how far I'd come since those days back in Brixton, popping chains and selling Oxo cubes just to get by. Somewhere, up there among those ancient ruins, you might, if you're lucky, find a little piece of my mind. What the fuck?!

CH. 18

The Book Of Love

Coventry has an important place in rave history. I remember getting booked to play this club in Coventry called The Eclipse, which was such an iconic spot. All the big names played The Eclipse and this guy Sasha was breaking through there back then. I remember girls turning up at 5.30am just to see Sasha who wouldn't usually come on until 6am. They were fine-looking girls, too; all dressed up to the nines. I just couldn't believe it. 'Who the fuck is this Sasha?! What's going on?' Stuart Reid and Barry Edwards ran The Eclipse and it was just one of those places. A legendary spot.

The Eclipse did great tape-packs of their nights, which provided really good exposure for people like myself and I became a member of the family over time. I was really good friends with legendary Coventry DJ and producer Doc Scott and his missus Sarah through Amnesia House, which hosted Graeme Park, Greg Wilson, Bryan Gee, Daz Willot, Stu Allan, Ratpack and loads more. The Eclipse was rammed most nights, but even when quiet they kept it open. It was a great club. Amnesia House eventually moved to another Coventry club The Edge.

Amnesia was a massive name in the rave game, having set up one of the first legal club raves Sky Blue Connection in Coventry in 1990, eventually spreading out all over the Midlands and beyond. One of the first big parties I played in the Midlands was for Amnesia House at Donington Park, Leicestershire in 1991. There must have been 8,000 people there to see a very strong line-up that included The Prodigy, Altern 8 and Doc Scott. My MC that night was Bassman and he was immense. The only downside was that the evening was plagued by sound problems and Amnesia eventually stopped using the famous racetrack.

The summer of '92, I was booked to play Amnesia House's The Book Of Love. Organised by bosses Micky Lynus and his brother Bambam and fellow siblings Neville Fivey and Keiran, I was driven to the Book Of Love by another of my drivers, Gary Glimmer. I grew up with Gary. In fact, I think I tried to rob Gary, the very first time I met him. I was walking round with Tanya who was in one of those slings around my chest, when I saw this skinny white Irish kid. Ha ha. We became friends a little later down the line. I'm not sure if he knew it was me who tried to sting him. I remember getting locked out of my house once and Gary's dad turned up with a ladder. Gary was from an Irish family and I loved them. He was a bit of a lunatic, though. A real handful.

We'd already been up north to Newcastle and then down to Doncaster before hitting Brafield Speedway Stadium in Northampton for the Book Of Love. The Doncaster Warehouse was one of my favourite clubs. I remember the crowd were wearing masks and were covered in Vicks, trying to increase the rush of their Es.

By the time we got to Northampton, there were about 7,000 people at the Book Of Love. It was a barmy summer's night and the vibes were off the chart. Amnesia parties were always special. The stand-out moment of this particular rave was when promoter Micky Lynus got married on stage by a vicar in front of thousands of ravers. It was fucking insane. Grooverider played the role of father of the bride and Carl Cox and Fabio were there on stage. It was amazing, believe me. One of the those special moments. The whole Amnesia House family was there to see Mickey (RIP) get married. Mickey Lynus was a one-off.

Nev (Amnesia House)

"The Book of Love was a memorable day in the history of Amnesia House. 'I want to get married on stage, in front of 7,000 people at an open-air rave,' said my business partner Mickey Lynus.
   -   'Yeah, alright then.'
Frost played that day at Brafield and Grooverider played the father of the bride and gave Mickey's missus away. It was a mad, mad night, but blinding. We had Carl Cox, Top Buzz, The Prodigy, Fabio and

Grooverider there. Mickey is no longer with us, sadly, but that night will never be forgotten. It was fucking mad, mate!"

***

I was round this girl's flat in Notting Hill one night, due to play a club on Harrow Road, which was also in west London. We were lying in bed when I decided to get up to go play my set. 'Don't go!' she begged. 'I think something bad is going to happen!' Normally, I would have said, 'Behave! I've got to work,' but this night seemed different. Don't ask me why. Anyway,
 this girl really didn't want me to go. For some reason, I said, 'OK' and missed the party. It was very unlike me. I always made the gig. The next morning, I put the TV on. It was the local news: 'There was a police raid at a club on Harrow Road last night...' There was footage of people lying face down in the street as police emptied the club. How weird was that? 'I told you I had a feeling,' she piped up. Considering the growing hostility towards raves from the government, police and tabloid press I'm amazed I hadn't been involved in a raid up until that point. They were happening, but I just about managed to swerve most of them.

Although my first visit to Germany had been a weird one, having come face to face with the Neo Nazis, I would equally never forget my next date there.

The Tresor (meaning 'bank' in German) was a club in the financial district of Berlin. It was Adolf Hitler's old bank apparently, and at one time was full of plundered gold. You went down these steps into this vault. It was so cold in there, there were stalactites hanging from the ceiling. It was real eerie. This was where Hitler kept all of his wealth apparently and it freaked me out I'm telling you. It was like a location for a horror film. Or worse. There was a dungeon down there and iron bars around the DJ booth. Safe deposit drawers were everywhere in the vault. I would not have been surprised if a group of vampires had turned up, looking for some dinner. Very odd. Just the thought that Hitler had presumably walked across that floor, was very sobering.

During my set, this geezer DJ Rocky kept touching my arse. Now, I was trying to control my temper at this point, yeah, but I was getting really fucking angry. 'What the fuck?!' I was trying to be diplomatic, but had to tell him in the end. 'Look, I'm not gay, alright?! Leave my arse alone!' I wanted to punch him in the face, to be honest, but being a DJ whose name was getting known, all around the world now, I didn't want to jeopardise my reputation. Mind you if I hadn't have said anything maybe I would have had quite a different rep.

Set over, I decided to have a walk around Berlin. I was suddenly hit by the noise. There were fireworks going off everywhere. The streets were mobbed. It was the anniversary of the Wall coming down and people were going fucking crazy. It was so surreal. Five minutes before I'd been down in Hitler's vault, now I was sauntering over into the old East Germany for a look-see. You could still see the differences between east and west, alright, even though it had been three years since the Wall came down. East Berlin looked like the seventies, whereas the western sector of the city looked very modern and cosmopolitan. There were still little bits of the wall left and so I grabbed a few rocks and stuck them in my record box to take home. The air was thick with firework smoke and there were people everywhere, getting pissed. It was so surreal imagining what their lives must have been like just a few years earlier. How must it have felt to see that wall go up, never mind come down? Imagine the bulldozers knocking that thing to shit... This was a wall that went up in the middle of the night as the people of Berlin slept. A wall that divided a city and so many families and loved ones. I spent most of that night reflecting on what these people must have gone through. I couldn't quite comprehend it.

I gave Ganga that piece of the Berlin Wall when I got home and she pushed it back at me as if it was possessed. 'That's the devil's work!' she informed me. 'Get it away from me! I don't want it in the house!' I took me ages to stop thinking about Berlin. It had a real effect on me.

CH. 19

Jungle

The music definitely appeared a long while before the name. The music and its vibe just crept into the scene especially when MCs started to feature more in hardcore dance. You could hear the start of jungle in tracks like *A New Direction* by Wax Doctor, *Livin' In Darkness* by Top Buzz and *What Have You Done* by One Tribe (featuring Gem), produced by George Kelly. I remember the great Grooverider owning the dancefloor at Rage with Naz AKA Naz's *It's Started Again*. I was digging out tunes by Satin Storm, Krome & Time and loved the gamechanger *Up Tempo* by Tronik House, which came out of Detroit.

Rebel MC was right there at the start and he was dropping the term 'junglist' in reference to citizens of a certain borough in Kingston, Jamaica. There has been much debate as to the first jungle single and many tunes have been heralded as the original and we could be here all day with that, so let's just say that there are many who can claim that mantle. So, what was jungle?

Jungle was influenced by reggae and many early tunes were essentially Jamaican tracks that had been sped up and mixed, but there was more to this scene than that. The 'Amen break' drum fill from the Winston's 1969 track *Amen Brother* that typified so much jungle and drum and bass had also appeared in some eighties' hip hop, as well as hardcore techno. The *Amen* break is the most sampled piece of music in history and my DJ friend and sometime driver Alex Hazzard was one of the first to sample the entire break. Most jungle releases had that technological side of dance too, born as it was from old skool.

So, as one path splintered off from hardcore into happy hardcore, the other led us to the dark side: jungle.

Of course, I was drawn to jungle. I was a reggae boy and had grown up around sound systems and chatting on the mic. When the dance scene splintered, there was no doubt which camp I was in. I was deep into the jungle, mate. For many, jungle was Marmite. You either got it or you didn't. Very few people had a passing interest in it. You either loved it or you hated it. Jungle was intrinsically linked to black culture and the mood of it pushed a lot of white folk away, back into house, techno or happy hardcore. But for those who loved it, jungle was heaven, mate. Of course, for a while, it was a part of rave and the beats would come in and out of sets, but by 1992 it was established as a scene, in and of itself. Acts like Shut Up And Dance, DJ Hype, Micky Finn and Johnny Jungle (Pascal) and many more had been putting out proto-jungle tracks as far back as 1990. I loved *Bang The Party* by Kid Bachelor and the Congo drum vibe to this music. The reggae vocals gave this music that jungle edge. Now it had breaks too and the Reinforced boys really developed that jungle sound and pushed it on loads with intricate productions and melodic riffs that we all fell in love with. I loved A Guy Called Gerald's *28 Gun Bad Boy* too and the records put out on Mark X's Kemet label. Kemet was based in Tottenham, Congo Natty's neighbourhood and between them, they raised black consciousness in jungle music. The boys at Reinforced Records, Moving Shadow and Suburban Base were also key to this growing movement. Club nights such as Telepathy were now solely jungle nights, as was Roast and AWOL (A Way Of Life) in Angel, Islington. 1992 saw the first Jungle Fever, put on by the guys at the influential London pirate Kool FM. Jungle MCs were now established with Moose, Flux, Navigator and the incredible Stevie Hyper D, working alongside us DJs. AWOL wanted me to be a resident there, but they expected all their DJs to remain exclusive to the club on the nights they played, and I was used to doing 2-3 a night and so I passed on that one.

The vibes at these events were different to the old-skool raves. The audience was now predominantly black, even though a fair few jungle acts and DJs were white. The vibes at these dances could get a little rough and boisterous, just like the music. I loved it, man. I fucking loved it. It was a link straight back to my sound system days as a box boy. For many black kids, jungle was the moment when rave finally made sense. This was speaking to *them*.

Tippa Irie

"There were some from the reggae community who didn't take jungle seriously, but I did and Nigel was at the forefront of this new scene. As an artist it's important to keep your eyes and ears to the ground, to see what's going on, especially if you want to be a part of something unique and that's what Nigel did. He had a genuine passion for what he was doing and it showed."

A massive moment in dance history occurred at Rage (at Heaven) when Fabio and Grooverider eventually graduated into the main room during the summer of 1992. That was big news. The second circle of rave was starting to take control from the old guard. That was how it felt. We knew this community was expanding and shifting. For me? Jungle. Every time. Happy hardcore was not my thing at all and I wasn't a house DJ and so I was seeking out all the latest tunes. I was deep into the jungle.

Fabio

"I was playing Rage with Grooverider when I first started to feel the jungle coming through. We started upstairs at Heaven, in the bar area, playing Belgian techno and all that. Then this mad techno started to give way to this more urban music, with mad breakbeats going off; Lennie De Ice's We Are E and tracks like that. Techno with breakbeats that were speeding up. It was a frantic sound. It went off in a different way to house. It was more energetic and people were properly havin' it. Then a few jungle tunes came out on Ibiza Records, Living Dream and Reinforced. Jungle came from that moment I guess. You had people like Slipmatt, Dougal, Vibes, SL2 and that lot staying with the hardcore, while we – Grooverider, Rebel MC, Jumpin Jack Frost and Bryan Gee – followed the jungle. Jungle was darker, more serious, yet warmer, being in many ways a tribute to reggae and dub.

When they decided to move us into the main room, at Rage, it felt like jungle had moved on a notch. It felt validated as a scene with many new nights popping up to play these tunes at. Older parties were now having to choose which way to go. Many nights now had specific music playing in certain rooms of clubs. The old-skool mix was being abandoned.

Jungle had serious vibes and there were a few hairy moments when it kicked off. There were a number of incidents where gangsters were trying to rob promoters and there were of course gang-related problems too. You would often hear gunshots being fired, but for whatever reason it made you feel alive. I was attracted to the danger. But make no bones about it, they were dangerous times back then.

I remember playing the Wax Club, which was on a Hackney estate and believe me, this place should have been designated a no-go zone. This was gangster-ville. I walked in and it was grimy, man. I have kids now, and there is no way on earth I would play a place like that now. No way! Not a chance. But we were very young.

Everyone played Telepathy at Marshgate Lane. Groove and I, Frost and Gee, DJ Ron; we all played it. The night I will never forget was when DJ Rap played there. Now, this girl was gorgeous – a former glamour model – and white. This club was rough and black. Rap was the only white person in there. As soon as she walked through the door, all eyes fell on her. I took her to one side and said, 'Did you come here by yourself?'

- 'Yeah, so…?'
- 'Are you sure about this?'
- 'Course I am.'
- 'Wow! You are so brave.'

Now, some guy had OD-ed on the dancefloor. He had collapsed and, sadly, died after having a fit. They had just cleared his body from the floor when Rap, in such a rush to get started, took to the decks. The first track she played, after this dead body had been shifted? Mr Kirk's Nightmare. Fuck me, what a faux pas. This was a tune that featured a telephone conversation between a police officer and a father, whose son had just died from a drug overdose. First my jaw dropped, followed by my head, which entered my hands. I tried to get her attention, but she didn't see me. My god."

This was a transitional time, from techno to breakbeats. One path showed jungle, the other happy hardcore. As there was no time-stretching equipment back then I just couldn't get on with the chipmunk vocals and all that. I was following the breaks. However, people were starting to use Akai 9500s, 1000s, 3000s and then EMU and so the sound was definitely developing from those sometimes very basic jungle tracks and although some of it was very, very good, a decent amount of it was shit. Bryan Gee was making major waves too with his A&R role at Outer Rhythm who were releasing the most amazing music.

Rage at Heaven was the place to be in the West End at that point. I distinctly remember Goldie being there with DJs Kemistry and Storm. Goldie was mad for the music, having been introduced to the scene by his girlfriend Kemi (Kemistry) after he moved to London from Miami. It took him a while to get used to this breakbeat-driven scene, apparently, but once he'd locked in, he stayed in. It was through Kemi that Goldie met the Reinforced boys Dennis 'Dego' McFarlane and Mark 'Marc Mac' Clair who had been making music as 4hero. Graf legend Goldie ended up doing some of his awesome artwork for Reinforced and helped sign a few acts to the label that went on to inspire so much.

Jayne Conneely (Storm)

"I remember the first time Kemi and I met Nigel. The South Bank show had decided to make a new version called The Young South Bank Show featuring underground youth culture and Kemi and I were asked to come along to be interviewed. We also played out a new version of the theme tune.

When we arrived, we were introduced to Judge Jules and Jumpin Jack Frost. We were so excited to meet Jumpin Jack Frost as he'd been one of our heroes and we'd heard him play many times as ravers. Kemi and I kept nudging each other, we were so happy."

Goldie would whistle through his gold-plated teeth during those nights at Rage and danced like a mad man. You just knew that this man was an artist when *Terminator* dropped. *Terminator* was a jungle anthem recorded by Goldie under the name Metalheadz in 1992 (he also recorded under the alias Rufige Kru). Goldie's *Terminator* marked the moment jungle started to evolve through time stretching which gave it its futuristic sound. That tune brought me to my knees. Goldie's use of that beatbox sound formed the core of that powerful masterpiece. We slowly became friends around that time. Goldie had something special and this *Terminator* track was a game changer and through its success, he became a real force in jungle. Woah! That tune was on another level. My god, people were shocked when they heard *Terminator*. I remember hearing a certain record executive lost his job because he'd had the opportunity to sign Goldie, but passed it up.

I first met Goldie at Rage and he was a proper character. Very loud and very animated, Goldie just let the music flow through him. The vibes just swept him up.

Fabio and Grooverider were continuing to boss the main room at Rage, having graduated from the bar and so this was an exciting time for jungle. Jungle was becoming more forward thinking as the breaks evolved into the music. Labels like Reinforced were releasing some really good tunes.

Telepathy started in 1990 at Marshgate Lane, Stratford, east London and it was an important night. Telepathy entered jungle folklore from the off as it became a haven for those wanting something a little darker than rave. Just like Rage, you had to be there every week and Telepathy was a weekend spot. Lots of DJs cut their teeth at Telepathy and it was a busy night. I played there one New Year's Eve and there was a really odd vibe there. It was grim, mate. I found out later that someone had died. It was a terrible atmosphere.

I loved playing Telepathy with Richie Fingers, Ratpack and Randall. Even if you were playing up north, you still made sure you got back down into town to play the last spot at Telepathy. I met this girl Georgia at Telepathy and I first started properly taking drugs with her. I had dabbled before, but now I was increasing my intake. Georgia and her friend Jill were known as Buzzing Bees 1 and 2. Jill had some decks and she often played some tunes back at hers once we'd left Telepathy.

I never really got into E, but I took my first one with Georgia and Jill at Raindance (Jenkins Lane). It was my birthday and I had just finished a back-to-back with Fabio. I took this half a pill and after an hour or so, everything went fluffy and light. I remember Delroy said, 'You look happy!' I don't think Delroy and Prince had ever seen me like this before. I was known for being a bit moody, but this particular evening, I was feeling so happy and was jumping around all over the place.

I had also started hooking up with this girl Lisa in Leicester around then too. Whenever I played up north, I bumped into her. She was beautiful and she loved to party. There was never a shortage of women.

Telepathy and Rage were essential to the jungle community. Thursday night was Rage and once you'd finished at Rage, lots of people would head for Steppers in Brixton. Rage finished at 4am and Steppers – originally an old reggae club – would open at 5am, playing on until midday. Tony and Louise would entertain all those souls who didn't want to go home. Not just yet. Jungle was creating a buzz.

***

1992 saw me finally deal with my father. My dad Frankie was an alcoholic and had been for some time. It really affected me and people still laugh when I say that I don't really like drinking. I will end up drinking if I'm doing other stuff, but I honestly don't like alcohol that much, and one of the reasons for that is Dad.

Dad would often go missing for days on end. Sometimes I would have to go and find him. I once discovered him sitting in the middle of the traffic at Clapham Junction. A guy came up to me and said, 'Are you Frost? And is that your dad?!' Dad used to be such a charming, flamboyant character who dressed sharply. Now, he was looking like a shadow of his former self. It was heart-breaking.

I would often go round to where he was living and have to remove him from bad influences who were pulling him down with them. It was like kidnapping your own father. My sister and I would take turns looking after him to stop him getting any worse. This went on for quite a while until we eventually got him into sheltered accommodation. It ripped my heart out to see him in that state. But we all made sacrifices in order to see him through it. It was one of the most difficult things I have ever done, but we got there in the end and slowly he started to recover from the demon drink. I was just glad to do my bit.

I went to help at Centrepoint again on Christmas Day, 1992. It was almost as if the more successful I became, the more I felt I had to put something back in. With the exception of that spat in Canada and the promoter who refused to pay me, I had managed to keep my temper under control. It felt as if I was slowly turning my life around. So once again I donned the Santa hat and dished out the breakfasts to those with nowhere to go. That same year I saw the leaflet 'Help sponsor a child' drop through the letterbox. There was something about this plea that touched me and right there and then I decided to get involved. You were encouraged to send a monthly donation to help with a child's education in a third world country, but I just paid the whole year straight off. Good things were happening to me and so I decided to spread the love.

Petulo Seven was born on the exact same day as my daughter Tanya. He was seven years old and lived in Malawi, Africa. I got sent

Petulo Seven's school reports and he even wrote me letters updating me on what he'd been up to. I got really involved in his life and loved receiving mail from this kid who lived thousands of miles away. It filled me with pride to see how well he was doing. I sponsored Petulo for two years in total and I hope he's doing well for himself now.

My little brother Gary was still suffering at this point too. We saw friends of Gary's, who were going through the same thing, lose their lives. It was so painful seeing my little brother in constant pain. It affected me a lot and made me realise how lucky I was.

***

1993, saw me fall foul of drink. An energy drink. My particular poison at the time was Lucozade; the unofficial drink of UK rave, so much so that they later released the drink NRG in tribute to the song of the same name by Adamski.

We were at a petrol station in Swindon one evening and I'd just gone into the shop to buy some drinks and snacks when I slipped on the icy forecourt. I went right back; my legs stuck up in the air like something from a Laurel and Hardy film. Everyone was laughing at me. However, I had landed on these glass bottles of Lucozade and when I got into the car, I heard the gasp. My back had been cut to ribbons so badly, there was a flap of skin just hanging off me like wallpaper.

CH. 20

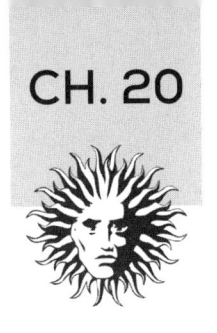

The Old Frost Returns

As much as I tried to escape the road life, working in clubs was a hazardous occupation back then. There were drug dealers, gangsters and violent thugs all over clubland. I had a beef with this guy for a bit and it all came to a head one night at Roast (Linford Film Studios) when a few words we exchanged turned into a tussle that spilled out onto the dancefloor. I will call this geezer Don. Anyway, it wasn't until I returned to the decks that I felt something wet on my back. I lifted my shirt and this girl screamed. I'd been stabbed. I hadn't felt a thing, but there was blood everywhere. I ended up in A&E after that and got some more stitches, only weeks after the incident with the Lucozade. I had also been stabbed (not too severely) a few years previously, at one of Tin Tin's events.

This feud with Don went on for a quite a while and me being me, I wanted revenge. Don was from the drug-dealing world and I spent quite a bit of time trying to track him down, but he was lying low. But if you wanted to find trouble back then, you didn't have to look too far. Then a couple of mates suggested I get a gun for protection.

One of the guys who hung out with me in north London, back in the day, along with Ranger, Matthew Sterling and Charlie B, was Cass. Cass was an older head and I really respected him when I was younger. Cass was really into his music and if he said something was good, you took notice. Fast forward to 1993 and I got a call from my older sister Samantha, who was seeing Cass at this time. The story Samantha told me wasn't good. Wasn't good at all. She was very upset.

'I started seeing Cass and lent him some money, yeah? But now he's saying he's not going to pay me back!' Samantha was sobbing. 'He also said that I could go tell my brother if I wanted to!' I was fucking fuming.

'You can go tell your brother? What?! What the fuck?!' I was pacing around the room, my heart rate going through the roof. Why was Cass trying to get me involved in this? He knew me and should have known better, yet here he was, taking money off my sister and having a dig at me in the process. Maybe he thought I wouldn't want to get involved, now that I was a DJ, but he couldn't have been further from the truth. You mess with my sister – and by proxy, me – then you're playing with fire, bruv.

I got on the phone straightaway and got Mikey Bullforce to meet me in east London. A childhood friend, Mikey cut an imposing figure. This was a man who often carried a shotgun beneath his long mac.

We eventually found Cass's house and decided to 'Lloyd' the door in. Lloyding a door in is an old burglar's trick where you snap a piece off a plastic video case or credit card or something, which you then slide up and down inside the door. Then you push the door and it clicks. You're in.

Cass was in the house when we arrived and he was very surprised to see us. There was a girl standing by some suitcases in the hall and she seemed very startled and started screaming. 'It's OK love, we won't hurt you! We just have a little business to sort out.' This girl was preparing to go to Miami in the morning and she was terrified that she was going to get hurt during whatever was about to happen next. I think she sussed by our entrance that this wasn't going to be no male-bonding session. I was so angry I was pacing around the room. The fucking cunt!

Mikey Bullforce was a bit of a ladies man and while I was pacing around the room, working myself up into a frenzy, he started hitting on this girl. I couldn't believe it! 'Can I get your number, so I can give you a ring when you get back from Miami?' I'd had enough.

I pulled out the 9mm…

This was the gun I'd been given after that feud with Don. It came from up north and… I don't know. I just wanted one. I felt, at that time, as though I needed one for protection after seeing the club scene get a little too dicey. Guns were around in those times and I was mad for wanting one. But there you go. I had a gun and it was now pointed at someone.

As soon as Cass saw this piece, he started shaking. 'I thought we were mates Cass… We used to hang out. What the fuck is going on? You take money from my sister and then disrespect me? Fuck that!'

I wanted his bank card so I could get my money back, but he wasn't playing ball, so I gave him a couple of whacks and he suddenly found the money alright. Dickhead. 'You ever fucking do anything like this again and I will fucking have you! Do you understand?!' Cass nodded. The girl was sobbing in the corner. 'Sorry, love, but we had to do this. I'm not having it!' The thing is, I felt that I had to do it. Had to. That was how things worked. You couldn't just let people fuck you over, not when it involved your sister… nah! You're going to get hurt. We left the house and walked back to the car. 'Do you think she'll call?' Mikey asked me.
- 'Who?'
- 'The girl…'
- 'You kidding me?! Fuck!'

I was very embarrassed by this incident, though and didn't tell a soul about what had happened. It was just like in *The Godfather III*: 'Just when I thought I was out, they pull me back in.' That's how it felt, I really didn't want any of this shit spoiling my career. But I felt I had no choice. There were a few incidents like this around that time and slowly, the old ways started creeping back. The bad boy was taking hold again.

Goldie

"What I am about to tell you, is complete load of lies. A Pinocchio story I made up just for the sake of it, while sitting in my rocking chair, here in Thailand. It's a pre-fabricated tale, if you like.

The first time I ever saw Frosty was in a converted cattle barn at a rave in Hull. Frosty was playing with a towel over his head, going nuts. He was playing some real hardcore dance music. Almost gabba. Frosty used to play really hard.

Nigel has been here since day one. Frost, Fabio, Groove and Randall. They've been doing their thing since it started. Part of the fabric really.

I have a lot of time for Nigel. I don't know how he's got around to writing a book, as most of the people in it, should have been arrested. But we've had some tumultuous times. Nigel has always had my back.

Grimy? Yeah. Crazy? Yeah. Frosty used to walk around with a machine for a time back there. He was always packing. A bit of a madman, really. If it wasn't for music, Nigel would already be dead. Somebody would have ironed him out. It would have been a gangster bloodbath. A really bloody scene from The Godfather Part II.

Nigel has been responsible for a lot of people really losing their shit over the years. We've been through a few scrapes over time too, but as I have said, he always had my back. He's one of the few people that when it came on top, was there by my side.

I was seeing Kemi at the time and we used to live on the 18th floor at 124 Dorney Tower in Swiss Cottage. This is a bit of a mad one, proving that life is often stranger than fiction. Things were blowing up for me at the time. Kemi and I went on one of our first holidays together to Spain and we asked this guy Gus to look after our crazy-as-fuck pitbull Massive.

So, Gus rang us while we were on holiday and said we'd been broken into. I was destroyed, mate and came straight home. Everything was gone. Two exclusive Stüssy leathers gone. One was a 'Stadium' and the other was a box jacket 'Kangaroo'. They took loads of clothes, my chunky Miami Vice Motorola, but they left Gus's PC, which was weird. They took the TV, amps, cassette deck; all gone. I was fucking livid.

I went up and down this block with my pitbull asking everyone if they knew who took all this stuff from my gaff. I was baffled.

I called on Andy on the bottom floor. Andy had nine Rottweilers and was bang on the smack and so I confronted him and it was a little like Russian Roulette. This guy was a bit of a madman, but I called him out and he bottled it. 'It wasn't me, Golds!' I believed him, actually.

So, I phoned Nigel. 'I've had my gaff cut out, mate.'

- 'Yeah, whatever G. I will come over and we'll sort it.'

I remembered that Pete Nice from Internatty was working for BT at the time and so I got onto him. When you had a mobile back then, 23 years ago now – your mobile was tied to your BT number, so the Motorola I had was still active and I could get the bill to see if they'd called anyone. So, I called Pete. 'I don't know if I can do this,' he told me. Anyway, he managed to do the dirty and there were four numbers on the bill. Wow! So, I called the numbers, tracked them to addresses and called Nigel. 'I've got some addresses, mate'

'What?! I'm there.'

One of the addresses was also in Swiss Cottage and this gaff was owned by a yardie. I asked him a few questions and found out that this place was a crack house. It was some mad place; a first-floor mezzanine flat just over the park from Swiss Cottage. So, Frosty and I marched over towards this gaff. Frosty just smashed the door in and we were inside.

We saw this yardie first and then this girl ran out and jumped over the balcony, man. She was gone, hobbling down the road. I started shouting, 'Where's my fucking phone?! Where's my fucking gear?' I collared one of these other fellas and said, 'Who's been over to my gaff? I've been cleaned out.' Frosty looked like he was going to beat the fuck out of this fella. I was trying to play good cop, bad cop and I was speaking to this bird there while this other guy was shitting himself. I think Frosty pulled something on him to scare him.

Next thing, we found out that some kid who regularly went there, had been talking about this stolen stuff. This kid was a fucking little crack head from Archway.

So, we've gone back and regrouped now and I've worked it all out. I've found out that it was this little crack head who was seeing this guy from the crack house's sister. This guy was a fella called Carl and I met him in Camden High Street once and I said, 'If you ever get into trouble, check me at 124 Dorney...' Eureka!

We had this second number too and so got the address for that. This place was a house that had been made into four flats, and I swear to God, Frosty and I climbed up this fucking tree and were watching this gaff for about two fucking hours. Suddenly, this black bird went in and we were like, 'Fuck!' We rang every bell and banged the fucking door and people were getting angry. 'Why are you banging the fucking door?' We eventually found her flat and said to this bird, 'Look, we need to know where your boyfriend is because he's fucking about and he's got my gear.'

We got his address and went straight there. We knocked on his door, dragged the geezer out, beat him on the side of his head and walked him into the middle of the road. I said, 'The game's up, mate. Where's my fucking stuff?'

- *'It was Carl, mate. Carl got me to go to your flat. We did three gaffs that morning, filled up the car and took the stuff somewhere to sell it on. I will take you to him, I swear!'*

- *'How are you going to get him to come out of his gaff?'*

So, we're thinking now. I gave this geezer a tenner. 'Go and knock him up and tell him to get you some weed. Say that you're going to go with him. Now, if you fucking tell him, the game's up, mate.'

I brought some back-up with me and had one in the front garden, one in the back garden and one in the car. So, I said to this guy, 'You make out like it's casual and when you see us, you run.' There's the code and all the honour of course and so no one likes a grass do they? So we decided we wouldn't mark him out as a snitch.

They came out of this gaff and they're walking down the road when we grabbed Carl. We smacked this other guy in the face before he ran off. We then grabbed Carl and put him in the car and I ain't gonna tell you what happened next, but he was very forthcoming.

'Where's my fucking stuff?!' Five minutes in and he's coughed. 'I got the stuff and sold it to this hire company…'

So, we've gone to this shop and I've gone in there with a fucking baseball bat and smashed the place up. The guy behind the counter looked shocked and claimed he knew nothing about my gear.

- 'Listen. Two black guys came in here, dadadada… and you need to refresh your fucking memory!'
- 'But we don't buy stolen goods, we never have.'

It turned out that he had sent these guys somewhere else up the road and lo and behold my TV was in the back of this gaff and I've got nearly all the gear back, plus a few bits and bobs.

I found out in the interim that this fella who had bought our stuff had a court date in King's Cross. Carl had folded like a pack of cards and grassed on this guy who still had my leathers.

So, we bowled down to King's Cross Court Rooms to see him. I contacted his brief beforehand and said, 'We're coming to court and I want my leathers.'

This brief told us, 'He actually got nicked in one of your coats.'

- 'Make sure you bring the fucking leathers.'

So, his brief came up to us holding my jackets, while this other guy was in the dock. We were like, 'Heyyy!!! Here we are! Give him a round of applause!' We were ordered out of the court of course.

So, I had the leather that was found in the car he was nicked in – logged as stolen (from me) and the one he was wearing. Job done and thanks to Nigel for all his help. Nigel was always there when it came on top. We have become very good friends over the years and we're always making plans for Nigel. Cheers mate."

CH. 21

Let's Start A Label

Bryan had learned a lot as an A&R at Outer Rhythm and had signed some big acts, including Moby, Dave Angel, Joey Beltram and Outlander. Bryan had a real eye and ear for spotting talent. But then suddenly, the parent label Mute went bust in 1993 and Bryan was laid off.

1993 was a great year for jungle and I loved tracks like *Return To Atlantis* by LTJ Bukem; a dub classic, which showed just how sophisticated the music could get. I also loved Rebel MC's *Junglist* on the Congo Natty label with Pete The Bouncer on vocals. That track absolutely smashed it. Then there was the 'Bristol sound'.

There was a big box of demo cassettes at Mute and Bryan took them with him as he was clearing his desk. One of them had been handed to him by two house producers known as Absolute 2 and it really stuck out. Bryan rang me one day and said, 'Come on over and have a listen to this little lot.' He seemed very excited about these boys from Bristol. Bryan was originally from Gloucester and so he had a personal interest in this bundle of demos.

It was jungle, but it had moved on a bit. These tracks had a real science fiction sound. It was wicked. The artists were two guys called Krust and Roni Size. I had never heard anything like it before. Crazy! Bryan found their phone numbers and got on to them straight away and soon we were off to Bristol to meet them. We had a vague plan: to start a label.

Big, Bad & Heavy

Bryan Gee

"I was preparing to leave the Queen's Park offices at Rhythm King when I found a load of demo tapes. Now, these demos were coming into the office 24 hours a day and they were 99% shit. You could get real uninspired listening to all this unknown stuff. However, every now and again, a gem would fall through the cracks. I missed out on a lot of big artists, because I simply looked at a cassette and had absolutely no interest in listening to it; it was just a name on a tape that didn't mean anything to me. Then, years later, they might make it big and you're like, 'Didn't this guy send this to me?' Ha ha. This song could be number one in the Billboard Chart now and shit like that. We all fucked up at this, though, because there was simply so much music coming at you. However, you had to take a punt now and again, and sometimes it worked and often it didn't. But I loved the tapes that Roni and the boys sent in and so I took them away with me when I left.

I still wasn't 100% sure about this jungle music from Bristol and so I decided to play some of it to the guys at our DJ agency Groove Connection. Fabio, Grooverider, LTJ Bukem, Micky Finn, Frost, Kem and Storm were all there when I played this tape.

The reaction wasn't great, to be honest. Frost liked it and so did Bukem, but there wasn't a lot of interest in it. But there was enough, you know what I mean? I had a genuine love for it.

Nigel and I were not producers and so we merely viewed this music as something exciting to get involved with. So, we made dubplates from the cassettes and started playing them out. That was the great thing about being a DJ; instant reactions. The music got an amazing response. That was when we decided to start a label.

Our label was never going to be about a specific style as such, we just wanted to sign music we liked. We didn't want to be pigeonholed, we wanted to be diverse.

Nigel and I grew up on funk and so we had similar tastes and that's how we connected initially, through playing out James Brown, George Clinton and rare groove. Nigel liked what I liked, which made things very easy. It was cool that way.

These Bristol tapes had something about them. Frost was on it straightaway and so we decided to go to Bristol to meet Roni and Krust. Taking Jumpin Jack Frost down there was like taking Andy C or someone, now. Frost blew them away and we got a deal done straight *off. Roni and Krust were so up for it. We told them our plan and they were down with it. They were to be the first acts on this brand-new label.*

Roni, Krust and the boys were five or six friends who grew up together and they had this really tight bond and we connected with them straightaway because they shared our vision. When artists don't have a label or any direction, they're often just making more and more music that's only ever getting heard by their mates. However, we were able to give them a focus. 'Instead of just making music for the sake of it, we can let you know where you're heading.' The boys had a real end-point with us and proper deadlines. They knew if they finished a track, it could be played out at Lazerdrome or Universe, that very same weekend and so that really spurred them on.

Frost took a back seat with the label, to be honest and I'm not sure why as such, but that actually worked out really well and he was always there when I needed him. I liked being fully hands-on and enjoyed working with the artists. Frost was more comfortable taking a back seat as a creative."

Roni and Krust were younger than us and borderline hippies. They dressed like travellers or something; 'save the whale' types. But they were very easy to get on with and the music they made was special.

Back in London, Bryan was animated with excitement. 'We need to start a label, Nige. These guys have got something. Something big!'

I had no idea as to how to start or run a label, but I respected Bryan and if he thought it was a good idea, then I was in. 'OK, let's start a label.'

We were walking through Camden one morning, looking for inspiration for a name when I saw a shop called 'V Experience', which sold candles and stuff. 'V. That's it!' We decided on 'V Recordings'.

Our first release was the *Deceivers EP* Fatal Dose (V001) by Krust, performing under the name Kirk Thompson. With that release, V was born. We had a name, some artists and more than a little knowledge stored up through years of DJing and playing out. Chris at Music House mastered the track for us and put us in touch with Bobsey and his wife Carmelita, who owned a pressing plant on the North Circular near Wembley. This plant was like something out of the seventies and had a real reggae heritage and it was from that factory that our first release was born. 1993 was the year we started making and releasing music.

Roni and Krust started to come and visit us in London once their names began to grow. They would play out in London a lot and always stayed at Bryan's house. I remember them turning up early one Sunday morning and I was like, 'What are you doing here at this time?!'

- 'We're going on a Greenpeace march.'

Roni and the boys were such lovely guys and Bryan was like a big brother to them, but I think they were a little wary of me. They had loads of other Bristol connections such as Die and Suv and they all made music; banging out tunes at a hell of a rate. Their sound was really developing and I played as much of it as I could. Krust showed us how to make beautifully intense tunes that lasted 12 minutes or more with *Soul In Motion* and *True Stories*, both of which set the benchmark in production. I also loved *11.55* and *Music Box* by Roni and Die with its neat drums and sexy basslines. One of my sets at Universe was composed entirely of this unreleased Bristol jungle. *Metamorphosis* was one of my favourites and it was totally blowing everyone away. 'Wooah, what the fuck is this?!'

Roni and Krust's equipment was quite basic, but their sound was developing at a rapid rate as jungle started to hit its peak in 1994. I loved Roni's *It's A Jazz Thing*, which had a distinctive riff that hit me like a funky train to the head. People called it the 'Omar tune' or 'electric boogie' as MC Moose named it. I had a disagreement with Roni over this track, as I wanted to release it, but he didn't think it would work. But we did release it. And it did work.

***

'Have you heard this remix of *Music Box*?' Katie asked me one morning, while at Bryan's house.

- 'What remix?'

Katie was helping us out with V and she had this white label. 'Give it here!'

I took this piece of vinyl and examined the sleeve. The track was called *Sorry. Not Sorry*. I stuck it on the decks. Now, this tune was a blatant rip-off off Roni's *Music Box* and I was fuming. That track was a game changer and to take it and mix it without permission was not happening, mate. I made some enquiries and eventually tracked down the offices of this label called No U-Turn.

I got to the Baker Street building, where No U-Turn was based and kicked the door of the office in. This guy Nico, who ran things, looked very shocked. 'What the fuck do you think you're doing?!' I shouted at him. 'That's our fucking tune!'

This Nico fella was apologetic and I think he knew he had to cough up some money to get rid of me because I was fuming. He also agreed to stop pressing the bootlegs. We were just starting a label and we didn't need this sort of shit.

Me and my girl Robyn Pelka.
I miss her so much. RIP

Tokyo with my boy DJ Shintaro

Niagara falls, back in the day

Receiving the best DJ Award at the Elevation Awards 1992 with Fat Freddie M

With Sammie and Prince

Me and Brian Gee

Credit: **Ron Boudreau**

In Jamaica filming the code red video with Super Cat. Me with DJ Ron & Jamaica's most loved actor Carl Bradshaw aka Jose from Smile Orange

Tour bus life

With Bonnie, Louise, Paul Shoey, Sam from Njoi and Dudley (DUDLEY RIP)

Groove connection: Bryan Gee, Fabio, Micky Finn, Grooverider and Sarah Sandy

With Bryan Gee on a V shoot

Jah Shaka. This man is one of the reasons I do what I do

Fabric 1999 with Goldie and Derek Moose

The original Harder They Come flyer

Minus 10 in Toronto; all in the mink

Viva Las Vegas

Tour life with Sgt Moose

Rest in peace Pete Mariner pictured here with a stunning carving he did of me. I was totally blown away when I saw this

Studio settings

My dog Levi (RIP)

With my brother, Grandmaster Roc Raida (RIP)

At the castle with my good friend Mr Dave Courtney

Brooklyn, New York with my boys Digga and Trigon

Me and Fabio

Matrix. Credit: Nic Wons

With Die and Duffus in Ibiza

Two nutters on the rampage

In Los Angeles with my girls

CH. 22

9mm Of Pain

I was quite happy living in my bachelor pad in Oval. I had it the way I wanted it and I could think back there, do you know what I mean? It was my sanctuary.

Then one Saturday afternoon, some police dropped by. 'Is there anything you would like us to mark?' they said, peering through the crack in the front door. Here I was, a young black guy with a nice flat and as they were chatting about looking after your possessions by marking them with a UV pen, I couldn't help feeling that they were giving me the 'once over'. Maybe they thought I was a drug dealer or something, who was living the life in this posh neighbourhood.

Three days later, I was walking back from my daughter's house when I was struck by just how quiet the street was. It was eerie. This was a busy road normally and yet there was this strange silence. It was weird.

I carried on up to my front door and as the key entered the lock... 'POLICE! Get down!'

I stretched out on the floor, face first, as armed police cuffed me. God knows what this looked like to the neighbours. I was in some serious shit now.

The handcuffs were put on and I was marched into the living room. They had been inside the flat for a while and had found something in my wardrobe.

A PC walked into the living room with my 9mm and a box of bullets. They found £1,500 in cash. I was screwed. All these items were found in the same place, which was a real schoolboy error, overlooking the fact that I had a fucking gun in the house. They took my jewellery and money and I never got any of it back. The police took it and, surprise, surprise, it was never documented. Just disappeared.

They drove me to the police station and I just stared out of the window. That was it! I was fucked. My career was fucked. The party was over. I had dropped straight back into the old life again over this fucking gun.

The gun was rare apparently and that made it hard to trace, but I wouldn't let anyone else take a bullet. I took full responsibility although they tried to cut me some deals if I told them where I got it. They also wanted to know if I was a drug dealer. 'The gun's for protection, man. I'm a DJ. I move in dangerous circles and it's never been fired. It was just there in case I need to scare someone.'

- 'Is that so?'

They eventually let me out on bail, but I was fucked, mate. Not only that, but I decided not to tell a single soul about what had happened. I didn't want *anyone* to know. No one. I didn't want anyone thinking I was trouble.

I couldn't sleep for weeks. I just felt so jumpy. My mind was racing at a hundred miles an hour. Why the fuck had I got that gun? Why did I leave it in the wardrobe with the fucking bullets?

I got the front door fixed, but I was pretty sure that my neighbours had seen what had happened as the police had closed off the road. That was why it was so quiet. It was a major police operation and so I'm sure some neighbour grassed me up. I didn't want to be in that flat any more.

I guessed I was looking at 4-5 years inside for possession of an illegal firearm. Fucked. The police kept phoning me up, asking me if I wanted to name any drug dealers in order to get my sentence reduced, but there was nothing I was prepared to tell them. 'Fuck off, bruv. I ain't telling you nothing, yeah?' I sounded brave maybe, but I was actually shitting it.

I was so jumpy and paranoid in that flat that I started to spend a lot of time with Lisa in Leicester. I had been seeing Lisa, on and off for a year or more, and she was always happy to see me. She had this posh place in the countryside and came from good stock, and so it was nice to get away from London and all the madness.

My lawyer worked hard for me and the case kept getting delayed and delayed and so I had a lot of time with which to worry myself half to death. I didn't even tell Bryan. I just bottled it up inside and hoped it would sort itself out somehow.

Lisa's father was a millionaire casino owner who had died in a helicopter crash and so she had this lovely home. That place was perfect for trying to forget about the madness I had just created for myself.

It was while at Lisa's that I decided to make some music, to distract my feverish mind. I knew DJ SS (Leroy) and Idris who ran Formation Records in Leicester and so I decided to hook up with them to take my mind off the court case. So, I often spent the week working with the boys in the studio during the day before going home to Lisa in the evenings. With my family life back home in London, ticking away, this truly was a double life. But then my life had never been simple.

Lisa was stunning and worked as a buyer for British Shoes. She was getting me these free Timberlands and shit, which was nice. We got on really well actually and the tunes I made with Leroy were eventually released as the *Underworld EP* on Formation Records in 1994. I was really proud of it.

So, that stupid business with the gun led me into a horrible court case, which eventually saw me making music for the first time. Weird how things turned out. I did three releases on Formation and this was something I was determined to carry on with back in London.

There was this hungry young producer back then called Karl, who also went by the name Dillinja; he'd released this wicked tune *Lionheart* with a guy called Burt. I'd been to his studio a few times, but nothing had really come of it, but now I was eager to carry on making music. I just knew this kid was going to be something special. The way he manipulated bass was awe-inspiring.

1994, and jungle was a massive thing by now. Coming from a sound system culture, jungle was always something I lived, as well as played out. But now, it was something I was making too. I asked Dillinja if he wanted to do something else and, as always, his studio door was open to me. I can't thank Karl enough for what he did back then. I will never, ever forget it. If I hadn't been given that opportunity I don't know what would have happened to me.

I loved the rare groove track *Foxy* by Mademoiselle and I knew I wanted to sample that. That was the starting point for this new track. I also loved this *Reggae Hits* album that was lying on top of my stereo at the time and so I took both records to Karl's studio. The tune was done in just under five hours. I kept listening to it, over and over, and I couldn't shake the feeling that I had a tune. A *tune*! I felt proud of the other tracks I'd made, but this felt different. This jungle track had a vibe that was infectious, complete with soulful harmonies and a brash reggae vocal: *'Big, bad and heavy, any sound test me tonight, dem ah go bury'* from *My Sound A Murder* by Jigsy King and Tony Curtis. The title *The Burial* was directly connected to the lyric. I didn't want to blow my own trumpet too much, but this track had me excited. *The Burial* was to be released under the name Leviticus, which I was using as an alias.

Music House was the place to get your dubplates cut back then and it was known as Jungle HQ. You would get your advanced acetates cut onto 10-inch vinyl so you could play it out. Everyone would wait in line at Music House to get their dubs. Chris at Music House was essential to the UK dance scene down south. You would walk into Music House and see Grooverider, Goldie, DJ Rap... loads of faces. It was like a community centre for jungle. We would swap tapes and listen to each other's music. We would recommend or slag off various promoters and club nights. It was a useful place to hang out. Sometimes you could be there for three hours or more and if Grooverider was before you, then forget it. He would spend hours getting sorted. I would sometimes jump the line by claiming I had a flight to catch.

This music-making lark was initially to keep my mind off the upcoming court case as any minute they could have called me in and so I wanted to leave a legacy to come back to. I was advised to plead guilty, but with mitigating circumstances, to soften the blow. I was terrified. Not of jail, but of having nothing to come back to once I was out and so I became more and more proactive with the music. This fear drove me on and making music soon became an obsession.

I wanted to perfect my mixing too. I remember DJ Bizness teaching me the art of 'turntablism' one afternoon. For hours and hours, we would perform this trick over and over again. I was learning to love a challenge and wanted to up my game.

***

Life was buzzing with regards to music, but everything else was turning to crap. The bad boy I'd tried to kick into touch, had taken control again. I was now getting involved in things I really should have avoided. I guess, looking back, the club world was just another version of the streets. The same problems and temptations were there, only magnified. The problem was actually inside me. When things kicked off, I immediately reverted back to the Hangman.

I was a full-time DJ and label owner and was very, very busy. I was also stressed because it was still really hard to fit family life into my schedule. Plus, I had this court case hanging over my head. Making and releasing music allowed me to ignore all the other grief that I seemed to have absolutely no control over. Or at least that's how I saw it then. V had to work or I really was screwed!

***

1994 was regarded by many as the year jungle peaked. I remember this young producer M-Beat hitting number 8 in the charts with *Incredible*; that track with General Levy blew me away. Shy FX also crept into the Top 40 that autumn with *Original Nuttah* (featuring UK Apache). I first heard *Incredible* at Music House when Junior Hart (UK Apache) asked me if I wanted to hear some of his new tunes (from his label Renk Records). Shy FX was another brilliant young producer and I loved his *Gangster* (featuring Gunsmoke). Jungle truly was emerging from the underground with loads of compilations being released and raves happening all over the place. People now identified themselves as junglists and would wear camouflage and shit.

V Recordings was really getting noticed at this time. Roni, Krust and Die were incredible and they just kept producing this amazing material, which we couldn't get out fast enough. Bryan was great at nurturing the talent. Bryan was like a football manager, the Sir Alex Ferguson of jungle. Roni and Krust just got better and better as their confidence grew. Bryan seemed to see things in people that they hadn't even recognised in themselves. Roni and Krust were very kind and wouldn't hurt a fly. I loved those boys to bits, but it took us a while to get used to each other. We had different outlooks, if you know what I mean.

All through the early days of V Recordings, I still hadn't told a soul about my impending court case. No one. Bryan, my family, not even Lisa from Leicester knew. I was starting to lose it. The stress was getting well on top.

This *Burial* tune I did with Dillinja was sitting on the shelf all through this crap. I played it to Bryan one morning and he was quite shocked.

'It sounds alright, that!' Seeing Bryan's positive reaction really gave me confidence.

Getting the mix right was vital to a track and this tune needed to be loud and so I sent everything to DJ SS in Leicester (Formation Records); the guy I made my first record with. He did the final mix and I got Stewart at Copymasters in Fulham to master the track and got the dubplates cut at Music House. I played the DAT of *The Burial* to Grooverider, Micky Finn, Kenny Ken and a few other DJs in the waiting room at Music House one afternoon. Everyone loved it! Groove boomed out, 'I'm taking a piece of this!' Everyone there wanted a cut. Raaahhh! It looked like I had a hit on my hands. It was an amazing reaction and I got so much love for that tune. Micky Finn, Randall and DJ Ron all wanted a copy.

'We're going to have to release this track,' Bryan said. We'd already had interest from some labels, but we really wanted to take this one on ourselves and so we decided to set up a new label solely for jungle. We called this new record label Philly Blunt after the cigar associated with smoking weed. The momentum was really building with *The Burial* and we knew it would blow.

I wanted *The Burial* to be a double A-side and so the flip was a track featuring my sister Yolanda singing on it. I got her to agree to do a vocal, but didn't tell her the lyrics until minutes before we started; I wanted it as fresh as possible. 'First you say yes, then you say no...' It was recorded at Roller Express in Edmonton where Finbar had a studio. A young aspiring producer called Optical engineered it.

The Burial was making a lot of noise and everywhere you went that summer, from London to Tokyo and Sao Paulo, you heard it. Dillinja went on to become 'the king of the bassline' shortly after, when he released some monster dub tunes.

Before we could release *The Burial* properly, we had to pay off Barry Manilow. *The Burial* contained a sample from Barry's *Copacabana* and so his people were straight on to us. We also had to buy the rights to *Foxy* by Mademoiselle so we could use the bassline, but that didn't matter as we were pressing more and more of this tune that was to become the crossover track of the summer. When you walked through the Notting Hill Carnival, you heard this track on all the sound systems and even mainstream radio stations.

It was such an honour to be asked to appear on David Rodigan's show on Kiss. I used to listen to Rodigan as a kid, back in the seventies when he was *the man* on Capital. The first single I ever bought was a track I heard on Rodigan's show in 1979: I loved *Barnabus Collins* by The Lone Ranger. David Rodigan and Tony Williams on London Radio were the best at that time for reggae and dub.

David was the first major DJ to play *The Burial* and this was to a reggae audience not a jungle crowd. It was such an honour. We then a had a chat on air about the song and how it came about. I will never forget the moment when David Rodigan played *my* record. The interest in that tune went through the roof after that.

I remember being asked to play a PA of *The Burial* at Elevation by Funky, who ran Moondance. I thought, 'Yeah, I could do that.' As my sister Yolanda did the vocals I forced her into doing hours of rehearsals back at my place. PAs are tough and a lot of it is out of your hands and so I wanted her to get the performance right. I was like a slave driver that day. 'Again! Again!' To be honest, I thought she'd either freeze or fuck it up. That was a common thing for experienced singers and that was something she most definitely wasn't. But you know what? She smashed it! It was amazing. She stood there and sang my tune in front of 2,500 people. I was so proud.

We licensed *The Burial* to so many compilation albums. It was massive. I eventually sold the rights to London Records and it made vast amounts of money all of which I ploughed back into V Recordings, although I did treat myself to a watch. We also rented a proper office space for the label. That track gave us such a platform to build on. With *Burial* and *Warning* by Firefox we now had Philly up and running, alongside V. Everything was looking up except for this impending court case.

Nick Halkes (XL, Positiva)

"As the scene started to fragment, I moved from XL to EMI to start up the electronic label Positiva and signed Adam F, around 1994.

Bryan Gee and Frost gone had down the breakbeat path and Coxy had his techno angle and many followed the happy hardcore route. Frost was there building jungle into drum and bass and our paths certainly crossed. I don't know why I didn't try to sign Leviticus, as it felt like one I should have had a pop at. There were so many good records out then, though, so maybe we'd taken too many on at that time. But The Burial would have been a good one to sign."

I went on a short trip to Miami while on bail, just to clear my mind. I went to stay at my auntie Evelyn's on New Year's Eve and spent the warm evenings at this strip club called Rolex. I spent three weeks in Miami in all. My head was buzzing with all this court shit and I didn't want to be anywhere that reminded me of it. Just by chance, I was asked to play New York at the legendary Limelight around this time. So, DJ Ron and I flew out.

I got to the hotel, unpacked, went to the venue and as I walked in, I felt very uncomfortable. The Limelight was a massive deal, yeah? But it felt grim in there and then I noticed the upside-down crucifixes. What the fuck?! I wasn't having any of that. So, I got a cab back to the hotel and went to visit some family there. I then got the first available flight out and didn't even say goodbye to Ron. I wasn't getting involved in that shit. That was the devil's work.

DJ Ron

" I always make a beeline for the decks when entering a club, but I remember Frost getting quite spooked. He was like, 'What's all this?!' He was pointing up at some upside-down crosses or something. There was some Satanic symbolism at this place and I kid you not, he ran out of the club. I was left standing there wondering what to do next. So, I thought I'd slide out of there as well. He was determined not to play, though. He was not happy!

We both had family there (New York), however and so we used this trip as a chance to see them instead."

CH. 23

The Proper Jungle

A legend of the UK jungle scene, Congo Natty had some hit singles under his belt from his days as Rebel MC; Congo changed his name in the early nineties when he embraced Rastafarianism. Congo was instrumental in forging the reggae-influenced dance of jungle and many saw him as the figurehead of the scene. Congo's *Code Red*, under the name Conquering Lion, was an absolute banger and so I was very chuffed to be asked to join him on a trip to Jamaica to shoot the video. If nothing else, it was another chance to escape my problems back home as my court case loomed large.

Congo Natty (aka Rebel MC)

"Frost and I are the same you know. We're from the same part of the urban jungle, see? I'm from Tottenham, he's from Brixton and he was a soldier. We're coming from the road, yeah, and music saved us. We got to channel our energy into music.

I was a junglist from birth. Junglist is who we are, it was always jungle. What I did before Congo Natty wasn't classified as hip hop or anything although it had breakbeats and a heavy bassline. Rebel MC's Wickedest Sound is jungle to me.

1994, I was planning a trip to Jamaica to shoot the video for Code Red. Jungle was getting a high profile at that time and so I wanted to assemble a team to take with me, yeah? I had signed to Island Records and the boss Chris Blackwell wanted to get us into the real jungle, yeah? Suzette Newman was his right-hand woman and she agreed as part of the deal with Conquering Lion that we would bring jungle to Jamaica; the home of our influences. So, I had to get my bredrins involved, so that we were a representation of the scene, as junglism is about brotherhood. So, Frost, DJ Ron and I – a good cross section of the jungle community – headed off into the jungle. The real jungle.

It was crazy to be getting a blessing from these Jamaican artists we met over there. It was an enjoyable time. A blessed time. We were met by the island fraternity and treated very well. Carl Bradshaw was there with us, acting as a guide.

I was moving to Rastafari during them times and so to me jungle was a revolutionary movement and that trip represented the start of something special."

It was a joy to be taking time out in Jamaica with Congo, DJ Ron and a few others. Carl Bradshaw was our host when we arrived and this guy was considered a national treasure in Jamaica after appearing as one of the leads in the 1973 classic *The Harder They Come* as well as the starring role in *Smile Orange*. Gamers can hear Carl on Tuff Gong Radio in *Grand Theft Auto IV*. As well as Carl, we also had notorious dancehall bad boy DJ Super Cat as our guide in Cockburn Pen; a very ghetto part of Kingston, Jamaica. To make sure we had safe passage through this sometimes dangerous territory of backroads and shacks, Carl spoke on our behalf whenever any locals started getting curious.

We had great fun filming the video with Super Cat and the boys; to bring jungle to Jamaica was an honour. It felt like a proper moment in UK jungle.

We spent a memorable night at The House Of Leo, which was a lively local dance. I was loving it out there, man. The sun, sand and great company was a million miles away from the UK. This dance was rammed and like all good parties it was eventually stopped by the police who searched everyone there. These police were called the 'Acid Squad', and they had these red stripes on their uniforms, like they were part of the army or something. Our hosts were well pissed off.

We had been joined by local legends Junior Reid, Ninja Man and Beanie Man and they really weren't happy with the hassle from the police. In fact, Beanie Man was arrested and as he sat in the police truck waiting to go back to the station, he started waving his hands in the air at us. He was crazy! He was released the following morning.

The Proper Jungle

DJ Ron

"Frost and I went to video shoots all over the world. We went to Jamaica to shoot the Code Red video and we had a great time there. The beach, the nightlife... we also met many greats from the reggae scene. We were young guys from the inner cities travelling the world now. It was amazing.

We were with Junior Reid at an outdoor reggae clash, when all of a sudden, hundreds of police turned up. They were just literally arresting people for no good reason. They had these open-top lorries and they were piling people into these vehicles. 'Everyone in the party – get in the lorry!' Junior Reid calmed us down. 'Don't worry, they'll run out of lorries. This is actually quite a regular occurrence.'

We were shooting the video in Super Cat's hometown, in his own backyard when a cordon of army-types, in green uniforms turned up. It was eerie because we couldn't see their eyes. One of them was sat on the back of this jeep with an automatic machine gun. That put the fear of god into me. Everyone went silent. We went to ground, frozen. We daren't do anything, because we didn't know what the outcome would be. They eventually moved on and we carried on with the shoot. This seemed a little crazy to be honest."

That trip was amazing and I got to spend time with loads of characters including Joe Lick Shot, the legendary MC, who could make any noise with his mouth, including machine guns. We also hung out with Captain Barkey (RIP), the famous dancehall artist. It was a joy, man.

Back in the UK, the court case rumbled on. Delay after delay just kept me on edge the whole time. I still hadn't told a soul about what was going on. My drive to establish this legacy to come back to after my time inside was getting stronger and a publishing deal with EMI was signed when I returned home from Jamaica. I guess I hoped that all these deals would enhance my reputation in front of a jury. But having been in the relative calm of Jamaica, the UK seemed to be getting me down again and so I lost myself in some remix work for Driza Bone and Jamiroquai. Driza Bone had a massive budget for the recording of their album. They would send a car to pick me up and take me to the studio every morning, where I would work with producer Aston Harvey, who would go on to set up The Freestylers.

I then arranged to go back to Jamaica for one final break, as I knew the court case was very, very close. I played four gigs in the UK on New Year's Eve before stuffing the boot of the car and heading to the airport with a mate of mine. New Year's Day we were walking along the beach in Montego Bay.

We hooked up with some of the faces I met on the video shoot with Rebel, while we were in Kingston. Captain Barkey and Tony Matterhorn of King Addies' sound system were great company at the Cactus Club. On the way back to the hotel that night, our car broke down just outside Kingston. Now, this was bandit territory and we were getting a little worried. You get robbed in those parts, you get me? Then, like a knight in armour, Beanie Man turned up to give us a lift back to the hotel. I was so relieved to see him.

I had missed a court date while I was in Jamaica and when I returned, there was a warrant out for my arrest. I knew it was coming up, but I just wanted to have some fun instead. So, as soon as we returned, I handed myself into the police. It was *on*.

CH. 24

HMP Brixton

'Nigel Thompson, you have pleaded guilty to possession of an unlicensed firearm…' My heart was racing. The blood was draining from my face and my legs were getting wobbly. Everything I had worked for was going to be destroyed by an act of sheer stupidity. I was never actually going to use that gun, but I had it in my house. Now, I had to take my medicine.

'… and we hereby sentence you to…'

Fuck!

'…four months in prison.'

What the fuck?! Four months? Was that it? I had been worrying myself half to death over this and they gave me four fucking months?! Yes!!! I was over the fucking moon, mate.

I was taken to Brixton prison, where I knew loads of the boys from growing up. 'Raaahhhh! What are you doing here, Frost?' they shouted when I came onto the landing in the morning. I could do four months here, no sweat.

As I have said, the bad boy was back and although I was relieved to get such a slim sentence, I'm not sure if it did me any good with hindsight. It felt like I had cheated the system somehow and maybe a longer stretch would have had more effect on me. But this felt like a gift from the gods. Four months? People sometimes went on holiday for longer than that.

Of course, everybody who needed to know, knew what was happening by now and so Bryan kept me in the loop with the record label whenever he came to visit me in Brixton. I was so happy to get rid of this monkey that had been clamped to my back for the past 18 months. I was walking on air, mate. I was so relieved.

I remember approving artwork for the Leviticus single, while in Brixton. London Records didn't know I was in jail and it was due for release while I was inside. 'Yeah, I want that Versace face as the cover, but I want it to be a black guy, yeah?' Bryan seemed to know what I meant. In fact, the 'sun face' turned out so well, we used it as a logo on every V release. The reason for the sun? Semiotics again! Just like with the name Jumpin Jack Frost being familiar, so did this Versace-esque face, which was already incredibly well known, all around the globe. You get me? That logo came out exactly as I imagined it, when I did these little sketches in my cell.

Of course, I'd rather not have been inside, but being in Brixton was about as good as it got. Then, one of the screws came into my cell one afternoon with some news. 'Tommo, you're going to an open prison in Kent, son.' Shiiiiiiit. I did not want to leave Brixton.

This place in Kent was like a holiday camp. We smoked weed, watched boxing matches, smoked weed, played table tennis, smoked weed… You get the idea. That place reeked of weed. I remember watching Nigel Benn fight Gerald McClellan on the big TV, just visible through a fog of smoke.

This open prison was an old army barracks with dorms instead of cells. Olinka, Bryan and Delroy regularly came to visit and would always bring me stuff that I could sell on to the other boys, as well as letters from my very close friend DJ Rap. I would knock out all these phonecards they gave me. The inmates would buy one off me and then give me two back when they got their 'canteen'. I had a lot of phonecards.

There was this guy in there called Budgie and he was a mate of Micky Finn's. Now, inside, you're quite protective over friends of friends and so when this other fella started calling Budgie a grass, I got really pissed off. 'Budgie is no grass! There is no fucking way that Micky Finn would hang around with a grass! Shut your fucking noise, yeah?!' Anyway, this dude kept going on and on about Budgie being a grass, so much so that I was starting to think that Budgie was in danger of getting done in. Now, the last thing I needed was to get in any more trouble, but this guy was really pushing it. Then one day, I snapped.

We got this guy and gave him a right going over. We put a pillow over his head and poured boiling water over him. 'Aaaarrrggghh!!!'

- 'Budge ain't no grass, yeah?! Now shut the fuck up!'

This guy was really shaken up, but he kept his mouth shut after that.

The open prison was a bit of an anti-climax to be honest. To be really truthful? I was bored in there. They called these places 'a shit and a shave', as it was just counting down the days really. I spent eight weeks there getting stoned, but thank the lord I'd got it done with.

Grooverider and Delroy came to pick me up and it was lovely seeing some friendly faces. The hardest thing about being inside, however, was not being able to listen to music. Now, that was hard!

When I got out I had loads of bookings stacked up through Groove Connection and Bryan had done a great job of keeping the label running. I'd been doing a show on Kiss FM just before my time inside and it was on a rotational basis. As luck would have it, the week of my release timed perfectly with my next show on Kiss. Because I'd been inside, I hadn't listened to a lot of the tunes I played, but still, I was back in the chair.

I met up with Micky Finn at a party one night and I told him how I honourably defended his name inside, by protecting his mate Budgie. 'They were calling him a grass, Micky.'

- 'I'm not surprised Jack,' said Micky. 'He is a fucking grass!'

DJ Ron

"Nigel and I had a connection because his half-sister Samantha went to my school. I recall Nigel coming to visit her north of the river, with his friends. They were quite antagonistic, to be honest.

A friendship formed years later, when I started playing more regularly, at places like Telepathy when the jungle scene started to lift off. We were at the centre of it all. The first time I met Frost properly was when I was DJing for Telepathy at Marshgate Lane. Ratpack were on before me and Frost after. I remember him coming up to me and he was all like, 'Nah, nah, I need to get on the decks, now!' Many people were a little wary of Frost, but I stood my ground. 'I'm still playing, bruv.' Ha ha. He didn't look happy.

There were a lot of similarities between Frost and myself; our backgrounds etc. My parents were from Guyana as well and it was something we shared when we spoke. I spent a lot of time with Rebel

(MC) and Frost by virtue of doing videos together. Rebel and I were friends, having spent our youths growing up together before the rave scene. Certain types of people tended to gravitate towards each other by how they spoke and what they liked and we all became friends.

We were entertainers, but we were still from the street and I remember that when Nigel went to prison for a spell, I was one of a few people from the scene who would go and visit him. I would bring him all this stuff. We were looking after him while he was there.

I moved to this flat in Old Street for a while and I used to have people from the scene passing through on a daily basis, like a hangout spot. You could chill out there and play Sega Saturn. Frost was out of jail and was the only one from outside of the east London circuit, who would come to my flat. Then I got an office on Goswell Road, also in the Old Street area. We considered ourselves quite entrepreneurial back then, which was cool, because we were from the block, you know? We saw what we did as a business and through all that we remained friends.

Frost can be a fiery character and he does what he wants and gets it done. We got on because I was one of the few people to say, in private, 'Nigel, you've gone too far there, mate.' A real friendship. The relationship may have been formed in the rave scene, but it wasn't solidified by it. We looked out for each other as human beings."

***

I was back in Northern Ireland soon after getting out and it was great being out there again. I loved playing Belfast.

I was out there with Flux and his mate Danny The Dog; so-called because he loved the ladies. The party at the Royal Ulster Hall was wicked and when we finished, these fit girls came up to us and started giving it the bunny. They were proper hot. I could see Danny The Dog was interested. 'Why don't you come back to ours?' they said. We didn't need asking a second time.

Flux, Danny and I got a cab with these two girls and we were off, mate. It wasn't long after setting off on this journey that the scenery started to get quite moody. This felt like a particularly dangerous part of a fucking dangerous town. The cab stopped at a certain point and wouldn't go any further and so we had to walk.

We walked through some flats and on the side of one building was one of those giant murals. It was of a IRA member, wearing a balaclava. There were British soldiers standing on the roof tops of the tower blocks with high-powered rifles.

It was about 4am as we walked past this house with the lights still on and music playing. 'That's our boyfriends' flat,' they said.
- 'You what?!'
- 'Oh, don't worry about them, they'll be asleep soon.'

We walked through the front door of the girls' house and were greeted by an IRA coat of arms on the wall. Some after-party this was!

We went upstairs and Flux quickly disappeared with this girl into one of the bedrooms, while I got acquainted with the other. Danny The Dog was not happy. He was in no-man's land. I got up to go to the toilet when I spotted Danny in the hall. Danny The Dog was so annoyed at missing out on the fun, he was watching Flux and the girl through a crack in the door. 'What the fuck are you doing?!'
- 'I had to get some sort of entertainment,' he said.

I went back to my girl in the living room, in fits.

After a while, Flux's girl came down the stairs, really angry. 'That mate of yours? He was meant to be fucking me and I was like, is that all you've fucking got?! Is that the best you've got?! Fuckinell!'

Flux looked well rattled. 'Ssssshhh!!!' he said to her. We were cracking up.

This girl kept going on. 'I'm not having that. Is that the best he's got?! Fuck!'
- 'Sssssshhhh!!!'

I felt it was time to go. So, we sneaked out of the house and walked down the street until we hit a main road. We then cabbed it back to the hotel. I have been in some truly dangerous situations where it has kicked off, but that night was weird in that I felt we had avoided some real trouble. I had a strange feeling about those girls and looking back, that evening could have got very messy indeed.

CH. 25

Rest In Peace

In some ways, 1994 was a majorly positive year – prison to one side for a moment – with *The Burial* doing the business and V Recordings going from strength to strength. But where there was light, there was also shade.

I was up in Leyton, east London, with Delroy and Mickey P one day, when I got a call from my sister Yolanda. 'Ganga is going to die. They are going to turn the machine off!' she said, in hysterics. 'Die? Machine? What the fuck?!'

This was out of the blue. I didn't even know my grandmother was ill. I was in total shock. Ganga was never ill and I just hadn't seen this coming. The light had gone out inside me. 'I need to get to the hospital. Now!' Delroy drove me to St Thomas' Hospital in Westminster and it was the longest journey ever.

My mum, aunts and uncles were all there when I arrived and I knew by their expressions that she had gone. Ganga had died. I just broke down.

Ganga had been the head of our family and had always taught us right from wrong. She could be hard on us, but she wanted us to treat people with respect. She wanted us to live by her values and the great example she set. I can't fully put across how important she was. Her influence is still with me today. Because inside, I always felt that I was a good person. My actions might have suggested otherwise, but inside, I didn't feel bad. Maybe I was delusional and just wouldn't face up to the fact, that I was letting people like Ganga down. She would not have been happy with my actions had she known.

I demanded to go in to see her. The nurse opened the door and I bowled in. An hour ago, we had been laughing away in Delroy's car... now this. I couldn't believe it. I held her hand and kissed her head.

Mum caught me as I walked out. 'Are you playing out tonight?' she asked.

- 'Yeah, why?'
- 'You need to make sure you do it,' she said. 'Try and carry on with life.'

Mum knew that I was the sort of person who, once they'd hit rock bottom, struggled to get back up. By working, I might be able to deal with things better. I had to restart my system before it was too late. I was so fucked up, though.

Whenever I was down I would always go to Bryan. Bryan always knew exactly the right words to say, and even if he didn't, he seemed to calm me down. I was in state of suspended animation and in dire need of help. We played some tunes together worked on a mix with all these strings and whatnot. I guess it was an anthem for Ganga.

Roast that night was one of the best sets I have ever played. I hadn't told anyone of what had happened, but I just kept focused, although I was in bits.

The funeral was surreal. I was so upset. First off, I wouldn't go into the church, then I created a real scene with people holding me back as I was screaming so much. I had lost the plot. Outside in the cemetery I tried to start a fight.

Life would never be the same without Ganga. She was gone. I just couldn't accept it. I still love you Ganga.

It was weird because I was really hurting at that time and I don't know if Lisa from Leicester was aware of this, but she rang me one morning with a bit of news that really cheered me up. 'Nigel, I have a present for you.'

I went up to see Lisa, where she presented me with this beautiful bundle of wrinkles. I named this Shar Pei Levi, after Leviticus and we soon became inseparable. I loved that dog. 'He was the runt of the litter,' she told me.

- 'The runt?! Is that what I am?'

I don't know how Lisa knew, but that dog came along at the exact right time. Thinking about it, I don't think I ever saw Lisa again, but I will always thank her for that. I loved that dog so much although I almost choked when I saw a vet's bill to get him a new knee fitted, just a few months later. £900! I wish I'd gotten him insured.

I moved back into Olinka's flat full time, now with Levi by my side. The Oval flat was a no-go since the police raid. So, we were a family once more, which was nice.

Olinka, Tanya and myself went to Florida that summer for a holiday. We went to Disney World and The Epcot Centre where I was bewitched by this lecture they did on digital shopping. They said that in the not-too-distant future everyone would be buying their stuff from a computer. I was really inspired by this and kept thinking about it all the time. When we got back to the UK, I would bend everyone's ear about this 'online shopping'. I bored Bryan senseless with my vision of V, selling all its records from a computer one day. 'We need to do this!'

I had a million ideas a day, but Bryan was always the one who actually made them happen. Without Bryan I would never have got anything done. Once I'd finished with an idea, I moved on to the next one, while Bryan got to work on the previous project. We worked well together.

I wasn't aware of my state of mind back then, but I was depressed. I had been for a long while. The music, bad boy behaviour and everything that went with it, masked it and made it worse. By and large, my friends and I didn't talk about these issues. We shelved them and carried on, allowing situations to get much fucking worse.

CH. 26

Rumbles In The Jungle

I looked up from the decks when I heard all this shouting. What the fuck was going on? SMASH! Some guy in a balaclava swung through the window of this club on a piece of rope. SMASH! There was another one. SMASH! And another. It was like being in Die Hard or something...

I was out of prison, back on Kiss, playing out and in the office at V. I also had to catch up with my family. It was hard keeping all these plates spinning. I went back to V Recordings for the first time in a while and this girl Katie was there, working away. She had been there on and off for a while now, but we needed her there all the time now as it was getting so busy. I had been seeing Katie, on a casual basis, since 1992. She was a lovely girl. Cypriot. It was cool being back in the office and slowly, but surely, I was getting right back into the swing of things with foreign trips booked and records due for release.

Jungle was a properly established scene by 1994 and the jungle look had started to incorporate Versace, Moschino and Gucci. I had these lovely Versace shirts with patterns all over them and some glasses with the coins at the sides. It was a Puff Daddy look. Champagne was now the drink of choice at these parties and cocaine and crack were now commonplace. People would smoke crack inside these clubs. Jungle nights could be dangerous and drug dealers and gang members would sometimes clash at nights like Telepathy in Stratford, Lazerdrome in Peckham and Hackney's Wax Club. They were still top nights, though, but there was serious criminal activity behind the scenes with gangs asking for protection money from promoters and label bosses. The

Midlands and Manchester were very rough gigs, back then. Manchester was known as Gunchester for obvious reasons.

Deana

"I was 14 in 1989 when I started going to acid house raves. I was never someone to go to pubs or clubs, but there was something about raves I loved. I'm from the Midlands and I went to many of the big raves around Birmingham and Leicester. I was hooked. Then when the music started to splinter, I followed the jungle path. I was a junglist.

The jungle dances, especially in the Midlands – Birmingham's Q Club and Starlight – and further up north, could be quite feisty affairs. There were lots of gang problems and you would often see the lights coming on in the club that would show a mass brawl going down on the dancefloor. Leicester boys fighting with Birmingham or Manchester. It could be quite brutal, but being a girl, with loads of male friends, I avoided all that.

These dances could be quite scary to the outsider if you didn't know how to conduct yourself. I have seen plenty of champagne bottles smashed over people's heads and armed police raids, the lot. Birmingham had the Johnsons Crew and the Burger Bar Crew and I went out with someone from Johnsons for ten years and things would get quite rough.

I went raving so much that I used to see these places as our little playground. If a dealer offered us drugs, I would tell the bouncers – this was before the professional bouncers etc. and when ravers took care of it – and they would take the drugs off the dealer and hand them to us. We would then sell the drugs inside. I moved down to London in the mid-nineties, where things were calmer.

Things could still get dark down south, but jungle wasn't as moody as it was up north. I had a friend come down from Manchester one time and he couldn't believe that people were hugging each other. 'What's going on here then?' he asked. 'Why is everyone hugging and kissing?'

- 'That's what we're like down here!'

We would often take our own bottles of Disaronno and champagne to these dances. You would see DJs and MCs receiving blow jobs by the stairs while smoking weed and doing coke. Then, in the mid-nineties it became kinda acceptable to smoke crack inside a rave.

When crack first appeared, I would chop up any rocks we were 'given' into £20 stones. We made so much money from that. We had these little rolled-up £20 notes in our pockets that we threw onto the floor when we got home. Crack was money. Selling it was one thing, doing it was another.

I remember going to SW1 with some boys from Peckham one night and there was a queue all the way down the road. These boys I was with didn't need to queue and so they went straight in, but we were just behind them and got stopped by security. As we were explaining that we were with these boys, I overheard one of the bouncers talking about my friend who had already gone into the club. 'That lad had a gun,' he said to his mate.

Once inside, I found the boy. 'Are you strapped?' He was. He dropped the gun into my handbag and walked off into the crowd. I was quite drunk by this stage and I walked into the smaller of the rooms and asked the DJ if I could leave something in his record box. He said OK and I dropped my handbag and walked off. I returned a half hour later and this DJ was standing there with his hands on his hips. 'What the fuck did you put in my box?!' That was the mentality back then. I remember a guy getting shot in a Leicester club. He was OK and his mates carried him out to safety, but it could get real rough."

Jungle could be moody in London, but up north things were getting way out of control.

I was playing out at this club in Birmingham at the height of jungle and you could sense a dark vibe. DJs can often feel when things are brewing, but I carried on. Birmingham and Leicester had some pretty lively nights during that period and I was always on the look-out for trouble. Then it kicked off.

SMASH! I looked up and saw a bloke in a balaclava abseiling in through the windows like the SAS or something. What the fuck?! Then SMASH! Another one crashed in. During these moments, the dancefloor shifted and a huge hole appeared where people had been dancing. I just ducked down and crept out. It was like being in the middle of a siege or something.

Manchester was a gangster town at the time, with lots of gun crime. I was alright up there due to my family connections and knew a lot of the people involved. I remember meeting the famous MC Top Cat in Manchester when I was 10. I was at Hendy's house on Clarendon

Road (Whalley Range, Manchester) and Top Cat was there; he was friends with Hendy through the sound system scene. That was a major moment for me. Years later, Hendy was shot and killed.

I had always spent a lot of time in Manchester with my cousins and that continued during the nineties when the gang problems got totally out of control.

Mark Edwards

"I grew up with the sound system culture here in Manchester and when I was older I used to put shows on. Nigel would always be coming up here and has never stopped to be honest. Nigel had a very close association with Manchester with a big following here. He always drew a crowd.

There were a lot of problems here in the nineties with gang problems and back then even Nigel had to be careful. Jumpin Jack Frost was a name, yeah? Nigel had more money than most kids were getting; he had all the nice clothes and jewellery. The more unscrupulous would tax anyone slightly influential, including myself. A lot of people carried firearms around then. The illegal firearms shipped to Manchester and Liverpool from Ireland. They were easily accessible.

By the mid-nineties, Manchester was in the grip of a proper gang war. We were now a long time gone since the raves in the fields. People were dying.

There were certain people who didn't like him, but Nigel knew enough of the right people. I would protect Nigel if there were any gangs causing problems. I would ensure he left a dance safely. We were not gang affiliated, see. But if you made money, then you were a target. 'I want what you've got!' The DJs always got the girls and not all of these girls were single of course. Sometimes these girls were seeing gangsters. That could be a difficult situation, right there."

Manchester raves were fun, but boisterous. Some nights in Manchester had seen ravers shooting guns into the sky during certain tunes. People would come onto the stage and take the mic from terrified MCs. Sometimes DJs had their headphones snatched from them as ravers used them as makeshift mics. It could get dangerous up there, you get me? You had to stand your ground or stay the fuck at home.

DJ Ron

"Frost and I were of a similar ilk and so we got bookings in controversial places, like Manchester. No one else would play there and the agents were moaning. DJs from down south just wouldn't risk it and yet he and I would often play out there.

Moss Side was a volatile place at that time and they were so grateful to us for going up there. I recall walking into the party once and hearing gunshots going off as I was going in. However, no one was running out. 'OK, so I'm going to carry on walking in here.' It was like the Wild West. People would hold lighters up at gigs or raves, yeah, but up there they had aerosol cans they would set fire to, so they were like flame throwers. Bang! Bang! When they asked for a rewind, it was mayhem with pistols going off. We were the only ones playing there and then that went wonky for a while.

I remember doing a rave in Birmingham and some guys from Manchester were refused entry. As Manchester was a no-go area for them, they hit places like Birmingham, Leicester and Stoke. Manchester was chaos, mate!"

Manchester gangs such as Gooch Gang, Cheatham Hill and Doddington were at war in the nineties. I'd known some of these people since I was a kid, so I was in a bit of a privileged position, really, and wasn't that surprised when I was asked to headline a party billed as a 'truce' between all the various gangs. It was a total honour to do it.

The truce party was to be held at my Uncle Berry's West Indian centre on Carmoor Road. Uncle Berry was such a role model to young black men up there and my connection with him was significant. That party was so important in trying to halt the violence at a time when people were getting shot left, right and centre. The night itself was a joy, yeah? There was no bad feeling and everyone had a great time. It felt as if something had lifted from the scene. I was so proud to have played a part in that, although the peace didn't last for as long as we'd hoped.

Dave Stone ran the label Sour and he organised a coach trip to Manchester one time, to take a lot of the jungle community up there. Now, this time here, it was me causing sparks to fly.

So, reggae artists influenced jungle, sure, but the scene was much more than that and had lots of influences from England, Belgium and

USA. However, this night up in Manchester had all these reggae MCs dominating the night and to be honest a lot of them were not that great. Everyone and his uncle were getting involved on stage and the junglists were getting pissed. I was making eye contact with some of my peers and they were equally fucked off by this reggae takeover, but no one was willing to do anything about it. So, not able to take it anymore, I stepped up, grabbed the mic and gave them both barrels. 'Fuck this shit! You're ruining jungle! You've pushed us so far.' I slated all the MCs. 'What's going on here? Jungle is much more than just reggae! Fuck that!' However, diplomatic and professional I tried to be, there were always moments when the mask slipped. What can I say? That was Jumpin Jack Frost. A big ball of uncontrollable energy.

Conrad Edwards

"My father was a youth leader in Manchester and worked at the West Indian Centre, organising summer schemes and football matches. Nigel was always spending time with us up here.

I remember Nigel disturbing a beehive when he was about 12 and they chased him down and stung him. Nigel was always hanging out in the Moss Side precinct when he was older and so he knew a lot of people here before he made it big.

I remember when I first heard the name Jumpin Jack Frost being mentioned and a friend of mine said, 'Bloody hell, that's your cousin! Nigel's bloody famous!' I couldn't believe it.

I organised one of the first jungle parties up here and Nigel played at that. It was at my father's club on Carmoor Road and was billed as 'Reggae Vs Drum & Bass'. There were so many people there and they took the place apart. It was years ahead of what was going on in Manchester at the time.

I used to carry Nigel's record box for him for a while and I couldn't believe it when girls would come over for an autograph. 'Wait a minute! What?!' I just couldn't get it into my head. 'Nigel is famous!'"

CH. 27

Drum And Bass

What was the difference between jungle and drum and bass? I saw drum and bass as an extension of jungle. As jungle started to evolve, and new reggae samples started to become scarce, the music became more technological. The technology allowed time to be stretched giving drum and bass its slick production and effects. The roughness of jungle started to fade a little. The audience started to change as a result with more white faces appearing at parties.

Drum and bass saw musicians such as Goldie going way beyond jungle, with emotional and sometimes cosmic material. For some, the more expansive dnb lacked that raw jungle vibe, but for others, there was only so far jungle could go. It has often been said that dnb was a way of clearing the clubs of the violence and aggression that jungle had become notorious for. Dnb had floaty female vocals and multiple layers of sound. Dnb didn't feature the rough MCs so much and was often picked up by indie artists who used elements of the more 'coffee table' dnb. I guess if one record summed up where the scene was going, it was Goldie's 1995 drum and bass masterpiece *Timeless*. This double album moved the music into the mainstream and was seen by many as a classic album, up there with Pink Floyd or something. *Timeless* was a monster, yeah? It had beautiful vocals by Diane Charlemagne on *Inner City Life* and I loved *Angel* and *Kemistry,* the tribute to Kemi. I remember hearing Doc Scott's 'The King Of The Rollers' remix of Rufige Kru's *Ghosts Of My Life* around then. I lost my mind when I heard *The Unofficial Ghost* for the first time. I was obsessed with music at this point and it was so emotional to me as well as therapeutic.

Big, Bad & Heavy

Adam F's *Metropolis* was like being trapped inside a *Bladerunner* set and *Circles* made us dance like lovers in the night. It wasn't the same vibe as jungle, but dnb had to happen in a way, for the scene and the music to evolve.

***

1995, both V Recordings and Philly Blunt were doing well. So much so, I decided to head to the music conference Midem in Cannes to try and set up some licensing deals. All the music industry bods met at Midem to do business and it was a great excuse to party. I hooked up with this gorgeous French girl and got fuck all sorted for the label, however. Ha ha.

Back in the UK, we heard a rumour that some Japanese label had released some of our tracks without our permission. Now, this got my blood boiling. It was moments like this that the old Frost reared up. I could feel the rage brewing. Some cunt had been making money from our music and they were going to pay.

We did a little digging around and found that these guys were linked to Smiley Culture who was my uncle's cousin and this caused a bit of friction between us, but my good friend Little Andy managed to smooth things out. However, these fuckers still ended up with the money.

There was a serious undercurrent of criminal activity back then and I was trying to work out what the fuck we could do about it, when we received some information about another prick who was selling our records to shops before they were released, thus making a killing on the side. We were pointed in the direction of a record shop in Archway, north London.

I took Mikey Bullforce, Rob Blake and a few mates down to this record shop. The mission: to get the owner of this shop to spill the beans. I was calm to begin with. 'I would like you to tell me the name of the person who has been selling our music on the side? Tell me that and we will go. Yeah?'

- 'I don't know, mate!' he said.

I knew he was lying. 'You fucking lying cunt! Tell me who's been fucking about with my music!' This guy still wasn't budging.

- 'If I knew I'd tell you.'

I was fucked off now and so we started smashing the shop up. One of my mates leant over and emptied the till. 'I don't know!!!' My friend stabbed the shopkeeper in the hand. 'Aaaarrgghh!'

'I'm going to ask you one more time. Who?!' Suddenly, the front door banged open.

'Nobody move!' Fuck me, it was the police. I really thought we were done for now. The police asked us what was happening and I took control. It seemed as if someone had heard the commotion and had phoned the feds.

'These guys have been selling our music without permission, officer and although we're trying to do things the right way, sometimes we get people stealing from us.'

It seemed as if the information I was giving them tallied with something else they were interested in and the police then started on this shop owner who had hidden his bleeding hand from view.

I am pretty sure the police had these guys under investigation as they didn't seem at all bothered by us. We were told to leave.

It later turned out that a guy who worked for Sony's distributor was making a killing by nicking and selling their records on the side, including Mariah Carey and other major acts signed with Sony, and of course V. This prick had been stealing records that hadn't been released yet and selling them directly to stores. A massive court case ensued.

Somehow, we got off scot-free that day. However, that altercation proved that the old Frost was only ever seconds away from reappearing. When the anger took hold, it possessed me. I couldn't control it.

***

Money came, money went. I had a grand in an envelope at this one party and when I went to the back office at Roast, to get my night's wages, I realised I'd fucked up. I went to slot the money in with the rest and realised I'd lost the lot. It had fallen out of my pocket and onto the stage. Someone was having a great fucking night. Fuck! I was sick, man. I looked everywhere for that envelope. A mate offered me some weed and a bottle and I calmed down for a while, but when I awoke the following morning, I was PISSED! A fucking grand! It really was a jungle out there, yeah?

CH. 28

The Darkest Jungle

As you've gathered, I have never really been a one-woman man. I have always had my head turned by the ladies. For the most part I got away with it, but I was well and truly caught out around 1995. Cold.

I woke up one day to find Olinka, and a girl I was seeing, both downstairs waiting for me. 'What the fuck?!' Olinka had been though my phone and found the messages and had rung this girl up and invited her over for a showdown. Fuck me!

My grandmother's death the year before had sowed the seeds, but now I really was in trouble. I was kicked out of the house by a furious Olinka.

I knew it was all my fault, but this split really broke me. Suddenly, all the ego and bravado fell in around me, leaving one very weak man. I was done in.

I moved into a place on Brixton Hill and just shut up shop. I became a recluse. I was so fucking moody I didn't speak to anyone. Not a soul.

It was just before this dark phase that I ended the casual relationship I had with Katie in the office. We were never that serious, but when I started seeing this girl Sharon, I could tell that Katie was pissed. Sharon and I didn't last either, but Katie did a really stupid thing.

Katie was in charge of my money and had £10,000 of it for safekeeping. Then she went missing. I finally managed to track her down and strong words were said. When I went to get this money back, she said it had gone. 'What do you mean it's gone?! It's not a fucking tenner! It's ten fucking grand!' Katie had taken it. I blew my top.

I grabbed her and threw her to the floor. Now, I would never hit a woman, but I did manhandle her. She lay on the floor crying and I just didn't know what to do. In the end, she returned £5,000, but that was all that was left. Then she disappeared and I never saw her again. I really liked Katie, but I had hurt her and she had taken revenge. Sharon had been very supportive too, but I couldn't blame her for getting out. I think I loved her, but I never said anything. I was too cool for that shit. So, Olinka had finally ditched me. I couldn't blame her.

I was getting more and more depressed. My mate Duffus would take me to gigs and I would just sit in silence. I was empty. It was all my fault. I couldn't blame anyone else.

I remember bumping into Grooverider one day. 'You alright, bruv?' he said, trying to catch my eye. I just shrugged. I had lost interest in everything. Bryan took me to one side when I saw him next. 'Why don't you take some time off? Just leave everything to me and come back when you're ready.' I took him up on his offer and went straight back home.

That dog was about the only thing keeping me going. I wouldn't even listen to music or watch TV. I just sat there, smoking weed while staring at the wall. I was the architect of my own disaster, but that didn't help really. I was in a very dark place. Well, I had lost it.

I remember walking down the road in the pouring rain, wearing a T-shirt and shades. I think the neighbours were a little scared of me. I wasn't eating properly either and had lost a lot of weight. I made sure Levi was fed, though. That dog saved me right there. I had to feed him and I had to take him for walks, even if I was wearing shades in the rain. I remember my sister Yolanda trying to talk me round, but a light had gone out and it took a long while for it to even begin to glimmer again.

I was a selfish prick who only reacted to people once they'd been hurt. As soon as Olinka dumped me, I wanted her back. More than anything in the world. Prior to that, I was seeing girls all over the place.

Yolanda Thompson

"Nigel became very depressed when he split from his child's mother. He wouldn't come out of the house unless it was to walk the dog.

My mum was very worried and took him to hospital so the doctors could give him counselling, but he ran off. He would disappear as

The Darkest Jungle

you talked to him, just drifted off like he wasn't listening. He was very withdrawn and it was very concerning for all of us. He was getting thinner and thinner and more and more depressed."

This went on for the best part of a year, and at my worst, Mum had planned to take to me to hospital to have me sectioned. Now, I can't believe that I was like that. Even when I played gigs, I was very, very moody. I just couldn't smile anymore. However, I needed that time out and gradually I got to a point where I could socialise a little, with people who knew me well. It was a lesson in life and it was up to me as to whether I learned anything from it, or simply carried on as I always had.

Then, just as I was getting back on my feet, an angel was sent from heaven to save me. That angel? Eric Cantona.

I was sitting at home watching Man Utd play Liverpool in the FA Cup Final in 1996. My mum was so worried about that game, in fact, my whole family was. People had been trying to reach me for days, but I wasn't answering the phone or the door. They were so worried that Liverpool would win this game, as they didn't know how I would cope. Then something truly magical happened when Eric Cantona scored the only goal of the match, thus winning the cup for my beloved Man United. I just felt this great weight lift from my shoulders. I got up and screamed and pumped the air and it was the weirdest thing ever. Had Eric Cantona saved my life? Fucking yeah!!!

I just lifted out of that gloom. It was amazing. I felt euphoric. That Monday I went into the office for the first time in ages. It was clear that Bryan had done an amazing job in my absence. There were two new girls in the office too called Shirley and Tracey. I was so out of the loop that they seemed to know more about what was going on at V than I did. Still, I had no one to blame but myself.

My show on Kiss carried on and was going from strength to strength. My jungle/dnb show was one of Kiss's top shows and I loved doing the handover from the Rap Show, which was on just before mine. Then one day, I saw these two beautiful girls in the studio, producing the rap show. This girl Jay was amazing and we started talking a bit. Then we started seeing each other. Jay was an amazing boost to my self-esteem and she really helped me get back on track. I was slowly starting to emerge from the darkness.

Kiss had a football team for a bit and that helped me no end in returning to normality. I had always loved football and was captain of

'Yellow House' at boarding school. I was so proud to coach a team of younger kids who really weren't that talented or confident. But through hard work they got to quite a decent standard and I was so made up for them.

If I wasn't playing football or playing out, I was at home with Jay just chilling. It was great having a kickabout over east London way with Grooverider, Pete Nice, Randall, Killa and Flux. I rediscovered my love of football by playing in the park with those boys. I remember we played in a charity match for a kid called Daniel De-Gale who is sadly no longer with us. We narrowly beat Choice FM that day, in a close encounter. Randall and I formed a great striking partnership.

After that charity match we played Choice again and thrashed them six nil. My good friend Spoony scored all six.

I first met Spoony back in 1994 when we were setting up the office for V. Spoony used to repair old computers and we met through our mutual friend DJ Ron. Spoony was becoming a massive name in the emerging UK garage scene and had a great show on Kiss. He was also a very good footballer.

We carried on with kickabouts in the park after those two games, as football was so therapeutic for me and really helped me through those dark times. I guess you'd call it male bonding. But there were still signs that I hadn't fully recovered, such as the small 'Saturday Night Special' or '22' I carried around in my ruck sack. What the fuck? I may have been getting better, but I was still fucking crazy! I remember Groove looking into my sports bag and seeing this piece. 'What the fuck have you got that for?!' I really wasn't right in the head at that point. Maybe I needed professional help beyond Eric Cantona.

Jay Davidson

"I was a producer at Kiss in 1996. I was a hip-hop girl, really, not a junglist exactly, but I went to a few dances. I was a producer of Max & Dave's Rap Show from 7-9pm and we would always hand over to Nigel at 9pm.

We would face each other in the two studios through this glass and I could see that Nigel was eyeing us up. I thought he was into my colleague Deborah, to be honest, but I later found out it was me.

Oh my god, jungle was huge then, it was like the energy around grime now. Nigel was a ghetto superstar, and was just full of energy and so excited about life. He was charismatic, charming and funny; but he was also a rude boy. Nigel was a road man; still a guy from Brixton who still lived that life to some degree.

I met him just as he had emerged from his dark phase in 1996. I wasn't interested in Nigel, but he pursued me. Frost kept dropping hints to all these people that he liked me. He wore me down in the end.

Nigel was very spontaneous and his life seemed chaotic and haphazard, but he still got shit done. This was fine if you had nothing to do, but sometimes it was just too much. There was no balance to his life. It was chaos!"

Bryan had started up a club night in my absence and it felt like a dis. I know that I'd been away and whatever, but that was how it felt. I thought we were business partners, yet here he was working with Oliver and Edo and Dave Stone to put on Movement at Bar Rumba. I was upset about that. I felt left out and thought it was a fucking liberty to be honest. I'd considered confronting Bryan about this, but Jay talked me out of it. I never said anything, though. I am not good at talking things through, I just let them build and build until they explode. Then I do something stupid. Both Bryan and I had poured blood and sweat into this thing and yet here I was, out in the cold. They didn't even ask me to play at this night and I was kinda pissed about it, to be honest. I had put every penny I had into this business. But I let it slide.

Bryan and I still had V. We were still like brothers and he tried his best to get me out of the gloom and depression that had engulfed me. Oliver and Edo quickly became good friends too. I was thankful that I'd emerged from the shadows and so that was enough back then, really, plus I had a few foreign jaunts planned to help keep my spirits up.

***

I was going to 'bleach it'. I wasn't going to sleep. I had to get up early to get a flight and was so excited I decided to stay out and have some fun instead. I was going to Japan for the first time and I was buzzing.

I decided to hit the Hanover Grand, this Wednesday night, yeah? I popped my chains on and went out into the West End. I had a nice little hip-hop look going on and was feeling good. I bought some champagne and started chatting to these American girls. It was one of those nights where you just felt so excited and everyone seemed to feed off it. These girls invited me into the VIP area and we had a really good laugh. I was talking to this one girl and I couldn't really see her face because of the hair that hung in front of her eyes. At one point, she brushed her hair back and I realised who it was. Mary J. Blige! I nearly fell over, for fuck's sake.

I had such a laugh with Randall and Digital in Tokyo. It was the first time I'd played there and it was like touching down on an alien planet. I was gobsmacked.

Tokyo was mad. You'd go to parks and see rockabillies, then dreads and punks. We would see these vending machines selling schoolgirls' knickers and stuff. What the fuck?!

I remember the gambling arcade we were in, started shaking at one point and I was so amazed. 'Did you feel that?!' Randall shouted excitedly.

- 'Yeah, cool innit?!'
- 'Cool? It's a fucking earth tremor!'
- 'What? I thought the building was doing it.'

I thought that Japan, being so technologically advanced, had buildings that could simulate earthquakes as part of a game or something. I thought the arcade we were in was doing a little shake.

The gig that night was wicked. The crowd were really into jungle. There was so much love for the music inside The Liquid Rooms.

Randall had been to Japan before and he loved it there. I remember sitting on this bullet train when we travelled from Tokyo to Osaka and Randall looked over. 'Just wait 'til this takes off!' Boosh! This thing just glided away. This was the future.

Before we left, we visited Electric City in Tokyo. This place had so much technology. I bought two limited edition gold-plated Technics decks and a mixer to match. I also got a keyboard for the studio we had built for the V Office.

When we got back, we had to face Customs. 'I'm not declaring this lot. It's going to cost a fortune,' I said to Randall.

- 'You can't smuggle that lot through,' he said.
- 'No? Fucking watch me!'

I threw a coat and a jacket over the boxes and sailed straight past. Fuck it! Randall did the exact same thing.

CH. 29

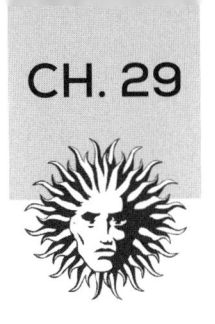

Critical Mass

Movement at Bar Rumba (Shaftesbury Avenue) was going from strength to strength and then, when it went monthly at the Brixton Mass, I found myself guilty by association. Mass was located opposite The Fridge, which was run by Ralph, who sent Little Andy to my office one day to summon me to the club so we could discuss this new night. Ralph was my elder – I knew him growing up – and he wasn't someone to cross. 'What's this Movement thing, Frost? Why didn't you come to me with this?' They were not happy that Movement had opened up a rival venue, literally across the road from theirs. In fact, he was fucking fuming.

It was not an ideal situation, but I couldn't deny having anything to do with this as it would have left Bryan and the boys in a whole heap of problems they would not have been able to deal with. Ralph knew me and so was going to be softer on me than he would have been with the other lot. 'Why didn't you come to me with this thing, Frost? Now you're setting up a rival thing, over the road from us…' He was really pissed and as an elder to me, I had to pay respect. Somehow, I managed to smooth things over, although we did have further meetings over the matter. I didn't let on to Bryan, Oliver and Edo, I just let them get on with it. For now, the wolves were kept at bay. I will always feel a little disrespected that I wasn't involved in Movement, but that said, Bryan kept V alive while I was going through that dark period. For that, I will be forever grateful.

V was booming. I remember being in Music House when Ed Rush played me *Funktion,* which he'd recorded with Optical. Ed described it as something 'different' that I might just like. I ended up signing the record there and then. It was a fucking banger, yeah?

Roni, Krust and all the others on V had been doing so much good music since my breakdown that Bryan suggested doing a compilation album and with that *V Classics* was born.

V Classics was released in 1997 and it was big. We had Roni Size, Krust, Die, Goldie, Dillinja and many more on that album, which really went on to forge the V name.

Around 1997, I would often spent Sunday nights at Twice As Nice (at Club Coliseum) in Vauxhall. Run by my good mate Steve Gordon, I loved Twice As Nice. UK garage was just kicking off and the smart dress code and beautiful women really appealed to me. Twice As Nice was a legendary spot right there and it had that little gangster edge to it.

The *V Classics* album was getting us noticed. Patrick Moxey from New York signed us to his Payday/Ultra Records label following that album's release and we were soon in Manhattan chatting to Patrick and his team. Moxey had a pedigree in hip-hop and had looked after Guru, Gang Starr and people like that and he was really feeling our sound. His promotions guy Gamal had loads of great ideas on how to promote us out there.

New York was great and we spent loads of time shopping in Brooklyn, where they still had all the big shops you'd see in Manhattan, but with much lower prices. I hated getting cabs out there. Yellow cabs are like black cabs in London, in that they will not stop for a black man. Fuckers!

Bryan, MC Moose, Ray Keith and I did a mini tour of the US – organised by our agents Gerry Gerrard and Steve Goodgold – not long after our meeting with Moxey. Gerry was a big cheese who worked with major rock bands like Nine Inch Nails and this tour sounded like the real deal. In reality, the tour saw us staying in a string of cheap hotels in seven or eight cities, but you had to start at the bottom over there.

Thanks to Gamal, we had interviews set up in every city and so that helped. We were the support act for a hip-hop collective known as The X-Men or X-E-Cutioners. Big up to Roc Raida (RIP), Sinister and Rob Swift. Raider was my main man and Sinister was my boy too. Swift kept himself to himself, though, which was fine.

The tour manager was a girl called Robyn Pelka and we became really close on this tour. Not close, as in seeing each other, though. We just became really good friends. Robyn was of Polish descent and she was my home girl. Robyn was a recovering heroin addict and a witness in a high-profile court case over there at the time and so she was sent on tour with us to get her out of New York for a bit.

Robyn was like my little sister and she would stay in my room with me. Bryan and Moose would tease me about her, but there was nothing going on. We were just so close, like brother and sister.

Every city we arrived in, there were members of the press waiting to do interviews with us. We met these two girls in San Francisco called DeMarie and Laura B. Laura was particularly bangin', but Bryan was ribbing me about her because she wore baggy flares. 'I know she's bangin' underneath all that,' I told him.

- 'How do you know?'
- 'I just know.'

We went out in the evening and woooooaahh! Laura looked amazing. Bryan's jaw hit the floor. I was enchanted by this girl. I vowed to see her again when the tour was over.

That tour was a wonderful experience and it allowed me time to put some distance between me and my depression. I couldn't be down about things over there. It was sunny every day and I was touring that enormous country promoting an album on my own record label. I was blessed. The only downside was when Bryan left his passport on the plane (tucked inside the glove compartment on the back of the chair in front). We had to wait for hours for that plane to be cleaned before we could actually see LA. We played Raymond Roker's Science later that night.

I was also booked to play this JuJu Beats festival in the desert, while we were there. This festival was amazing; slap bang in the middle of nowhere. I met these two lovely girls at JuJu who I'd bumped into at Mass the year before. It was lovely seeing Alexis and Vanessa again in this desert, 30 miles outside LA.

I remember Clayton from Hardware handing me this track *Messiah* by Conflict and it was a *tune*! I was the first person to drop that track in the US. It was so great seeing those girls that whenever I heard *Messiah* again, I instantly thought of Alexis. We became close friends after that. The moment that track dropped it felt like being in a church and the vibe was off the charts. There must have been 10,000 people in the desert sun. It was real hands-in-the-air shit.

A real moment on that tour was driving into New Orleans from the airport. We'd been picked up by this guy Donny who was acting as our guide as we entered the city. We hit this stretch of road in New Orleans that was flanked on either side by swamp, when the car suddenly screeched to a halt. 'See that?' said Donny pointing out through the windscreen. There, in the middle of this road, was a fucking alligator! The cars were honking and making a noise, but this creature was not moving. It was while we waited for this fucker to clear the road that I had another reality check. How had I ended up face to face with an alligator in New Orleans as a touring musician? I don't think the 14-year-old me would have believed this. My life had changed beyond all recognition. I had a girlfriend in California in Laura B and Robyn was my little sister from New York. Plus, I now had a network of new friends in the US. It was crazy!

Junglists Platoon consisted of Scooba, Subflow and a few others. They were the first to get jungle going in the US and we first met them on that tour. Years down the line, they would always hook up with us whenever we were in LA. They sorted us out with weed, which always helped. LA was also home to my close friends Jodie, Erin, Nexy, Essassin, Rob Machete and Big Sam (who owned the LA record store Temple of Boom). I loved LA.

When we finished the tour, I hooked up with Laura B again in San Francisco. I stayed at her house and while she went to work during the day, I would go exploring the city. It was an intriguing and fascinating place, but San Francisco had *so* many homeless people, many of whom were begging, that it could be quite overwhelming. Laura B worked in the film industry and we were tight for a bit, but after a week or so, I had to go.

Soon after we got back to the UK, we got a call from Twilo, the biggest club night in New York. They wanted Bryan and me to do a monthly residency. Now this was good. Raahhhhhhh!!!

New York became a second home for a while. Konkrete Jungle in New York was another great night to play and was the longest-running drum and bass night in the US. I did a mix CD for the promoter Mac; a life-long servant to drum and bass and a man who deserves a lot of love and respect for what he's done for the music in America. Bryan and I would head off every few weeks to the Big Apple to play out at Twilo, this amazing club.

I remember deciding that I wanted a mink coat around this time. I was aiming for that pimp look from the old-style movies. And so we went to the fur district where I found this lovely mink bomber jacket for $2,500. 'Fuck it! I want it!' I had no cash on me and so Bryan put it on his credit card. I wore it as soon as we got out of the shop. I was the shit! God, this mink jacket was amazing. Not only that, but wearing that mink was the only time I managed to get a cab to stop. Money talks.

We would shop at Jimmy Jazz, Dr Jay's and Macy's in Brooklyn, which were a lot cheaper than the stores in Manhattan. Bryan loved his Maurice Malone back then. We also bought stacks of bootleg videos and shit.

Bryan Gee

"I remember that mink coat because I bought it! That was Nigel, through and through. He liked the fluff and that. This big, white mink was brighter than anything I had ever seen in my life. I said, 'Are you sure?' when he pulled it off the rack. The gangster thing was in back then with Puff Daddy and all that. Nigel would have had a mink hat to go with it, if they'd had any.

He wore that mink out at Bar Rumba and he lit up the entire club. It was like a golden fleece or something, it was so bright. Everyone else had bomber jackets on, but that was Nigel. He loved his clothes and style. Everything had to be the most expensive: glasses, belts, shoes. It had to be the real shit. Nigel had always been like that.

We went to Dekalb Avenue in Brooklyn when we were in New York. This place had all the hip hop stuff and we were crazy for all that. We bought CDs, tapes, hats and belts. We would often spend all day Saturday there with MC Dynamite, just looking for stuff."

I remember getting a flight back to the UK from New York with techno legend Frankie Bones and house DJ Disciple in '97 and we were so pissed. I was smoking weed in the toilet on the plane and we were making such a noise. It was around this time that I started to party a little harder. I had a lot more money in my pocket and I was determined to enjoy it.

Gamal did a wonderful job promoting our album over in the US with loads of press in the nationals. He also hooked us up with some cool brands too: Zoo York, Maurice Malone and Tommy Hilfiger. All these labels started giving us loads of free stuff. It was quite surreal actually. We were off all over the place, from LA to Ilford!

Big, Bad & Heavy

Andy Nicholls

"I used to be a raver when I was younger. I used to headbutt the ceiling to the bassline, when Jumpin Jack Frost came on. Then, years later, we got to meet through a mutual friend and I became his driver for a bit. We had loads of adventures.

1997, I was driving Nigel along the A12 to Clacton for a gig. It was a stormy night with heavy rain coming down. My friend was in the front seat and Nigel was in the back. We were on the dual carriageway where there was this slow gradient going down that went back up overground. To the right, were these gaps, so police could u-turn. Well, such was the torrential rain, we aquaplaned straight through the gap and into oncoming traffic.

I had no seatbelt on and because the impact was 137mph, I bent the wheel into the steering column. It was a big crash. I came around and everything was red. Dripping red.

I remember asking Nigel if I was OK. Nigel said, 'You're going to be fine,' and phoned for an ambulance. My leg hurt, my jaw and face were swollen; my teeth had punctured my mouth. Nigel had a gouge taken out of his arm by a window handle.

I went to hospital and as I left, the police were phoning Nigel a cab so he could go and do his gig. Ha ha.

I had an X-ray and got a cast on my leg. Three hours later, the mobile rang. It was Frost. 'You coming to Ilford? I just met DJ Ron and he's going to take us to the club.'

- *'What?! I'm in hospital, mate! I've just been in a car crash, remember?'*
- *'Just discharge yourself.'*

I must have been mad, but an hour later, there I was in DJ Ron's car, squashed into the front seat on my way to an Ilford club, with a swollen face, plaster cast and a trouser leg missing. My lips had been stitched and I couldn't talk. My kneecap was shattered and there was blood all over my clothes as I sat down by a wall in this Ilford club, waiting for Ron to take me home. Not many people survive a head-on car crash, never mind going raving straight after. Still, at least I hadn't become the driver that killed Jumpin Jack Frost. Small mercies I guess."

***

Critical Mass

My loyalty to Man Utd was getting more and more obsessional. There was an FA Cup game at the start of 1997 against Wimbledon at Selhurst Park, which saw me lose my mind.

My daughter Tanya was getting older and so I decided to indoctrinate her in the ways of the Red Army and got her a shirt with Giggs written on the back. When I managed to get tickets to Selhurst for the Wimbledon game she came with me.

United were losing one nil with just injury time beckoning when Peter Schmeichel went up for a corner.

I was standing there, wishing for something to happen; just praying that the lanky keeper could cause some chaos in the penalty area. The ball came in, Schmeichel turned and... wow! He scored with an overhead kick! I went mad. I think I lost my mind for a bit. I was going mad. Fuck me! Injury-time bicycle-kick winner from a goalie. It didn't get much better than that.

Then disaster! The ref ruled the goal offside.

I couldn't believe it. I went fucking nuts! I was screwing, man. What the fuck!!

I'm not sure what happened, but the next thing I knew, I was on the pitch and two stewards were trying to get me off. Our seats were near the touchline, but somehow, I had managed to run right onto the turf and I'm not sure what it was I was trying to do. Who knows, maybe if those stewards hadn't stopped me from getting any further, there would have been a strangled referee. It was crazy.

They wanted to take me away and arrest me, but it was only the sight of Tanya crying in her seat saying, 'That's my dad!' that convinced them to give me a break. Tanya kept asking me, 'What were you thinking?' The truth was, I didn't have a clue. I just went mad. United lost.

OK, so I was hardly a role model for the young, but I did take a young MC called Kerry under my wing around this time. Kerry was a real livewire. I loved her spunky, get-up-and-go attitude, but she was a becoming a liability to herself and was getting into trouble with court fines etc. I ended up paying her legal fees while giving her the odd lecture to try and calm her down. Kerry had lost her dad and she was finding it hard to cope. My mates couldn't work out what I was doing with her, but I saw something in her and got to know her mum really well. Sometimes, in this business, you need someone to put an arm around you, and on that particular occasion, the arm belonged to me. We are still friends to this day and I am very proud of her achievements.

CH. 30

Mercury In Our Blood

V was flying. *V Classics* was a hit and now we had *Planet V* taking shape. Roni Size was blowing up too having just signed with a major. Talkin' Loud (part of Polydor) released Roni's new album *Newforms* and it was something else, man. Roni, Krust, Die and Suv were smashing it, plus they'd done some tracks for *Planet V*, which we were delaying for release as Roni had just been nominated for an award. The Mercury Prize.

I didn't know much about the Mercury Prize and when I read the shortlist – Radiohead, The Prodigy, Beth Orton and The Chemical Brothers – I didn't think Roni had much of a chance, to be honest. Jungle/dnb never really got much love from the mainstream. Goldie's 1995 *Timeless* album had been the biggest thing to emerge from the scene up until that point.

I had become very tight with Goldie and often played his nights at the Leisure Lounge in Holborn. Goldie was sponsored by so many labels at that time and he was a tabloid regular too. Tommy Hilfiger was the label back then and Goldie always gave me first dibs on what he'd been sent. DC shoes used to send him 4-5 pairs of trainers a week. My daughter Tanya got so much Hilfiger stuff her nickname was Tommy Girl for a while. Because I was in New York so much I'd bring home bags of clothes for her.

Just like Goldie's *Timeless,* two years previously, *New Forms* by Roni Size Reprazent had started a wave of interest in this underground music again, prompting the Mercury Prize nomination. We were proud to be with Roni, Krust, Die and Suv and the boys at The Dorchester Hotel for the ceremony. I had a lovely £500 suit and a case of cigars.

I tried to persuade Bryan to get dressed up, but he wasn't having any of it. 'I'm going as me,' he said. Because we expected The Prodigy or someone to win, we just thought we'd have a laugh and celebrate being there with our friends. Giles Peterson was with us at our table as he ran Talkin' Loud, who put *New Forms* out and we all had a right laugh that day.

When they announced the winner – Roni – we just looked at each other in shock. What the fuck?! Oh my god! We went crazy. I lit my cigar and just sat there puffing away, unable to take it all in. These guys that Bryan had found in an old box of cassettes were now the most talked-about people in music. Life was never the same after that day.

We joined Roni and the boys on stage and couldn't have been prouder for them. Not only that, but this Mercury Prize winner was due to appear on our upcoming album. We were all winners that day.

For someone like myself – a bad boy from the underground – to be up onstage at The Dorchester, looking out at the British music industry... Well, what can you say?

Movement was on at Bar Rumba that night and so it was the only place to be. The Mercury win was all over the radio and TV and everyone was talking about it. It appeared on the radio as we cabbed it to Bar Rumba. It was on the television in the back office of the club. It was in the papers on the way home that morning. Drum and bass had only gone and popped up into the mainstream. It was fucking insane!

This was a win for anyone who had ever wanted to make a tune whether it was in a studio or at home on a computer. That win was for the whole scene and it couldn't have happened to anyone lovelier than Roni and the boys. The game had changed.

Roni Size

"I first remember the name Jumpin Jack Frost from the rave flyers I used to collect. Krust, Die, Suv and I would go to raves like Fantazia, Dreamscape and clubs like The Edge. You would see Frost's name right there at the top, along with Ratpack and Micky Finn and people like that. So, we knew Frost by name although we didn't quite know his face.

Bryan Gee was working at Rhythm King as an A&R and he was given these two tapes by Paul Wilson and Andy Watkins who were largely responsible for the Spice Girls records. I knew Paul and Andy (Absolute 2) from Bath and they took me to this studio in the late eighties/early nineties to make some music together.

Paul and Andy eventually passed some tapes on to Bryan at Rhythm King and he loved them. So much so, that when the label folded, Bryan took these tapes with him as he saw some future potential in them. We eventually got a call from Bryan and he agreed to come to Bristol to see us. He was starting a new label called V Recordings and Jumpin Jack Frost was his partner. We didn't know Bryan so well, but we knew Frost of course.

We got invited to London to have a meeting with Frost and went to see him at his place in Brixton. I remember Krust, Die and me walking around Brixton and it was pretty dark, these times, so we were lucky that we were with 'made' people. Frost lived in a basement flat and it was well shady, but with an amazing atmosphere. Nigel was there with three others. Nigel did all the talking and said he loved the tunes. 'I'm going to help you get this music out there!'

They were playing some gigs that night and they invited us along. There was me, Krust, Mark Ital from Iration Steppers, Bryan and H. Frost had three or four gigs that night and I remember him dropping our music at The Edge in Coventry. Wow! That was the first time we'd heard our music played out live. It was a real moment. Then we went to Birmingham and met Goldie. We finished off at London's Jungle Fever. It was the adventure of all adventures. We got home about 7am and we were shattered, but we'd just heard our music being dropped at these events and that was incredible. Our music was played through a proper system and once we'd heard this – and seen the reaction –

we knew exactly what we had to do with these tracks to improve them. Not only that, but Frost and Gee gave these tapes to everyone who mattered: Fabio and Grooverider, Rebel MC, DJ Ron and DJ Rap. We knew we had to sign with V Recordings. We stayed at Bryan's house all the time after that.

Being lured by a label outside of Bristol gave us some kudos. We were the new kids on the block and had something special. I always described it as the golden ticket and Bryan and Frost were the first to let us in through the door.

There is a great interview between me and Frost on his Kiss FM show, which opened the door to many A&R men. That show on Kiss should still be on. It was fantastic. Frost had a real ear for the music.

We would bring DAT tapes to London and the stuff we thought they'd like, never quite hit the spot. They would always go for something else. They really knew what they wanted.

V broke so many tunes back then. Playing out, Frost would drop dnb like my Music Box or It's A Jazz Thing at a Jungle Fever or Roast. Or he'd spin Krust's Jazz Note or Deceivers. They showed a lot of love for these boys from Bristol. I learned so much from Frost and Gee. They were flying back across the Atlantic all the time, and they had all the latest clothes and slang. I remember Frost kept saying, 'Yeah, that's runnin'' and when I used it back in Bristol, they were like, 'What? Runnin'? What's that?'

They were not only our mentors, but they actually cared about us. I could phone Frost at 4am, with a new bit of music and he would pick up the phone. Amazing friends. Not only that, but Bryan, Frost, (LTJ) Bukem, Fabio and Grooverider are my still favourite DJs.

I was getting a lot of approaches from labels after that initial phase and Frost and Bryan were quite determined that they were the best to be with at that time. They were right. There was Lucky Spin, Moving Shadow and RAM, but they put us straight: 'You'd me mad signing with them.' That said, they understood when Talkin' Loud came knocking. 'Yeah, they're a major...'

We were playing Montreux Jazz Festival in Switzerland when we found out we'd been nominated for the Mercury Prize. We didn't know much about this award, but we thought we'd go to make up the numbers. We were very tired when we turned up, but we were determined to eat and drink as much as we could.

My mates back in Bristol were like, 'What the fuck?! Who are they?' when they saw Frost and Bryan on TV. Frost had the sharp suit and the fat cigar and they really looked the business. This was no joke. The whole experience would not have been the same without them.

We played that night, but were very tired. We had a great time drinking and relaxing and caught up with some friends of ours as well. The food was very good. Then, ten minutes before the end, Photek come over. 'We've heard a few whispers that you've got it!'

- 'What?! No way.'

It was inconceivable. Then another guy repeated the rumour. I honestly wasn't interested.

The announcement was surreal. I had Chemical Brothers down as the favourites as they were so tight, but the judges took a fancy to us.

I guess we looked like no one else in the room and we were a little 'kicky', I guess. What a moment. Everything changed after that.

We went to Bar Rumba that night, having stayed at the hotel for a bit. It was a V Recordings night there of course and it was a stormy one! Ha ha. We were renowned for our parties, as that's what we did. We set the standard for work hard, play even harder."

CH. 31

Sex, Drugs And Drum And Bass

A major US tour was announced for Roni Size Reprazent soon after the Mercury was announced. Things were really escalating. The tour was Roni Size Reprazent with Planet V supporting.

There was no more Chelsea hotel and cheap roadside spots. We now had two million-pound tour buses and rooms at the Plaza, Paramount and Soho Grand. We were doing this one in style, yeah?

Moose was touring with us a lot back then, but he had a day job and was always having to ask for time off, as you just can't turn these opportunities down. So, Moose was constantly trying to explain to his boss why he wasn't coming into work. I guess, going on a US tour with Roni Size was a reasonable excuse.

These tour buses were amazing. The ceilings had mirrors and we had two big fridges, stuffed with drinks and snacks. There were satellite dishes on the roof and all that jazz. It was the shit, man. Our tour manager was Pip (or Sgt Pip as we called him) and our manager Simon Goffe came out for a few days, too.

The New York gig was wicked. I mean, Madonna was there! For fuck's sake. There was a lot of money invested in that tour and our names were getting out and about.

The tour bus was the place to be for the after-party. Girls would come back after the gigs for an hour or so. The fridges on the bus would be restocked and a Kentucky Fried Bargain Bucket of weed would be waiting. We would get through a quarter pound of weed in a day. Cocaine was appearing more and more at these times. It was sex, drugs and drum and bass. The girls would then be asked to leave before we went off to the next town.

The driver was amazing. This guy used to drive country and western stars and rock bands about and we just couldn't work out when he slept. Hats off, mate. The parties would then continue as we rolled down the highways.

We would wake up in the morning and the fridges would be full again. We just couldn't work out what was going on. We would do a gig, have an after party, go to sleep, wake up, enter another city, check into a hotel, chill, do a gig and so on… This was what happened every single day as we drove around America. I honestly thought I was dreaming.

Roni Size

"We ended up touring with V Recordings, right across America for two months. We had two tour buses and because of that we formed such a tight unit. We got on well with Bryan, Frost and Moose and had some great moments. There were no bad vibes on that trip. It was very special.

I was actually working all through that tour and so I didn't party so much, but it was definitely going on. I could hear it! I could smell it! A lot of Blunts were smoked.

It was while on tour, following the Mercury Prize that I realised the severity of where we were, back then. I was writing music, doing loads of interviews and dealing with the label etc. We did a lot for MTV around then, too. I was definitely the sensible one.

It was weird over in the US at that time, as people didn't know which bubble we were from. Then we met this cowboy waiter in this isolated diner in the middle of a remote town, who spotted us. 'You guys are Roni Size Reprazent!' How on earth?! We were all so shocked, and it was then that we finally realised that we were doing something recognisable.

I loved New York and it was so great meeting our idols like Guru and Method Man. I loved seeing all these famous landmarks for the first time too. I remember us all standing outside Trump Tower.

Having Bryan and Frost there made all of this so much more credible. Credit where it's due. They were a great support act. I remember going *on after them in LA and they had rinsed the place out. We knew we had a job on our hands that night."*

My good friend Robyn couldn't make that tour, but we hooked up with her friend Squishy. Squishy was a Las Vegas showgirl and a real wild character. Boy, did she like to party! I remember sitting in the tour bus as it was parked on Hollywood Boulevard and my eyes popped out, when I saw Squishy playing with some bananas. This was lunchtime and we were parked on a busy road while this girl was having sex with some bananas. Luckily, the windows were blacked out. I remember Moose coming on to the bus to get something before realising what was happening. He simply spun around and bolted for the exit. Ha ha. There I sat, snorting coke on Hollywood Boulevard, as a showgirl pleasured herself with some fruit. It didn't get much better than that.

There were so many women on that tour that Bryan and I started calling ourselves The Hot Boys! When we had after-parties at hotels we would get adjoining rooms to double the size of the party. There were so many women, and they know who they are. I don't want to embarrass anyone by mentioning their real names. But those parties were really fucking wild.

Once you'd established a reputation as someone who liked the ladies, word seemed to get out all around the country. You would get to Chicago and they would all seem to know that you were game. I don't know if there was a network of groupies who passed on information, but whatever it was, I wasn't complaining. It was incredible.

Back in the UK, Hot Boys HQ was the Holiday Inn, King's Cross. If walls could talk eh? We would party there for days on end. People would be banging on the doors and calling reception, but we just kept partying. Life at HB HQ was eventful, to say the least.

Bryan Gee

"We built up a proper relationship with Roni's Full Cycle and soon V was lording it as one of the biggest drum and bass labels going. Roni's boys had a new sound – a Bristol sound – and every tune was killing it and because of that, V was growing. Then of course, the majors started getting involved in jungle/dnb. It was like the grime thing now, where everyone wants a slice. Sony and London did a deal with us for Leviticus.

Then Roni got a manager when they signed to Giles Peterson's Talkin' Loud and they started looking at the bigger picture. The next level was beckoning.

I had mixed emotions when Roni signed to Talkin' Loud. It was clearly a cut-off point for us, in terms of getting music from our biggest artist. But wow! It was an amazing deal for them. Reprazent signing to a major allowed us to look at the bigger picture too. We had such a good friendship with the Bristol boys. Reprazent was a band that took drum and bass to a new audience. They played the music live with a double bass player, drummer and vocalist and the shows were electric. They blew everyone away. The energy at those shows?! Wow! They were the hottest ticket in town.

We lived so far underground we didn't even know what the Mercury Prize was. Roni just phoned us one day and said, 'We're going to an awards tonight, do you fancy coming along?' To us, it was a night-out with some free drinks; we had no idea what it was really all about.

We rocked down to the awards at this grand old place in Mayfair. This was our first experience of this type of thing. We sat at our table where we could see The Prodigy over there, and Chemical Brothers around the corner. When they read out the winner, we just couldn't believe it. No one expected it and so it was a genuine surprise. We thought The Prodigy would win with their comeback album. 'The winner is... Roni Size Reprazent!' We jumped up and followed Roni and the boys onto the stage, which was a really great moment. Frost had his dark glasses on. Ha ha. We looked like the freshest thing in town. It was like Brexit or Trump, in that no one expected it. Rahhh! Who are these guys? They were still pretty unknown, but we helped to gangster up the stage a bit to make it look rowdy. It was like the Wu Tang Clan had appeared.

We hit our club night Movement at Bar Rumba after for an afterparty. Movement was the place to be on a Thursday night. We had everyone play for us, from Andy C to Todd Terry who once did a drum and bass set there. 'Stick to your day job, Todd!' Everyone was getting involved with jungle and dnb, whether it was from a genuine love for the music or just to be associated with it.

We all went back to Bar Rumba as winners of the Mercury prize. Bar Rumba was crazy on a Thursday night anyway, but that win lifted the atmosphere ten times over. We announced the win at the club and it was one of the best memories. It was amazing. The Mercury win did so much for dnb. Goldie was the biggest name back then and was making a similar kind of noise, by bringing what he could to the scene and so the Goldie effect, followed by Roni Size and the Mercury Prize got some real recognition for the scene beyond the UK. We got completely mashed up on sambucas that night. We had a great time.

The US tour with Roni was crazy. Now, the Americans wanted to know about jungle and dnb. Reprazent asked me and Frost to DJ as openers for the shows and we couldn't turn that down.

As Reprazent was a band, we had to travel by coach, state to state, right across America. This experience made the bonding even better as we lived 24/7 on the coach. We would sleep in bunks, wait in line for the toilet and eat together. It was such a great way of seeing America, rather than flying everywhere.

Every night was party night. You would do a show, then go back to the coach with some groupies. Then, after an hour or two you'd be off to the next town. Then it was wash, change, have some food, do a soundcheck, show-time and party. Every day! It was proper rock and roll, man.

There were so many girls and Nigel was at the forefront of all this and instigated most of it. The Hot Boys had a real reputation that preceded us. You would meet some chicks and they would tell their friends and before you knew it, there were girls everywhere. So, we called ourselves The Hot Boys. Ha ha! We had started getting a harem around us on Thursday nights at Bar Rumba back home, but now word had got out in the US too. We lived off that rep for a bit. That's what you do when you're young. We were just doing what rockers did.

It was a great experience and one of the best times on the road I have ever had. Our MC, Moose and I flew to Japan at one point to join another tour, leaving the boys to do Canada before we came back to hook up with them again. How rock and roll was that? We left a US tour to go on another tour to Japan before going back to the US for the original tour.

Nigel was just this big character and a father figure to everyone on that trip. Wherever Nigel was, he was going to be one of the biggest personalities in the room. That was just standard. Everyone had that respect for Nigel and the way he carried himself. No one fucked with Nigel. Nigel said 'Shit', everyone said, 'Where?'"

***

I remember us stopping for some food at this one-horse town near the Grand Canyon and it was your typical hick joint. Tumbleweeds were actually blowing across the streets. Signs were flapping in the wind outside gas stations and all that. We went into this saloon and the waiter was wearing a stetson. For fuck's sake. He paused for a minute in thought and then he suddenly pointed at the boys. 'Are you guys, Roni Size Reprazent?!' It was crazy.

Bryan Gee had to leave to go to Japan just after we played Detroit and so I was on my own as we entered Canada. Now, Canada has a fearsome border patrol and I was awoken from my sleep, still in my pyjamas as we tried to leave the US. It must have been minus 10 when we left that bus so the authorities could search it.

We were so lucky. Our last party had been two nights ago and so the bus was clean for the only time on that tour. Was that planned? Not as far as I can remember. So, they let us through and we made our way to Montreal, which was fucking freezing. Then it was on to Toronto; one of my favourite cities on earth. The gig in Toronto at the Industry (run by Gerbz) was Reprazent, Planet V and Goldie who had flown in to play. What a night! That night went down in Toronto folklore as one of the most wicked parties ever. I have had a special relationship with Toronto ever since, once going on after Run DMC at the 10,000-strong Syrous festival run by Rob Lisi. This was a far cry from that first trip when I had to beat the promoter up to get my money. This gig at Industry prompted them to ask me back for a monthly residence too.

We met this girl Lily when we played LA on the last day of the tour. Lily was a journalist who wrote about Oasis and bands like that. She became a good friend of ours. Lily could be a bit moody and hanging out with her was a shame in that it kept other women at bay, who thought Lily and I were an item. We weren't. Lily was doing 'the Kevin Costner' from *The Bodyguard*; she was deflecting the attention I was getting. I guess that makes me Whitney Houston! I hooked up with actress/singer Michelle Gayle while I was in LA. We'd been friends for a while and it was lovely seeing her.

We met this guy Sal at our LA show, the final one of the tour. Sal ran the Viper Room. 'Why don't you play my club?' he asked me. I didn't really know what the Viper Room was, but it seemed dead cool. 'It's Johnny Depp's place. It's where River Phoenix died,' Lily told me. It did sound cool and so I agreed.

Sex, Drugs And Drum And Bass

I stayed in LA for an extra week after the boys had gone back home and so I hooked up with Alexis again, who had become a very important part of my life; she even brought her mum to one of my gigs. However, Alexis really didn't get on with Lily and I somehow had to make it work between the three of us.

Lily and I were on our way to a gig, when we bumped into the Wu-Tang-Clan outside our hotel Le Parc Suite. I remember Lily chatting to Ghostface Killah in the car park. 'You're so cute,' she told him. I took her to one side. 'You can't say that to him. That's Ghostface Killah!' She didn't have a clue who he was.

This guy Sal Jenko came to pick us up in his Navigator to take us to Venice Beach later that evening. 'There's a place there that sells fish and chips,' he said.

- 'Fish and chips?! Fuck that! I don't want fish and fucking chips!' What is it with the Yanks and fish and chips?

I got introduced to this white dude with a really long beard back at the hotel. It was only Rick fucking Rubin from Def Jam. Rick had dropped by especially, just to see me. We got on like a house on fire, and were chatting away for ages about the Illuminati or something. Then we met this guy in paint-splattered boots and dirty old jeans later that night, after my set at the Viper Room. He had this beanie on and looked like a proper bum. It was Johnny Depp. He looked like he'd just finished painting a shed. 'Your music's really cool,' he said. I admit, I was quite stunned. Then Sal suggested I play the Viper Room once a month, which meant that I now had residencies at Twilo in New York, Viper Room in LA and Industry in Toronto. We were in the US all the time after that.

I played Philadelphia with TC Islam and Afrikaa Bambaataa not long after that Roni Size tour. Afrikaa MCed for me, which was an honour, but for some reason, no one was dancing. They were all just sat on the floor. 'They must hate me,' I thought. When it ended they all got up and went mad. They were all on crystal meth apparently.

Before one trip to the US, I had my tooth taken out. Jay took me to the anaesthetist as I was such a chicken when it came to the dentist. Jay had real trouble getting me home after, as I was so out of it from the anaesthetic. Then, in the US, after so many flights and the effect of cabin pressure, I got this pain in my gums. I was in agony sitting in the hotel. It was a terrible pain. Throbbing! Moose followed me to this dentist in San Francisco to see this guy Dr Barcelona and they took my payment ($450) before they'd actually do anything. They soon found that a reasonable bit of tooth had been left inside my gum by the guy back home. I am a real coward when it comes to the doctors and dentists, but thankfully they sorted it. I had a pop at the dentist back home when I returned and got a pay-out. The guy in the US gave me a copy of the X-ray to present to this fucker in Tooting who caused it.

I'd had a lot of extreme painkillers when I left San Francisco and so when we got to Chicago, I was feeling very woozy. It was freezing cold, especially having left the heat of Frisco. I went to bed, the hotel heaters full on as I was shivering, and slept right through the fucking gig. Because I'd locked the hotel room door from the inside, no one could get in. I woke up the following morning as fresh as a daisy. So, the promoter had paid for my flights only for me to have a kip.

The press after the Mercury Prize win was amazing having appeared in the *New York Times* and *Rolling Stone*. I went to the Miami Music Conference that year and met Roger Sanchez and Tony Touch, which was amazing. Armand van Helden came over and said, 'You guys are amazing. I love what you're doing, man! I saw you in the *New York Times*!' You appear in the *New York Times* and people get to *know* you!

Interest in our album *Planet V* was bubbling too. I remember seeing all these stickers on lampposts while we were in Manhattan one time, saying 'Who is Cam'ron?' Cam'ron was an unknown back then, but I thought it was an ingenious promotional device and decided to do something similar when we got home. Thousands of 'Planet V –Coming soon!' stickers soon popped up all over London on our return. 20,000 of them, all over the place. With Roni's *New Forms* still shifting, we were waiting until the moment was just right to release *Planet V*. We had this great press officer in the UK called Laurence Verfaillie. Laurence was French and she had worked with Alan McGee at Creation Records and once sang backing vocals on a Jesus And Mary Chain tune. It was through her that we tapped into some really clever marketing shit.

Through Laurence we got simultaneous appearances in *Mixmag*, *Muzik* and many more of the dance titles of the time. Laurence was a PR genius and we learned so much from her. I still have her Gucci glasses at mine, actually (sorry love!).

I was also fascinated by US rapper and multi-million-dollar entrepreneur Master P, who had a record label, fashion line, film company etc. I loved the way he built up his brand. I spent so much time in the US, I was bringing all these ideas back with me to the UK.

Sex, Drugs And Drum And Bass

We hosted the Planet V album launch at Bagley's in August 1998, working with Oliver and Edo from Movement. Oliver and Edo were excellent promoters and they really got on with stuff while we were away in New York or wherever. The buzz in London for *Planet V* was amazing and this party was going to be massive. It had an all-star line-up and had to better the *V Classics* party previously held at The End.

That night at Bagleys set the blueprint on how to throw a multi-genre launch party. It was an amazing night.

***

July 5th, 1998 I played a gig at Camden Palace with legendary MC Stevie Hyper D. The following morning, I awoke to the news that Stevie was dead. I couldn't believe it.

Stevie was the best, yeah? I wasn't that tight with him, but I worked with him a lot over the years. I used to tell him to shut the fuck up when he started going off on one. Ha! He was a lovely guy. That boy was an innovator with the mic and where he led, others followed. Stevie was the first drum and bass MC to use 'double time' within the bars where he sped his lyrics up to twice the usual speed. Stevie was also the first dnb MC to release an album. Stevie played with a lot of the big names but was mostly associated with Nicky Blackmarket.

Stevie died from a heart condition at the age of just 30. The dnb scene was in total shock. A young family was left behind. So, the dnb community decided to help out with the funeral costs and we all clubbed together. Bryan and I donated a grand to the fund, as did many other performers and labels. We looked after our own, yeah? RIP Stevie Hyper D. You are missed, my brother.

CH. 32

White Lines And White Sand

There had always been a bit of coke going around, but after that tour of the US with Roni, my intake was going right up. Right up my nose.

1998, I did a mini tour of the Balearics with Carl Cox. I took my driver Duffus with me on this jaunt. It was a crazy one. The last night was a gig at BCM in Palma, Majorca which was owned by the legendary club owner Tony Palmer who had been big in northern soul as owner of Wigan Casino. BCM was where I bumped into this young dancer called Geri Halliwell back in '91. What the fuck happened to her?

Duffus and I ended up in Tony's office after the show and things soon spiralled out of control.

Tony was an extravagant character – he had a gold-plated Harley Davison for starters – and I remember him constantly disappearing behind this curtain in his office, only to appear a little later with a tiny saucer. The saucer was piled high with coke. He must have done this about fifty times that night, no kidding. Back and forth Tony went, with this little saucer. Fuck knows how much gear he had in there.

We were drinking tequila and were heads down in this powder when the dancing girls arrived. I was getting used to this sort of carry-on and so wasn't that surprised when these girls started doing lap dances. Duffus looked like he'd died and gone to heaven. Soon, it was a full-on sex show and the drugs just kept coming and coming; Tony disappearing behind the curtain like a magician or something. Every time he appeared with this saucer, his face looked more and more like Herman Munster. It got to the point where I couldn't take any more powder and so I disappeared with a couple of the girls.

Sadly, I never saw Tony again, but he really was a one-off. Rest in peace, my brother.

The partying was fun, but the drugs were getting out of control. The coke was now following me around the world. I was getting a real taste for it. Still, it was all smiles and laughs for now.

I couldn't tell my story without dedicating a tale to the island that started it all. I have been to Ibiza dozens of times and have so many happy memories of the place, which occupies a special place in every DJ and raver's heart. Without Ibiza, we would never have had rave.

There have been so many parties, girls and antics on that beautiful island. I remember going to Ibiza with my drivers Gary Glimmer and Duffus this one time. As soon as we arrived, we really went to town. We hooked up with Everson and Mark from Ratpack when we got there. We all had to share an apartment as everywhere was booked up and we were packed in like sardines into this crappy two-bedroom apartment. No air-conditioning. For fuck's sake.

Evenson had a big abscess on his face, which had swollen up like a grapefruit. We ribbed him a bit. 'What the fuck is that?!' We were really laughing at poor old Ev.

My mate Duffus had a bag of medical supplies and he gave Ev some tablets to reduce the pain. Slowly, the lump reduced and disappeared. Ev was very grateful. Then it was a case of getting on it.

There was something in the air that week. We bumped into Brandon Block who had just been beaten up by police for stealing a bus. Blocko had driven this bus from the airport all the way to San Antonio. It was a really slow car chase like the OJ Simpson one. I remember Brandon fell off his chair at the Star Bar and was sitting on the floor holding his drink that had remained completely untouched. We got royally on it.

We decided to sleep on the beach that morning as the apartment was so stuffy and I was awoken by Gary's screams. Gary was a mad Irish bastard and because he had fair skin, he had been burnt to a crisp. He looked like a strip of bacon. 'Aaaarrghhh!' Every time someone touched his skin, Gary screamed in agony. So, of course we kept touching him.

We encouraged Gary to take some coke and pills –

he didn't need that much persuading – to numb the pain and he was OK for a bit. He kept beating his chest like an ape because he couldn't feel the pain, but he was clearly very tender. As there was no air conditioning back in this shitty apartment, we somehow managed

RIP my brother Tenor Fly

And the beat goes on

With Hank Shocklee from the Bomb squad

South London Artist Leo Scott made this picture of me purely from vinyl

My brother. The don Víctor Mercado (Puerto Rico)

Minha família brasileira é tão querida para mim. My sister Mari Rossi far right

With my favourite photographer, Craig Boyko

With Shabba, Maddix, Smokey and Richie Lou. Brixton Boyz

Terminator is coming

My big brother, Paul Trouble Anderson

Me and Andy Bartman

On set at Privilege in Ibiza

With Brockie, Det and Skiba

Family. London, LA and Chicago connect:
DJ Clent, Joey Drago and Noir

With Katy B

With my friend and house music legend
Marshall Jefferson celebrating my birthday
in 2015

With my girl for life DJ Law

My fam for Life. Alexis (Noir) Gutierrez and Jose (Joey Drago) Gutierrez. Los Angeles

With Optical, Doc Scott, John B and Marky

This guy is one of the first people to let me play on his decks. RIP Junior Mac

With Blacker Dread and Congo Natty

Me and Prince

To live and die in LA

With my girls, Jodie and Erin in Los Angeles. Credit: Regal D

With my good friend, Claire Lydon aka Normalist

With my girls. Lady MC, Shirley and Jay

With Rob Machete at Respect in Los Angeles. Credit: Regal D

With Ron Tom and Omar

LA Love. Credit: Regal D

Classic shot by Nic Serpell-Rand

I have so much love for this man. Big love and respect Robert Stush

Me and my brother Alvarez

South Central Los Angeles. Watts Towers. Credit: Noir

New York City with my girl Vanessa Rey. I was stuck there for a week due to the volcanic ash cloud

Live in Toronto. Credit: Nic Wons

On set at Respect in LA. Credit: Regal D

to find a hotel room so Gary could lie in the breeze. He was OK after a snooze and a cold shower.

Then we started on the brandy. I remember bending Ev's ear about the online shopping seminar I'd seen at the Epcot Centre a few years before. I was still obsessed by the idea of online shopping. I think Ev was getting a bit bored to be honest and I couldn't see if he had his eyes open through his shades.

We were drinking in this bar, run by some local gangsters and they refused our money – being friends of mine – which was nice. I was all over the place and ended up copping off with the sister of one of the owners. Then Gary turned up, suitably refreshed for another go on the crazy train.

'Let's go to Space!' I shouted.

- 'Yeahh! Fuck it! Space! Space! Space!'

I'd been to Space many times, but as we made our way to the famous daytime club, I soon realised that I had taken a wrong turn. We were halfway up a mountain, when Space was located over near the airport. This was a right magical mystery tour. We were buzzing and my sunglasses were all bent out of shape. We went round and round on these bikes for hours. I came close to running out of petrol.

If there was one person you didn't want to see when you were on it, it was Grooverider. I hated seeing Groove when I was buzzing as he didn't touch drink or drugs. As straight as a die, I always saw Groove as an older brother although we were the same age. Groove was fine however and actually spent the entire evening with us and we were *mangled*. How did he do it? He played table tennis with us and joined in with all the conversations, stone-cold sober. There are crazier stories concerning Ibiza, some of which are damn filthy, but that jaunt always stands out as we were all together, the sun on our backs with a drink in our hands. It was like a normal lads' holiday I guess. We even had a sunburn casualty. We missed our flights home too, thanks to Gary and Duffus who got cosy with some girls, just as we were meant to be leaving.

***

I had developed a love affair with Japan and had a great time on my fourth visit there with Ed Rush and Optical. It ended up with me acquiring a Japanese girlfriend, which was an experience.

Amy played the harp or something in this very well respected orchestra over there and she was quite posh, I guess. We got on well, but she was INTENSE! This girl was demanding, mate. Everything I said was micro analysed. She got serious, really quickly.

I came home and carried on as normal, but kept receiving these love letters from Amy. She was really into me! Then, when her orchestra got a gig in London she wanted to pay me a visit.

I met her at this hotel and suggested we take a cab back to Brixton. As we made our way south I could see she had started to get quite nervous. 'You don't live around here, do you?' she asked, voice trembling as we drove through south London. Amy had no idea about the ghettos and I think she thought I lived in Chelsea or somewhere. By the time we got to my place she was terrified.

I had to calm her down and chill her out, but whenever anyone came up to me in the street, she would grab my hand so tightly. She was all over the place. I never saw her again after that. Good old Brixton.

I was in Japan one time working for this guy Towa Tei from Deee-Lite, which was fun. Later, I got to work with their lead singer Lady Miss Kier too and we became really good friends. I was getting quite a lot of remix work at the time, but I couldn't engineer and so I would get Dillinja in to help. I think he had started to get fed up with it to be honest. I also did some work for Jazzie B at his studio, which was like the USS Enterprise in *Star Trek*.

I got quite tight with Lady Miss Kier and we did a lot of shows together, as far a-field as Puerto Rico. We also collaborated on a tune; a cover of the John Coltrane track *Impressions*. It was part of a project called Fused Up, put together by Gavin 'Face' Mills. I knew DJ Face from way back and we didn't get off to the best of starts, when we played Heaven one time. I recall really wanting to slap him. He was well cheeky. Then we did a gig together at BCM in Palma, Majorca in 1991 with Frankie Valentine and we became good friends.

We hired session musicians to lay down the music on the first day and then the following morning we recorded the vocals. It worked like a dream and Lady Miss Kier was excellent, as was Brian 'Keys' Tharme who played the piano. 1998 was a really enjoyable time and Miss Kier and I would go on to do loads more things together.

The late nineties saw me playing New York, LA and Toronto every single month, as well as all the other gigs abroad. In fact, I was hardly ever in the UK. One particular trip that sticks out was Puerto Rico, mainly because I almost died.

The Hidden Agenda promoter Victor Mercado reminded me of myself. 'I want to show you the rain forests,' he said one morning.

- 'OK...'

We went up to this beautiful lagoon high up in the rain forests. It was so beautiful up there. There was a swing tied to a tree that went into the cool, clear water. There was a waterfall and an array of colours all around these stunning rocks, plants and trees. I dived into the water and the current was so strong. Then, after what seemed like seconds, Victor screamed.

'Get out of the water now!'

- 'What?!'

Panicked, I started making my way back to the bank when there was this roar like a jet engine. Whoooossh!!! It was a flash flood.

You couldn't see the rocks anymore as the water gushed over everything. If I hadn't gotten out when I had, I would have been brown bread. The water took everything with it and tossed it up into the air. It was fucking scary.

The previous night, a hurricane missed us by about 400 miles. That may sound like a distance, but it's really not in 'hurricane terms'. It was close enough to make the waves rise up that night as I was swimming. One wave tossed me 20ft into the air from the sea and I landed on my hip on the beach. My leg hurt so much from that powerful wave that it was a real struggle swimming against the current in that lagoon, in order to get out. Victor found it all most amusing.

The more I travelled, the more women I met. It was getting crazy, man; the ladies were all over me. The drugs were becoming a thing too. I was getting to the point where I always had a couple of grams on me and would be snorting coke on flights to places like Toronto where I worked for Gavin at Industry. I had known Gavin for a while by now and got loads of bookings through him. I got stopped at the airport in Toronto where they swabbed me. 'You've been doing cocaine,' they said.

- 'Yes. In England. But it's gone now...' I told them.

I had actually been snorting all the way across the Atlantic. They let me in, though, as I had a work permit. The girls just swarmed around me in Canada as I hung out with Steve the Wolf at Industry in Toronto. Life had started to get really crazy.

The most reckless flight I ever had was to Dubai in 1999, when I was booked to play this party for promoter Ben McDonald. I decided to take Charlotte who was Oliver from Movement's sister. I had no idea where Dubai was or what was considered right and wrong over there. I was wearing my Gucci leather coat and sunglasses. Charlotte was this gorgeous blonde girl. We looked like trouble.

I started on the gear as soon as we unfastened the seat belts. Back and forth to the toilets, we went. Then we had a few brandies before finishing off the second or third wrap. It was only when we stopped off at Qatar, and I saw the veils and hardcore Muslim vibes, that I first started to worry. What if I'd been caught? Fuck! This was a country that took no shit when it came to drugs and I hadn't a clue what I was doing.

We threw the wraps away once we arrived and I summoned all my mental strength – which was limited by the drugs and drink – to get through security. I turned to Charlotte: 'Everyone's looking at me!'

- 'Well, what do you expect? We're buzzing our tits off!'

We got through, met the promoter Ben McDonald and breathed a sigh of relief. Ben was a former pro-tennis player who got me some free pairs of Nikes. Result! Then, once we were in the hotel, I started to relax. So much so, I started smoking weed. In Dubai. I blew the smoke down the plughole of the toilet sink. I then sat in this restaurant, which was a sky dome affair, and chilled for a bit. I was clueless as to how close I had come to getting into some really serious shit.

We then went to the bar and spotted someone who looked just like Andy C. 'It is Andy C! It's me!' said the man who was sitting with his wife. Turned out that Andy C was on holiday. We had a great evening with those two and Andy came to the gig later too.

Charlotte came to LA with me on another trip and my friend Alexis took me to one side and said, 'Darling, you don't need to bring women to LA. We have plenty of girls! What were you thinking?' She was right, though.

In Switzerland one time, I was having a drink with these two dancers when they started talking in French, probably knowing I couldn't understand them. Then they popped the question: 'Would you like to come back to our room for a party?' I got up without finishing my drink. Well, I'm way too classy to go into details, but it was amazing and threesomes, as you might know, can be tricky. But this was wicked. Well, they were ballerinas. As they got dressed after, one of them whispered, 'I hope you never forget this night!' Well, there wasn't much chance of that. This was the way of things back then.

I had such a reputation with the women that Bryan took advantage of it one night in New York. Bryan had been caught with a girl in the dance who wasn't his girlfriend – who also happened to be at this club – and yet everyone assumed it was me she was with, as Bryan walked away, leaving me with this beautiful woman. I had Jay with me on that trip and she was furious. Yet it was Bryan who was flirting with her. 'Same old Nigel' went the story, but Bryan didn't correct them. He just stayed silent and let me take the blame. He clocked the play and I ended up taking one for the team that day, the old bastard!

CH. 33

Party Like It's 1999

1999 was such a year! Following the success of our massive Planet V party, we were asked to open a brand-new night club in Smithfield Meat Market in Farringdon. The club was to be called Fabric. It was Oliver and Edo who put us in touch with the owners of what sounded like a pretty impressive super club, already being touted as 'the best club in London'.

When we turned up for the opening night, the paint had just dried and they were still screwing in the light bulbs of this impressive venue.

I was standing there in my tied-waist Gucci leather coat and Gucci leather trousers, just about to play the opening night of what was to go on to be a legendary club. I was there that night with my good friend Tennessee who worked at the Cabaret Club in the West End. It was a multi-genre night with all sorts of different sounds being played (hip-hop, R&B, house), by a host of top DJs, but the main room was drum and bass. That launch party went down in history and from that day forth, Fabric's place in clubland was guaranteed. I was on a massive high when I left that club to get my flight to Belgium. I had just been a part of history, mate.

Could 1999 get any better? Well, I bought a Man United season ticket that year. The year they won 'the Treble'.

I had already been arranging gigs around Man United games, home and away, and so I thought I'd go the whole hog.

That season, I saw them win the League title and the FA Cup, while being off my nut on coke; don't know why I bothered actually as I didn't

Big, Bad & Heavy

see any of the action at Wembley. Then I got wind of a last-minute ticket to the Champions League Final in Barcelona.

I didn't have a hotel booked or anything, but nothing was going to get in the way of this. I was so nervous and excited and even missed Micky Finn's wedding to be at that match.

Bryan was a Chelsea fan and we always had this rivalry going. If I was watching United/Chelsea round his house, he would turn the telly off if Chelsea were losing. So, when United were losing to Bayern Munich with just minutes to go, I had all these texts from Bryan who was at Micky's wedding. Bryan and the others were loving it.

The closing few minutes of that game were the best I have ever experienced. We drew level and scored the winner to seal the Treble and I was so moved I was blubbing. An old man, maybe 60-odd, turned round and said, 'Come here, son.' We had this lovely hug amid all the mayhem.

As I had no hotel I partied the night away in the fountains with the United fans, acting like a proper loon. It was an amazing night. A dream had come true.

1999 was mad, bruv. I was playing New York, LA, Toronto and all over the place. I remember playing this concert in New York with the legendary Slick Rick. What the fuck?! At the time, the US was crossing hip-hop with drum and bass and so I was there DJing for Rick with five-time DMC champion DJ Kraze. My agent Gerry Gerrard and his assistant Steve Goodgold sorted this slot. Amazing. Gerry looked after a lot of big acts – like Nine Inch Nails – and he made this happen. I was on stage, playing dnb in New York City as Slick Rick's support act. I was over the moon. Wow!

I was seeing this girl in Brooklyn at the time and I was in New York so much she genuinely didn't believe I was from London. 'You're playing me!' she'd say, whenever I turned up.

Ordinarily, I would leave New York to hook up with Lily in LA. I loved clothes shopping at Barney's and Fred Segal and places like that. I loved Prada, smart shoes and diamonds. Lily would always tease me that I dressed like a queen. We would have dinner on the roof at Barneys, overlooking Rodeo Drive where I'd think about how far I'd come from those early days at Stassi's. I always stayed at Le Parc in LA and Alexis would often pick me up in her Wrangler Jeep to take me to the Viper Room.

The Viper Room had a cigar room out the back and I met so many people out there. Sharon Stone was there one night and she was deadly serious and stern, but she said hi. The manager Sal knew everyone and so he would often introduce me to people. It was mad really and I knew it at the time.

I remember hearing this mad remix of Goldie's *Rider's Ghost* while I was in LA. The track had been unofficially mixed by this record shop owner and house DJ XXXL. I had been friends with Sam (XXXL) for a while, going back to that first tour of the US. Had Goldie been alerted to this mix he would have gone fucking bananas, but I have to say, I liked it. I played the record on Kiss and in my sets and eventually Goldie got to hear about it. I suggested he release it as a remix but he refused. Later, he did make enquiries about releasing it, but nothing came of it.

Sam (XXXL)

"Well, I was a house producer (The Coastal Commission) at the time as well as a label owner; I was running my Pacific Coast House label out of the record store Beatnonstop on Melrose Avenue.

I was getting a lot of my inspiration for my production work from jungle and was going to see Frost a lot, up at the Viper Room. I was also listening to my mate's recordings of Frost's radio show '360 Degrees' as well as those hosted by Groove and Hype. Even though I was making house I was DJing jungle around LA as DJ XXXL. Soon I started booking shows at the Troubadour on Santa Monica with the Usual Suspects, Loxy, Ink and J Majik etc. I then started a dnb label called Crimescene.

The Doc Scott VIP of Goldie's Riders Ghost had really blown my head and I figured I'd have a crack at a remix too. At that time I had commissioned the Usual Suspects (right after Killa Bees dropped on Renegade Hardware) to do a remix of a tune I'd done called Flatline, which was really just a jungle booty of the old classic rave track Ephemeral by Tic Tac Toe. They sent me their finished mix and I wanted to go cut a dub to hear how it sounded. I figured I'd put the Ghost track I was still working on, on the flip to check that too and see how it was coming along.

I took the plate into work at Beatnonstop to listen to it the next day and quite literally as I put it on the decks Frost walked into the shop!

He got super hyped on the tune and so I flipped it and played them the Suspect's mix of my Flatline tune and he was going mental! I gave Frost the plate that day and later that night went to see him at the Viper Room; he was on a line-up with A Guy Called Gerald and Lady Miss Kier from Deee-Lite.

Frost left LA and I went back to working at Beatnonstop while putting beats together at night. Not long after that I got word from my boy Jakes that he'd got Frost's latest 360 Degrees during which he'd dropped the Suspect's mix of Flatline as well as the remix of Goldie's Riders Ghost. He sent me a copy of the show and I was speechless. Next thing you know I have Randall, Tech Itch and mad amounts of DJs banging down my door to get the tune. 'Frost is rinsing your track you know, pulling it up 2-3 times. It's smashing up the dance...BRING ME IN!'"

Things were buzzing back in London. I had been good mates with Goldie for a while and we would hang out at Ten Rooms, China Whites and the Cabaret Club, which was our favourite spot mid-week. We were hanging with Leah Wood, Rolling Stone Ronnie's daughter as well as Kate Rutherford, daughter of Mike Rutherford from Genesis and Mike & The Mechanics. I started seeing Kate for a bit. She had this beautiful place on King's Road and we had a lot of fun hanging out there. I was taking more and more coke around that time.

I split my time in the UK between gorgeous girls in London, plus the women I was hooking up with in every US city. We were putting on some mad after-parties in London and would continue to book adjoining rooms so we could really go for it. The Shabby Crew – and you know who you are – would party for two-three days straight. I remember being at one party when I had a nagging feeling that I should be elsewhere. Then I remembered. 'Shit Duffus! I almost forgot. I'm due in New York tonight with Roni.'

- 'I've never been to New York,' said Duffus, looking a bit jealous.
- 'Right then, you're coming!'

I took Duffus (a Cypriot) to this really black area of Brooklyn and dared him to check a girl out. Which he did! Ha ha. Duffus was flamboyant and I remember him pretending to be mine and Roni Size's manager throughout the entire trip and everyone believed the old bastard. We flew from New York to Toronto on the second day with Armand van Helden who was convinced that Duffus was my manager. He played the role brilliantly. I took Duffus to Brazil as well where he pulled this absolute stunner. I remember the following morning, he looked quite down. 'What's up Ray?'

- 'I'm going to have to tell my girlfriend about this.'
- 'You what?! No! Don't do that! Don't you dare! We're on the other side of the world.'
- 'This isn't me. I don't do this. I will have to tell her.'

He told her as well, the fool. Mind you, I am the last person to take relationship advice from.

We did this Planet V gig in Zurich – me, Bryan, Moose and Ray Keith – and I got chatting to these air hostesses, one of whom dropped her digits, so we could meet up later. They were really into seeing us do the gig that night and she rang as promised, later that evening.

So, we met with this air hostess and a few of her colleagues, including the fucking pilot! This guy was lagging, do you know what I mean? He was 'on one'. I slipped off with this air hostess for an hour before returning to the rave. Now, I left this pilot in the main room, while I was with this girl and the pilot was steaming drunk by now. He was pleading with me. 'Don't tell anyone about this, yeah? Not a soul! Just don't even make eye contact with me if you see me!'

'OK, but why all the drama? I don't even know you bruv. I will never see you again.'

- 'You will,' he said, rubbing his eyes. 'I'm flying you home.' Fuck!

The flight back had a different cabin crew, but word had got out that I had seen this girl. 'Which one of you got lucky last night?' asked one of the stewardesses. All the boys pointed to me. This girl appeared again later and came straight over. 'The pilot wants to know if you want to see him land the plane,' she asked. I wasn't sure how I felt about this, but I disappeared into the cockpit.

'Thanks for keeping schtum,' he said. 'I was lagging last night, mate.'

I was just staring out of the window at the clouds and shit as he pressed the buttons and spoke through this mic. Fucking hell. The last time I'd seen this dude, he was slumped on a sofa with a glass of tequila. That said, I watched him land this baby like a total pro.

I worked in Europe a lot too, playing for MTV Europe; my mate James Hyman was the producer there at the time. The shows were hosted by VJ Simone and I did quite a few sets for them. I was also playing for Goldie at the Leisure Lounge back in London. Goldie and I agreed to host a joint party in 1999 at the Café De Paris. I loved Café

Big, Bad & Heavy

De Paris and had always wanted to put on a drum and bass night at this exclusive club. Bryan Gee thought we were mad. 'What the fuck?! No way!'
- 'It will work, I'm telling you bruv.'
This joint party was amazing. We had loads of celebrity guests there, like Lennox Lewis and Nick Moran from *Lock Stock And Two Smoking Barrels.* It was probably the most exclusive dnb party ever; the dress code was 'super smart'.

Goldie and I both supported Man United and we went to see the boys lose 5:0 at Stamford Bridge together with Guy Ritchie. It was at Stamford Bridge that we met Joanne Beckham, David's sister. I got to know her quiet well. Then we bumped into Joanne at the MOBOs when D'Angelo was whacked over the head with a champagne bottle for hitting on some guy's woman. We sat at a table with David Bowie's wife Iman, Jerry Springer and Dwight Yorke. It was a really fun night. Goldie warned me away from Joanne, though, 'You go out with girls like that, you'll get the paparazzi going through your bins, mate.'

***

It was a Champions League game and Goldie and I travelled to the United home match together by train. We were on our way up north to see United play Juventus I think and Goldie was getting a lot of attention. Well, he was a star. Goldie was great at chatting to people and signing autographs. I remember that Noel Gallagher was on the phone to Goldie and he kept slagging us for being United fans. 'Fucking pair of you,' he'd laugh. 'Fucking United?!' It was good-humoured stuff.

We did some coke during the match and were having a few drinks and another line or two after when Goldie took a call. 'We've been invited to the players' lounge!' Fuck!

I was very nervous when we walked into this bar. All of the United team were there. Fuck it. I decided I needed some help.

I racked up a monster line in the toilets of the Executive Lounge at Old Trafford. Sniiiiiiiiiffffffff!!! I wiped my nose and marched back in.

The first person I saw was Roy Keane. Keano looked so serious, man. I lost it. I wanted to say something, but didn't want to risk it. I was feeling a little paranoid and was sure that everyone was looking at me, wondering who this nutter was. Then I bumped into my mate Devon from Brixton. What the fuck?! Devon used to work in the cab office where we sold our stolen cassette tapes back in the day. I'm not sure why he was there, but I was so happy to see him in the players' lounge at Old Trafford. If the schoolboy me could have seen that…

After the game, Goldie and I spent the evening talking to some girls we met, but we were too tired to do anything. We talked and talked and then crashed to sleep, which made a change.

On the train back, we were sitting behind this geezer, who kept looking round at us. Eventually, he started up. 'I used to go to school with a mate of yours,' he told Goldie. 'He's called J Majik now.' Goldie nodded as J was a friend of ours. Goldie rang him.

'This guy is saying he went to school with you, Jamie. Do you know him?'

- 'That guy is a cunt! He bullied me all through school,' Jamie revealed. 'He's a fucking wanker who made my life a total nightmare!'

Goldie hung up and smiled. 'Right, we can have some fun here.'

We gave this guy such grief on the way back to London. We totally ripped the arse out of him. All the way, back. 'You're a proper fucking cunt, aren't you?' We spent the whole journey, banging on his chair and nudging him. Karma's a bitch, right?

CH. 34

The Boys In Brazil

I went to Brazil for the first time in 1999. Promoters Oliver and Edo had found out that a guy in Brazil had been using their name Movement. 'We're only using it because we love what you guys are doing over there,' the Brazilians revealed. 'Why don't you come over and see us?' So Oliver and Edo went over to Brazil to say hello. 'You won't believe what it's like out there,' they said when they returned. 'The landscape is amazing, the vibe is off the chain!' They eventually established a working relationship with these boys through the label Trama.

Not long after, I got invited to go to Sao Paulo too. The touring had gone crazy from '97 through to '99 with the three residencies, plus all the random bookings, but I couldn't turn down a trip to Brazil.

This girl Mari Rossi showed us around Sao Paulo and we even went to see a football match: Corinthians versus Palmeiras. 'You have to support Corinthians!' she said. So, I bought this hooligan mask and wore it at the match. It was the kind of mask that Mexican wrestlers wore. I looked like a right nutter in this thing. The atmosphere at the game was incredible. At one point, police horses charged through the crowd, which had been releasing smoke grenades. It was crazy!

Mari became a little sister to me over the years. We became so tight and would always meet up on future visits to that wild country.

I remember wearing this wrestler's mask when I went to meet Patif and the guys at the record label. I think they were a little thrown by my mask, to be honest. I mean they could have been supporters of their rivals, I guess. I kept this mask on throughout the entire conversation as Patif, label boss John Paulo and I discussed record releases. Well, I was taking a lot of drugs by this stage.

John Paulo shook my hand as he left. The door banged shut and I leant across the table towards Patif. 'I want some drugs!' Patif looked a little taken aback. Drugs were rife in Brazil of course, but here was a man in a head mask cutting straight to the bone.

To get the coke, we had to visit a favela and although Patif grew up in these slums he really wasn't keen on going back. Still, we jumped in a car and headed off to the south side of the city. 'Where we are going, you can't wear this,' he said, tugging on the mask. I finally took it off.

Patif

"Nigel was so excited as we left the city and headed for the favelas. The nice buildings had gone, then the houses had disappeared also and soon we were in the slum areas.

We had to get the car through this alley that was barely wide enough and two armed guys stopped us at the end. Nigel was gripping the seat. 'What the fuck?!' he whispered.

- 'Well, you said you wanted some drugs.'

We went inside this warehouse and these armed guards took us over to these sacks. 'How much do you want?' they asked.

Nigel handed over the equivalent of £50 and they handed him a bag. Nigel's eyes were virtually popping out on stalks. It was like a bag of sugar.

'What the fuck?! You'd get one per cent of this for £50 back in the UK! Fuck me!' I took Nigel back to the hotel where Bryan was.

Come the night of the gig I really didn't think he was capable of playing any music that night. But he got to the VIP Room of the club and demanded some champagne. I said he had to tell them in advance if he wanted champagne as they had to order it in. However, I sent someone off into town to get some Cristal and Nigel drank the bottle in one go. 'Bruv, bruv, I want to play!'

Nigel was up there at the decks when a record jumped, so he threw this record into the crowd. It was a dubplate and fairly heavy. This dubplate sailed through the crowd and hit a female friend of mine, *in the head. She was OK, but a little overcome with shock. That Dillinja dubplate is now framed on her wall."*

***

It was a privilege to play the last night at Toronto's super club Industry. I had become part of the family there along with Gavin, Steve (The Wolf), Jenstar, Big Joe, Justin, Rob Lisi, Marcus and Harris. Mr C and I, spent ten hours on the dancefloor dancing like bastards that night. I was on MDMA and champagne and danced all the way through a Danny Tenaglia set, which went on for about ten hours. That night went down in Toronto folklore and I remember it as a very spiritual evening. I played at a massive rally outside City Hall there, when they were trying to outlaw raves. There were thousands there, bruv.

I didn't know it at the time, but I was getting towards breaking point. The drugs, booze and women were taking their toll, which was fine for as long as things were looking up. Most people would have bitten my arm off to swap places with me, but just because the damage couldn't be seen, didn't mean it wasn't happening. Oblivious to all this, the parties just kept rolling...

The Miami Music Seminar was always a good time. It started as a seminar and then morphed into a giant party where you'd hook up with everyone in dance music. The parties were legendary. I arranged to hook up with Duffus one year and he got there before me. I was in a cab from the airport when I saw Duffus walking down Collins Avenue. 'Frost, you old bastard!' he shouted.

I let Duffus stay at my exclusive apartment on Ocean Drive. They stocked the bar in these places with some high-quality shit. I had Cristal and all this waiting for us. I remember bumping into my good friend Todd Terry in the foyer. I had a brief chat with Todd as he'd been on my radio show just weeks before. Everyone went to Miami.

We had one after-party where I ended up with this girl back at the apartment and I remember thinking that something wasn't quite right. I looked over to the door, while this girl rode me, to see Duffus staring through the crack of the door. 'Hey fuck off, you old bastard!' He was off his nut.

The partying was getting crazy, actually. Drugs, champagne, girls. Lots of girls. I remember hooking up with Victor and his pals from Puerto Rico in Miami. They were a murky bunch. I was there with Bryan

Gee, DJ Ruffstuff – who we took around with us on his first trip to Miami – and DJ Marky. Oliver and Edo brought Marky over to the UK after seeing how massive he was in Brazil. This guy smashed it at Movement and so Bryan and I took him to Miami with us. I gave half of my set to DJ Marky and that night at Ultra, was the moment he made it in the US. It was a magical night. He smashed the granny out of that club, I'm telling you.

I remember going into this portacabin to get paid after and it was like something out of *Scarface*. There was money everywhere, and all the counting machines were hissing as they flipped notes over and over and over. I took $3,500 and gave Ruffstuff – who was on his first trip to Miami – $500 for being such a loyal soldier.

I was on a flight to Philadelphia with GQ after departing Miami and this girl just started chatting me up. 'Hey, you're cute! Can I sit next to you?' This girl Erica was the dead stamp for Beyonce. No kidding. She was hot. GQ kept looking over. 'You lucky cunt!' I kept sticking my tongue out.

Erica followed me to the gig and she came back to the hotel with us after. I bumped into GQ at breakfast in the hotel restaurant the following morning and he just kept sticking his tongue out at me, while I chatted to her. What a week that was.

***

V Festival was mad. I had this portacabin and a fully stocked fridge, but it was Gary my driver who emptied it. He was off his nut on the brandy and by the time I got off the decks he was lagging. The thing is, he had to drive me to Dingwalls later, to play at Goldie's bash. I remember talking to some Spice Girls and Simon Le Bon and his wife Yasmin at Dingwalls, straight after V. It was an amazing night.

Festival culture was starting to boom around that time and there were more and more of them popping up all over the UK and beyond. Festivals gave dance music a real boost at a time when some of my peers were finding things tough back then. UK garage was starting to make it big too and interest in dnb was nowhere near what it was, although I seemed to be doing better than most. 1999 had proven to be quite a year for me, save for one particularly upsetting moment.

CH. 35

Bad Moon Rising

On the morning of April 26th, 1999, I was awoken by the phone. I had got in at 8am after three gigs the night before and so I wasn't expecting the phone to keep ringing and ringing. Shattered, I went downstairs and picked it up. It was Sarah from Groove Connection and she was in a right state. 'Nigel! Kemi's dead!' I gulped. I couldn't believe it. DJ Kemistry (real name Kemi Olusanya) was Goldie's girlfriend in the early nineties. Kemi was dead.

Kemi and Jayne (Storm) were driving home after a gig in Southampton when a van kicked up a loose cat's eye on the road. The cat's eye then flew up into the windscreen and entered the car roughly where the tax disc was displayed.

Thinking it was a stone or something, Jayne pulled over as she could see Kemi's head was down and her hair was covered in glass.

After pulling over it was then that Jayne realised Kemi was unconscious after trying to revive her. By the time the ambulance arrived Kemi had passed away. Kemi was just 35 years of age.

Goldie and Kemi were still very close at this point and he was in bits. This was the girl who introduced him to jungle when he moved to the UK from Miami. Kemistry and Storm were also very well regarded in their own right. The entire dnb community was in shock.

So Goldie called me and asked me over to Jayne's flat. Goldie and Nicky, Kemi and Jayne's best friend, were already there and then Doc Scott turned up.

We just couldn't believe it. Everything had been thrown into chaos. We all just sat there, stunned. Kemi was such a beautiful soul and it was one of the saddest days for us all. We sat there all day going over memories of Kemi. Kemi was a soldier, yeah? The family had lost a daughter.

CH. 36

A Bad Heart

We were out of the country when the MOBOs happened and so we sent Shirley from the office to accept the award. It was an amazing moment when I heard that Shirley told the crowd: 'I am here on behalf of Bryan and Frost who are currently touring the US!' How cool was that? We'd got to the stage where we couldn't even make awards ceremonies. Ha ha.

We were partying all the time. We had a two-day bender in a Birmingham hotel after a Planet V night at the Q Club and we got adjoining rooms again and went mad. I was on a high anyway, as Dillinja had just given me *Nasty Ways* as an exclusive to play out and it blew the roof off the place. From that moment on, I was pumped. Dillinja always gave me his new stuff to play out and I was always grateful to be given that respect. Karl really valued my feedback.

This after-party was debauched. We seemed to attract so many misfits and delinquents who liked to party as hard as we did. A lot of these parties are a blur now. I remember girls going in and out of the rooms, and a coffee table covered in powder. These parties were *shabby*!

I was getting bang on the chang at this point, yeah? I was changing. I was not the same person any more. I was capable of doing some horrible things. I always felt that I was a good person at heart, even when I was younger and a bad boy. But now I wasn't so sure. I was becoming convinced that I was a bad person. With a bad heart.

Through all the partying, I had started to lose my sanity and was experiencing severe paranoia. I was depressed, but our successes had clouded things. I was being paid to do a job I loved and had women and drugs on tap, but there was something that didn't quite sit right. I was suffering from severe depression, I can see that now, but I didn't quite realise this fact, due to all the other things going on.

My cousin Jason was getting married that summer and I joined my family for what was supposed to be a happy day. Now, I wasn't even doing drugs that day, but when I started arguing with a friend of the wife's side of the family – after he'd upset some kids – I blew my fucking top. He looked at me and I started fuming. He was eating away at me. I wanted to fuck him up. Cocaine had taken a person who was prone to blowing up and doing mad stuff and accentuated it. I was now an extreme version of me. To be honest, I had lost control.

This argument spiralled and I went off to make a phonecall. Within 15 minutes, my mates had arrived. They had what I needed. A gun.

What the fuck was going on? I was going to shoot this guy? In front of my family? My mum and dad? At a wedding?! My cousin Eric and my stepfather saw what was going down and stepped in. This guy also saw what was happening and legged it. There I was on my cousin's big day, kids running around the place, waving a Glock 45. 'Where the fuck is he?!'

It was my fault. I was doing coke all the time, but the powder was going to town on me. I was a fucking zombie. It was like someone had turned the lights off inside my head. I didn't feel anything. I just played my sets and got on it. When things went OK, the depression was forgotten and ignored. When things turned for the worse, the problems came to the forefront and I just couldn't handle it. The bad times were now becoming more and more regular and of course the drugs only made the situation worse.

There were definite signs that I was starting to lose it and Bryan was the first to mention it. I remember Bryan blowing his top one day in the office. 'What the fuck are you doing?!' He walked over and wrestled this giant shark knife from my grip. This blade had all these serrated edges down the side and I'm not sure what I was doing with it or where I'd gotten it. Bryan locked this massive knife inside a cupboard and confiscated it. Bryan was the teacher. I guess I was the naughty kid. 'I'm keeping this,' he said.

I had started to become very withdrawn. I was socialising OK, while on coke, but other than that, I couldn't raise a smile. I spent loads of time with my dog Levi around this time. Just me and the dog. What the hell was happening? I had everything going for me as I flew around the world playing records – with a girlfriend in every city – and yet I was so unhappy.

I hated being on my own on tour. Touring was a lonely thing when you were going solo. On your own on the plane, on your own at the hotel. You got to the airport the next day, on your own. When I was with Bryan, he kept me in check. But I was falling apart.

I worked for Kiss for eight years and won two awards for best radio show. When Emap bought Kiss and moved it from the Holloway Road to Oxford Circus, I was in full-on party mode and just lost interest. They scheduled a meeting and I just didn't bother turning up. I never went back.

Kiss for me, was Steve Jackson, Chris Phillips, Matt White, Jazzie B, Fabio and Grooverider and Max and Dave; people like that. I felt that this new Kiss was too corporate and mainstream. It had lost its cutting edge. I just walked away. I was far too interested in cocaine at this point.

I was about to play Buzz Club in Washington DC, just three blocks down from the White House. That area was full of junkies, just walking around in a daze. Lots of crack there, as I recall. I was so out of it on coke, I just burst into tears back at the hotel. It felt like I was having a breakdown. I had Jay back in the UK and she really looked out for me, but I didn't treat her well. I was seeing so many other women. I was too distracted. She was there for me, but I wasn't there for her. I deeply regretted that. I have tried not to go into too much detail with regards to my relationships in order to protect the innocent, but I had two more children (Kaya Robyn and Dante) in 2000 too, which added to the overall stress. Things were building up to critical mass. I was barely holding it together. I was a fucking mess, mate.

CH. 37

September 10th 2001

The smell, man. It was like death itself. The city was just full of smoke and little bits of paper flying around on the breeze. It was a clear, blue day up above. Down below, it was hell on earth, man. I was fucking terrified...

I had been out in Seattle on September 9th, partying with promoter Marcus, a playboy type with a speedboat. Marcus lived on an island near Bill Gates and he was a real party animal. I loved playing Seattle as it had a great vibe there.

On September 10th I flew into JFK. I met hip-hop DJ legend Tony Touch for a bite to eat and a chat, before going back to the hotel prior to this gig I was doing that night with DJ Empress. I had set Empress up with some gigs back in London, the year before. She was like my little sister and we got on well. She was a wicked DJ.

We did the gig and Empress, my friend Karine and I, got so drunk. Karine and I then went back to the hotel after waving goodbye to Empress. Karine left at 6am and I went back to sleep.

I awoke to mayhem. I looked out of the window and saw all this smoke. Then there was a bang at the door. 'Everybody out!' What the fuck?! I got dressed and took my record boxes downstairs. I had to check out of that hotel anyway, and so I took all my gear with me. I remember running down the street with these two massive record boxes and my heavy Louis Vuitton sailor bag. I was sweating like mad.

I didn't know what was happening. I thought it was world war three or something. I didn't know that two planes had just crashed into the World Trade Centre.

The smell of the smoke was deathly. I can still smell it now. It stank!

I was trembling I was so scared. I was terrified. I honestly thought that a missile had been fired at New York City and in a way it had. Two of them! There were people running everywhere. Screams, sirens and this thick smoke.

I checked into a cheap hotel further uptown and just sat in this room, shaking. I had the TV on while I started on my weed. I would fall asleep and then get up, make some phonecalls and then smoke some more before falling asleep again.

I had a gig in Denver the following day and so not only was air travel shut down, but I also had to redirect my flight to London. So, I had to phone promoters, airline companies and my friends, but I couldn't get through to anyone as the phone lines were fucked. I racked up a £500 phone bill that day. I spent days in that room, just crying. I just couldn't stop crying.

September 12th, I got Jay to send a message to my mum to say I was OK. Mum had spent a day worrying herself to death after the Foreign Office told her that Nigel Thompson had been reported missing. It was another fella, but she hadn't known this. It was a scary time.

I just remember this smell. That stink of death around New York. There was stuff in the air, bits of dust and paper and it felt like you were walking through a movie set. Only it was real. The days following the attack were eerie, as there were virtually no flights and so the skies were empty. You realised just how much noise planes usually made now they were gone.

I finally got a flight home four days after the attack. I had lost a bit of myself in Manhattan at that time. My life was off the rails anyway and being holed up in that hotel amid all this destruction and despair, made me feel so empty. I had all these girlfriends, but I just didn't care for them as I should have. If it hadn't been for Bryan keeping me in check at certain points, I would have crashed and burned a long while before that.

I was trying to get hold of a dear friend of mine MC Question Mark who worked for American Airlines in LA who was often good for an upgrade, but he wasn't around. My mind was racing. The thought of flying home was terrifying. That flight out of New York was the most nervous experience ever. I remember an Arab type walking through the airport and everyone gasped. I did! It was that mad. 'Could he be a terrorist?' Something had been triggered inside us all. I usually got my head down real quick on a flight, but I just couldn't sleep on this trip. I

September 10th 2001

was shaking. The world had changed and I will never ever forget those days. I must have cried about 500 times during that week. It was if that awful attack had shone a light on my life; and I didn't like it one little bit. Yet, I was the lucky one. I hadn't lost anyone in those twin towers. But I was definitely breaking down.

DJ Empress

"It was such a big deal when Nigel and Bryan Gee came over to play Twilo in the nineties. The Sound Factory was a big venue and so V would play host to over a thousand people in there on a Thursday night. I first met him in 1998 and we became good friends from that day forward.

I first got into jungle aged 14, in 1994. I worked at Satellite Records on 342 Bowery (opposite CBGBs) and so got to hear all the latest jungle and drum and bass. I first heard jungle in that store and later when I was older I had free range to order anything in I thought would sell. By acquiring the music, I fell in love with it and I knew what all the regional centres liked; Boston liked the darker stuff while Atlanta, say, liked the funkier vibes.

I was learning to DJ in '94, but it would be four years later that I actually felt ready to play out. I just wanted to make sure I was ready (I was still only 18). I didn't think I'd ever be a DJ and play out, but it got to a point where I was hearing other DJs and thinking, 'I'm better than them. They're not even playing the songs I want to hear.' I loved jungle; it was this crazy cool, underground music with so many styles, intertwined: break beats, hardcore, reggae; so many elements. I was obsessed.

I met Nigel when playing Twilo around '98 and we got on so well that we played together in Toronto before I was invited to go over to London to play Movement at Brixton Mass with DJ Marky from Brazil. That was a massive deal for us, as London could be quite closed off back then. We played London in '99 when I was still 18. Nigel was so sweet, which was good, as many were quite sleazy. I always felt so fortunate and thankful to him for giving me an opportunity to play in the UK. The party was a Unique artists' Christmas party with Bad Company, Zinc, Andy C, Ed Rush and Optical playing. It was a tough crowd, ha ha! My first mix was a double drop and Frost bolted into the DJ booth and said, 'Again! Again!' My hands were shaking all over the place. He was so enthusiastic. I was firmly under his wing, from there on. A part of the V family.

There was something in the air that night of Sept 10th, 2001. We were at Konkrete Jungle and we got very drunk. We had so many shots and got totally wasted. Derrick Carter, Ritchie Hawtin and Jeff Mills were playing at Konkrete, this East Village club.

September 11th my boyfriend and I woke up so hungover. He worked at a nursery located in one of the Twin Towers, but he was so ill he decided not to go in. After all, working with children while nursing a hangover... not good. So we went back to sleep at around 6am. When we woke up, the world was ending. The phone was constantly ringing. 'Wake up! A plane has crashed into one of the towers!'

What I remember from that day, among so many memories, was the sky; it was so clear and crisp, not a cloud to be seen. There was a wind blowing east and from Brooklyn, where I was, you could see millions of these little bits of paper floating in the air. We were a short walk from the Manhattan Bridge and all this smoke, ash and paper was landing in Brooklyn. I will never forget that smell; it hung around for about a month. Thousands of people walked over Manhattan Bridge and the only cars allowed over were these black vans. It was so weird and shady. Total chaos in and out of the city, as we didn't know if there was going to be another attack."

CH. 38

Aftermath

I got back to the UK and just retreated from the world. I didn't sleep for two days. I just sat home with Levi and smoked weed. I couldn't help thinking about New York; the city that was now my second home. That place had been battered.

I was in a bad place before 9/11, but now I was walking towards the edge. But after a few days at home, I started partying again, thus parking the underlying problems that were not going to clear anytime soon.

The Cabaret Club was my favourite haunt. I was hanging around with Bonnie, Leanne and Alison, these immaculately-dressed girls. We would sometimes go to these posh restaurants and I would get into all my Prada and that; nice shoes and diamonds. I was out all the time in these upmarket clubs. Kate Rutherford was still about and so I spent a lot of time in Chelsea. We were living the life: wine bars, clubs, restaurants and drugs. Lots of drugs.

The drugs could no longer mask things, though. I had changed and couldn't get back to when I was happy. I had such crippling anxiety and was very insecure. I was hanging with these posh, rich people who I had no real connection with. I think I liked the fact that they hadn't known me before. With them, I was a blank canvas. Anyone who knew me, would have taken me to one side for a chat. I was now doing drugs with lawyers and doctors in this circle. I never felt like I belonged in this society, but it was better than being at home on my own.

I knew many people who had destroyed themselves on crack and so I had always avoided it. I saw people fall apart right in front of my eyes while doing that shit. So, what was I thinking when I started on the rocks. How fucking stupid. But there you go, now my life was heading for the rocks in more ways than one.

There are two ways of smoking crack. You can freebase a rock through a pipe or sprinkle into a spliff. I combined the two. Instead of splitting a rock into four to place inside a Blunt, I would put the whole rock in. A whole crack rock in a spliff. What the fuck?!

The smell of crack was weird. It was like someone had set fire to a load of chemicals. The smell was sweet, though and enticing and for a while it had me in its embrace. The high was like nothing on this earth, but it didn't last that long. Soon, you were looking for the next hit. Then the next. Crack was insane. It gave you something good and took it away so fucking quickly.

I had started hanging out with these two girls, who were a right handful. We would have a few drinks, smoke some crack and have sex. That's what we did. I had two girlfriends, (Melak and Gwen) both of whom would sleep with me and all three of us, were controlled by another: crack cocaine.

It could be fun, lots of fun. I had two girlfriends for fuck's sake, but the crack was in charge. I was spending so much money and just wasn't thinking. I would buy crack, have sex, then buy more crack and have more sex, and then we might phone someone up to get more girls over. The bedroom and living room would be full of drugs and girls. It was mad. I knew it was crazy there and then, but I just let it play out. I wasn't able to stop it, even if I'd wanted to.

My parties with Melak and Gwen were initially a weekend thing, but it soon started happening midweek. I was getting deeper and deeper into this. The need for crack was getting more and more desperate, so much so, I was starting to take money of the business. Bryan didn't know at first and so I partied hard, smoking away the record company's assets, as Bryan held the label together. This went on for about a year as the trail of destruction I left behind me got longer and longer. Something had to give.

I had always been an early riser, but crack put paid to that. I would get up at midday to find my dog staring at me. You can't lie to a dog can you? Animals know when something is up. Levi knew I was a mess. That dog knew I was not my normal self.

Sometimes there would be a girl in my bed and I would wait until she gave me a clue as to what her name was, because I'd nearly always forgotten it. I often couldn't even tell you where we'd been the previous night. Then I would eventually get up and take a shower.

Once I was up, I would take Levi for a walk as I always had. By this time, Levi was getting older and he would just stick by my side. I could hold it down quite well if I bumped into anyone and would act as if I didn't have a care in the world. I would be wearing some sharp clothes with a necklace and diamond ring and I was convinced that these would paper over the cracks (or should that be crack?).

I would then make a few calls and see what new music was out and maybe go to Music House to cut some dubs and then it was back to the house. As my crack use increased, I found it harder and harder to get out of the flat, as I would go through massive waves of shame and I would hate myself so much I could barely look at myself in the mirror. My soul was being eaten away every time I took a hit.

I had a giant fish tank and my favourite inhabitant was this big 'red devil' fish that would rearrange all the stones every day. It would make mountains out of gravel, this fish. I know because I watched it. For hours on end. Levi and this fish would have staring competitions that went on for hours and I would just sit there, watching them, unable to do anything else.

Sometimes, I would invite a girl over to try and break the routine. Increasingly, I knew I had to stop taking crack, but I was willing to ride it out for as long as I could. Pure madness and self-delusion were at work.

I saw Fabio at a club around this time and he gave me a few home truths. I had known Fabio since I was a kid and I valued his opinion. I knew he was right. I was out of control. 'Boy, you got to sort yourself out! It's glaringly obvious that you're not yourself. Sort it!' Why was I being so self-destructive?

I started off doing rocks all weekend in the east London flat shared by Melak and Gwen, but soon, I was doing rocks at home, on my own. I would do about 5-6 rocks in the evening, while I was out, plus half a bottle of brandy. I would then take a girl home and we would do more stuff. Then it was sleep, until I saw Levi again, looking up at me in the morning with a strange girl beside me in bed that I couldn't remember meeting. Round and round it went. The only change was at weekends when I hooked up with the two girls, and that was when things would go ultra-crazy.

People had heard what was going on. You buy drugs, the dealers talk and then you have friends asking you what all this shit is about.

'You doing crack now, bruv?' I remember Delroy and Prince sitting me down inside their car. 'What's all this we're hearing about you, Nigel? Fucking crack now?!' I would just nod my head.

- 'What do you want me to say?'

I would end up saying whatever they wanted to hear because it got me out of these awkward situations. Then I'd be free to get straight back on it.

I had lost the plot. I actually robbed two guys of their crack one evening. I saw these two regular joes buy £200-worth of rocks and simply took it off them in the street. Here I was, an award-winning international DJ and boss of a well-known record label, robbing people for crack.

Chalkie White

"I really lost my soul around 1993. I lost so many years in those days. I would do the gig and then get on it with the ravers for 2 or 3 days after. Then start again. I was getting into some serious drugs and was really bad for a long time. Then I hit rock bottom and that was scary.

Frosty had always been there for me. I saw him in Brixton one night, a while back and he pulled me to one side. 'You've got so much going for you, don't fuck it up, mate!' That meant a lot to me and I was able to get clean, due in part to people like Nigel who stuck by me. I have been clean for 15 months now and I can hold my head up high. Cheers Nigel."

I was with Melak one day, when I heard a BANG! Melak went downstairs to confront a very angry man. It was her boyfriend! I knew she had a fella, but it hadn't stopped us. I also knew he was a fucking lunatic. 'Who the fuck have you got up there?!' he shouted. Whack! He hit her.

I didn't know what to do. She was screaming. I was naked. I prayed to God that he wouldn't come into the room. The screams went on and on. I grabbed my trousers and pulled out my gun. In my drug-fuelled paranoia I had got hold of another piece. I was convinced that I needed this gun and I can't fully explain it. So, now I was in a potentially fatal situation. If this prick decided to walk into the room he was going to try and kill me, leaving me with no choice – or so I rationalised it – but to use this gun. Fuck!

I stood there shaking with this gun in my hand. 'Please don't come in here, mate! Just go out the way you came. Please don't come in!' This guy blew his top again and I heard the door go. BANG! He'd gone. It was the front door. I dropped the gun on the bed and gasped for air. Once I'd settled down, I got dressed and got the fuck out.

***

I ended up in downtown Baltimore after a gig in Washington around this time. This area of the city was so bad the cab driver wouldn't drop me off at first. 'I wouldn't advise hanging around here,' he said.

- 'It's OK, I want to be dropped here.'

There were dealers everywhere. I bought a $100-worth of crack and had a spliff there and then in the street. No wonder *The Wire* was set there, Baltimore was rough, man. There were people shouting and screaming on the sidewalks.

I walked down this road and stopped with a judder when I saw *them*. Coming towards me was a posse of six giant rats. They were as big as cats, I swear it! They weren't crossing the road to avoid me either. Fuck! I crossed the road and watched these 'rat cats' disappear into a storm drain as I lit another rock. These rats were not fucking about.

The thing with drugs is that the madder your life gets, the more drugs you need to deal with it all. I went to this crack house in London one time and ran out of money. I waved my empty wallet at this dealer and wondered what to do next. I said to this geezer, 'How about I swap you my gun for some more crack?' I went to show him the handle of this gun and he sneered a bit, probably thinking it was a replica. 'That gun's not going to work,' he said, or something like that. So, I went to take the gun out of my waist simply to show him and it went off. BAM! Fuck me, this bloke jumped. I could have blown my bollocks off. He was terrified. 'Here you go!' He handed me 20 rocks and I legged it. He honestly thought I was holding him up!

Fabio

"Nigel has always been very emotional. I remember when the first Gulf War was on and it really upset Nigel and he would talk about it all the time. We would be in clubs and Nigel would run home to watch the

rolling news. It really affected him. He was in New York when 9/11 happened and that scarred him for life. He gets very emotional about that too.

I remember being at my Swerve night one evening in 2002 and I'd had a few drinks on an empty stomach. I walked in and went straight to the toilets. I couldn't play, I felt so bad, and told DJ Bailey to take over before trying to get myself together. I collapsed in the toilet and when I came to. I heard someone say, 'Get him upstairs!' It was Nigel and he picked me up and carried me outside. I was really embarrassed and so I pretended I was unconscious. Then Nigel called me an ambulance. He was so concerned. I just needed some fresh air and to get my blood sugar up. I was fine, but Nigel had been so worried.

We grew up in a culture where young black men did not talk about emotions. Black men were unemotional, yet Nigel was genuinely concerned. He got my respect for that. It meant a lot to me.

I knew Nigel was going through a phase as there were lots of rumours flying around about what he'd been up to. Nigel was overdoing everything and everyone was talking about him. It was hard to take. Nigel was making a fool of himself.

I was at Movement at Bar Rumba one night and I said, 'You know what? You are my boy! But you are making an absolute arse of yourself, bruv.' Nigel was drunk and being very being loud. He wasn't happy.

'You what?!'

I said, 'There was one time recently when you did something for me and now I'm going to help you. You need to calm down. People are talking about you. The people really close to you, don't have your back!'

- 'What do you mean?! Who?!'

Nigel was very angry, but I carried on. 'I'm not naming names here, but you're missing the point, bruv. You need to get your shit together.'

Anyone who knows Nigel, will be aware that this was a brave thing to do. Nigel can be very aggressive. He can switch! There's a scene in GoodFellas where the boys play a joke on Joe Pesci and you know that he's not going to forget the laughs they had at his expense. You don't want to get on the wrong side of Nigel.

'Nigel, I'm your bredrin. You can take it the wrong way if you want, but one day, you will thank me. Your boys haven't got your best interests. They're

talking shit behind your back.'

He walked off, severely vexed.

I saw him two days later and he said, 'Thanks for that Fitz. I took it all in and everything you said was right.' Those two incidents made us very close."

I kept seeing both these girls and was smoking crack all through the week. After a year or more of crack I had started to look a total mess. I had an ingrowing hair on my cheek and I just let it grow into this wart, the size of a golf ball. I was convinced it was cancer and that I was dying as a result. I didn't care to be honest. I looked a complete and utter mess, but that was nothing compared to what was going on inside my head.

I hated myself so much. I think the drugs just allowed me to turn attention away from myself. As soon as I had time on my hands to think, I would start to cry. The drugs took that worry away, but in doing so they created more and more problems that the sober me just couldn't deal with. These things seemed manageable until something went wrong in the 'real world'.

Mum rang me one day, upset, because Levi was ill. Mum always took care of my dog when I was busy. I raced round to hers and found him lying on the sofa. I picked him up and got him in the car to the vets. On the way there, Mum said, 'Prepare yourself, son. It might not be good news.'

Levi was with the vet, when he looked over at me. His eyes then went blank. He was dead. It was if he had waited until I came home before he died. I was hysterical. I fell to the floor sobbing.

I lost it again outside and ran out into the middle of the traffic outside the vets, as cars beeped and screeched to a halt. Everything came crashing down around me. I didn't know what I was doing. A bloke came up to me on the pavement and I tried to strangle him. My sister got me into the car and I banged my fists against the seats and windows. I got home and crashed on the bed.

I played Fabric that night and was on the verge of tears when MC Rage dedicated a song to Levi. That dog was the one thing that had kept me anywhere near sanity. Now, he was gone I felt totally alone.

My sister Yolanda was living in my flat at the time with her boyfriend. I had put all of my electrical gear into a spare room and when I turned up out of the blue one day, I found out that her boyfriend had cleaned out all my stuff. The lot! Thousands and thousands of pounds of gear. I went fucking ballistic.

The next time I saw him, I tried to run this guy down in my car. He escaped unhurt, but I was out of control. It was bad enough that I had tried to run the geezer over, but I also had a machete, hidden away in the glove box.

Finally, a red flag was being waved in the V Recordings accounts due to all the money I'd been siphoning out and smoking. That was when I was called in for a meeting with Bryan and Shirley.

I sat down in the office and Shirley went through the bank statements. Bryan wouldn't even look at me. I had put thousands of pounds into the business, but without Bryan's efforts it wouldn't have worked, so he'd done more than his share. In fact, I was royally taking the piss. Bryan knew what was happening, but hadn't felt confident enough to confront me. Until now. Many people had noticed the change in me. I would get calls all the time from friends: 'People are saying you're addicted to crack,' they would tell me. 'You know where this leads. You've seen what it does…'

Bryan finally turned to face me. 'You look like shit, mate. What's going on? You're taking money out of the business. That's not our money, that was for the artists.' Bryan turned away and I could tell that he was really upset and angry. It was a hard thing for him to do, but he did it. 'You need to step away from the business, Nigel.' I looked at the floor. I had fucked this right up and now it was affecting my best friend who had been with me all the way through this. I was nearing the end of the road, but I hadn't gotten there just yet. I got straight back on the crack.

Bryan Gee

"This was a weird, dark time for me and it was a real strain on our relationship. I could always read Nigel, but when he was doing these drugs I found it hard to understand him or see what was on his mind. He was a different person. To be honest, I was frightened. I always felt we were brothers and that we had each other's back, but now I wasn't so sure. If I had a problem, I would go to Nigel and vice versa, but this was the only time where I wasn't too sure if it was still like that anymore.

Nigel had changed so much and kept a real distance between us. I sometimes felt like he wanted to attack me or something. I just wasn't sure. I didn't even feel comfortable in my house, you know what I'm saying? Nigel was in a dark place and I wouldn't talk to him as I couldn't tell what his reactions were going to be. I loved Nigel, so maybe I should have stood up to him before. I was too soft, I guess. I should have done more.

I knew he'd done wrong to the label and all that, but I found it hard to tell him. So I didn't say anything. I was too nice, maybe?

There were a lot of rumours flying around. 'Frost has been doing this... doing that....' This gossip wasn't good for the label and soon no one wanted to work with us. These rumours could have killed the label off. No kidding. It was already nose-diving. I was just holding the fort, trying to keep things going.

He was on drugs and when you're on drugs and addicted, you don't care about anything other than getting more. There was all this poison about. It was all negative press. Is a young artist going to want to work for a label where crack is making all the headlines? People had already gone cold on us. The aura had gone. Shirley and I would sit in the office worrying. Was he going to come to the office and take stuff to sell? 'Are we a target?' We were scared. I didn't know what was going on in his head.

That was a time of some real darkness. I felt a real dark vibe going on and was so worried about what was going to happen next. I'm a country boy from Gloucester getting caught up in all this madness."

CH. 39

AWOL

2004. I went missing.

I didn't tell anyone where I was going.

I just left.

Disappeared.

No one knew, not my kids, my mum, no one. I had two young kids at this point in Dante and Kaya, but I was in no fit shape to see them. I was gone, mate.

Gone.

I checked myself into rehab. It was that, or more crack. More crack would have ended up with a toe-tag and a gravestone not long after. I couldn't take anymore. I had to stop the madness. It had to stop.

Rehab was one of the most difficult things I have ever done. I found this place, deep in the countryside near Bournemouth and checked myself in. I didn't tell a soul where I'd gone.

This centre was secured, but of course you were free to leave at any time. I paid for my treatment, which wasn't cheap, as I felt I had no other choice. I unpacked my bags and sat on the side of the bed, wondering whether I was doing the right thing. I was also scared. I didn't know what rehab would entail. I mean, it wasn't going to be easy overturning the problems I had, but what choice did I have? I had to do something.

The great thing about rehab was the time. You had lots of time. Drugs seem to take time away and they distorted it. Being a DJ is not a 9-5 either. But being in rehab gave me space to think about things

Big, Bad & Heavy

for the first time in years. There was also a routine at this place and that was what I needed. It was a mixture of a 5-star hotel and boarding school.

The average day would follow a strict schedule.

7am. Breakfast and chores. You were expected to keep your room clean and your bed made.

8am. Medication. I honestly don't know what was in my medication, but I trusted them. I mean, I'd been smoking god knows what prior to this so I didn't ask any questions. I just gobbled down the pills. A nurse would then monitor your health just to make sure you were OK.

9am. Gym session. We would play various games and get the heart going before having a break. We would all have a chat and a wind-down after the exercise.

10am. Group therapy. This was hard at first. You had to be honest and totally frank. You could not hold back on anything. This was really hard for me, but I got used to it and it really helped. Every patient was a professional – there were no street junkies – and they all had issues with heroin, crack or cocaine.

We were all rebuilding ourselves from the ground up and hearing other people's experiences stopped us from feeling isolated.

11am. Journaling time. This was a time of reflection and thought. You literally spent an hour on your own, clearing out your mind of all the clutter. Who am I? Why do I do the things I do? How can I change the way I deal with things? This was also a time of regret. I regretted so many things. The way I treated people, the drugs I had taken, the fights, the knives, the guns... you are staring in a mirror and being asked to describe what you see. That was painful, man.

12pm. Lunch. I ate really healthily there and that helped to keep me positive.

1pm. One-on-one counselling. I was in tears for many of these. I was just pouring my heart out to someone. It was painful to do, but a massive relief after. I talked about my childhood, the area I grew up in, school, my family, the rave scene and the drugs... This was hard, but it had to be done.

I also underwent depression counselling, which was long overdue. If only, young men, black men especially, would just face up to depression and get it treated. Don't battle these things out alone, as I did. Seek some help.

Mum, Auntie Barbara, Cousin Jackie, Cousin Toni, Cousin Nigel, cousin Cora in Guyana

My brother Alvarez, Hekeimo the groom and my sister Yolanda at their wedding in Guyana

With the family in Guyana

My brother Alvarez, my niece, my granddaughters and grandson

With my sons, Dante and Sion

Me and cousin Debbie

With my grandchildren surrounded by love

Me and Dad

Me and my girlfriend, Rachel

I love my kids. Tanya, Ziesha, Kaya, Dante, Tori and Sion

With my cousin OG Trenton in Guyana

Me and my girlfriend, Rachel

Me and Mum

With my brother Alvarez, my sister Yolanda and my cousin Stephen

With my brother Alvarez and my good friend Julia Eastwood

Me and Rachel with Bailey and Sunshine

Blue Frost

Ibiza with Inter, Funsta, Bassman and Fearless

With my good friend of over 30 years Mr Andy Ansah

With Legends Gordon Mac and Norman Jay

Chef, GQ, Grooverider, DJ Ron, Me and DJ SL

With Lloyd Life, Robert Stush and Tina Bling

With the late great Tenor Fly (RIP), Topcat, Congo Natty and Daddy Freddie

Big, Bad & Heavy

The Respect LA squad. Credit: Regal D

Me and my boy, Duffus

OG Jarvis - Biology

Me and Jazzie B

The Clapham Common reunion

At the mural of me in Brixton with my boy Ripper and my sons Dante and Sion

Say hello to my little friend

Without music, life would be a mistake

Pimpin' ain't easy

Mad love to my Fight Klub family

Team Frost, baby! With Fearless.
Credit Craig Boyko

Watching Manchester United with my good friend Danny Carter

With Andy C at XOYO
🔥🔥🔥🔥

Best Jungle DJ Award (2015) and Lifetime Achievement Award (2017)

3pm. Sports. I had always loved playing football and this really lifted my spirits. You could also have acupuncture and all these different therapies. There was a pool, too. Then you'd shower.

4pm. Drug screenings. Obviously the centre was free of illegal drugs and had to be kept that way and so you were tested every single day.

4.30pm. Medication. You got more tablets before another medical assessment from the nurse.

5pm. Chores.

6pm. Evening meal.

7pm. Family therapy. You were encouraged to involve family members in discussion, but I just wasn't ready for that and so I would take another group session.

8pm. Social time. We would watch films and TV or play table tennis and other games. I would sometimes have a swim or go for a walk around the grounds.

9pm. Quiet time. You had a chance to do your homework, which was often writing essays on what we'd been discussing that day. You could also phone home from the phoneboxes in the centre.

11pm. Lights out. On the dot.

The extensive counselling allowed me to just stop for a bit and focus on what was driving all this. I had acupuncture and all sorts of therapy.

I was in rehab for two months, which allowed me time to feel sorry for myself while reflecting, reminiscing and crying. There was a lot of crying. Then it was time to rebuild my life.

I really needed this time out. In fact, after rehab I still kept out of everyone's way. I was out of the picture for a year or so without seeing anyone.

I hated myself so much, but probably no more than how others felt about me. I had let everyone down. I had two little kids for fuck's sake. It was the most difficult time of my life. I had no confidence or optimism. I was feeling better, but had no idea as to what to do next.

I ended up spending a few months living with friends in the countryside. They just let me do my own thing and it felt good to be amongst nature. I would go walking around the countryside, just thinking things through. I was starting to feel stronger and more hopeful.

Even when I returned to London, I kept myself out of the way before I could even think about making that next step back into my life. I was terrified, embarrassed and ashamed. I had disappeared off the face of the earth as far as most people understood it. I phoned my mum twice from rehab just to let her know I wasn't dead or something. Just hearing her voice made me feel so warm inside. I felt like I had let everyone down and I needed their love again.

I was shaking the day I finally went home to Mum's house. I stood outside for a bit, plucking up the courage. I'd been through so much and had put everyone who was close to me, through hell. I walked in through the front door and 'Woooooaaaah!!!' Everyone was so glad to see me. I hadn't seen anyone in nearly a year. My family and friends were great and didn't judge me or make me feel bad. We just had a great time catching up and of course I was interested in what they'd been doing, too. We had a great Christmas together that year.

I then arranged to meet Bryan. 'Fuck me, it's good to hear from you!' he said. He had upset me when he started Movement without me, but it was nothing compared to what I'd done to him. I had been a terrible liability. He was so happy to see me I just burst into tears. It was very emotional. I'd been a lunatic the last time we'd met. The shame I felt was debilitating. I was scared to show my face in the scene again, but Bryan smoothed things over like he always had. I couldn't thank him enough.

V Recordings had really recovered from when I left it on its knees. V had done a lot of work with the talent coming through from Brazil such as Patif and DJ Marky. I owed such a massive debt to Bryan and Shirley. I remember seeing an act Bryan had signed – LK – appearing on *Top Of The Pops*, and I was so proud and excited. Bryan had pulled off another coup.

Although Jay and I were no longer a couple, I burst into tears when I saw her again. The way I had treated her, really tormented me. She was crying too. We had a cuddle and made up.

Getting straight and clean was a long road, though. If I thought otherwise then I was going to fail. There would be bumps along the way and I needed to use all the strength I had to get over them. I'd heard stories of DJs getting involved in similar situations to mine, but they have never spoken publicly about it and so I won't name names. We all have our demons.

***

Ratpack were long-standing icons of the north London warehouse scene going back to the days of the squat parties. They were also one of the first acts to introduce prominent vocals and MCing over the beats. Evenson Allen and Mark Lipmaster will always be legends. Back in December 1991, Ratpack were travelling to a night on Leigh Bridge Road when they were caught up in a hideous car crash. Both Evenson and Mark were seriously injured and rushed to hospital, but Evenson's missus Sue Bronson wasn't so lucky. There was nothing that the paramedics could do and Sue died in the seat next to Ev.

Although beaten up and suffering from grief, Evenson carried on working as soon as he was able to. I had started dwelling on this, as I tried to piece my life together. This put everything I was going through into a sharp perspective. I had nothing to worry about, next to what Ev had been through and yet he played out with all the inner strength a person could muster, days after suffering such a loss. Ev was such an inspiring man who I admired so much as an artist and a human being. I can't imagine what he must have gone through and his bravery and strength came back to me, when I was at my lowest.

Bryan Gee

"Those dark times made us both stronger. Everyone was back in love with the label, which was great as you're only as good as your last tune. We were both much wiser and I was really proud of him for turning his life around. I couldn't have imagined him being this way back when he was in that dark place. He was now kinder, more mature and reserved. Nigel was calmer. Maybe that was a part of growing up.

Nigel was taking no prisoners back then, but now he was very open with people.

We didn't go back to the dark place, we just tried to deal with it and move on. I tried not to visit that place in my mind. It seemed as if we'd gotten through the worst and we were both better for it."

CH. 40

Rebirth

Confidence counts for a lot in this game. Many great DJs have failed because they lack that self-belief or maybe didn't get that little bit of luck you need. I was now at zero confidence. I wasn't sure I could ever play a record again. I know I'm not the best DJ out there, but I had something people wanted. Charisma? Maybe. Plus, I always had Bryan around me and this support network of Fabio and Groove. I also had Dillinja who continued to give me first dibs on so many tunes. Goldie deserves a mention too as I worked the Leisure Lounge with him so many times over the years. Many better DJs never succeeded because they didn't have that in their locker. Now, I was more or less starting from scratch.

    I had known this girl Amanda for years and I met up with her again during this period, post rehab. Amanda was funny, smart and very, very loud. She was a primary school teacher and always the centre of attention. She soon put me right. 'Oi, you fucking cunt! Stop moping and let's sort you out! I heard that you fucked everything up. But no more!' We were inseparable as Amanda got me back on track.

    Amanda got my confidence buzzing again. It took a while, but she reminded of who I had been and what I was capable of. We drove to Glastonbury Festival without tickets and just sat in the car, having a laugh. Amanda was great company.

    That Christmas, she invited my dad over to her house and bought him presents. She got me loads of nice clothes and this made me feel good about myself again. Confidence. It's just one word, but it's everything, believe me. Without it, you are screwed.

I got a call to play LA just after Christmas. Just out of the blue. 'You're not going unless I can come!' she laughed.

- 'OK, then. Come with me!'

My confidence was at such a low ebb at this point, that the idea of having Amanda with me, eased my concerns. So, we packed our bags and headed for the airport. I played for promoter Jeremy Fitzgerald who lived in the beautiful Marine Del Ray. Jeremy's dad owned the world famous Century Club in LA where I played. That trip did wonders. We met up with my good friend Alexis and her husband Joey and we had a wicked time out there. I remember dropping Amanda off in Compton. She was wearing a bright red dress and she didn't see the significance of where she was until I picked her up 15 minutes later. I wonder what the local Crips thought of that red dress. Ha ha. We had a great time out there shopping on Melrose and eating some lovely food. I showed her all around LA.

I will never forget what Amanda did for me. Never. Sadly, we parted ways after a while, but I will always be grateful.

I have been so lucky to have people like Amanda in my life. Amanda was like a dog with a bone when it came to my career. She turned everything around for me.

Bryan was another one, who had always been there. I'd been away so long I didn't know anything about all the technological advances that had occurred in the industry. 'You should go online,' Bryan suggested one day.

- 'You what?'

Although I'd been bewitched by that online shopping seminar back in Orlando all those years back, I'd been oblivious to it all when it finally arrived. Myspace? Didn't have a clue, mate. People had just started sending music files by AIM at this time too. But with help from Bryan I slowly started to get back into the game.

Bryan was instrumental in plugging me back into the scene that I had largely abandoned. I got fresh new tunes from V to play out and my boy Dillinja was continuing to smash it. I played so much of his stuff as I tried to get my career back on track.

My progress was slow, but just as the cliché goes, I simply took it one day at a time. I just didn't want to go back to how I was. I had to keep moving forward.

Grooverider was a proper friend. 'You're moving in with me,' he announced one day. Groove wanted to keep me away from temptation.

I was so flattered. 'I want to keep an eye on you,' he laughed. Groove put aside a lot of time helping me get back to normality after losing my way. Another great friend of mine, through all these years was Robyn.

CH. 41

Soul Mate

My friend Robyn Pelka from New York was a great source of comfort through all my crap. Robyn had been through all of this before as a recovering heroin addict. In fact, Robyn had been through far worse. Myspace was around at that time and we started chatting a lot online. Robyn had just beaten a brain tumour prior to my exit from rehab and so she knew how things were. Robyn also knew me and the things I'd done and so it was lovely being able to talk to her. Robyn and I had stayed close since that very first US tour. She was so important to me. She was family. My little sister.

When I had Kaya and Dante in 2000, such was Robyn's significance in my life – I gave Kaya the middle name Robyn. Dante had Delano; my dad's middle name. Robyn was a true friend. I used to remember her asking, 'Why do you hang about with me? I'm just a little Polish chick.' Robyn came over to London in the late nineties and we had such a great time. Robyn was always the first person I'd call when in New York. Robyn was one of those friends that bypassed all the crap. We just clicked and really looked out for each other.

I was playing New York –

Robyn's home town – in 2006 at this tiny venue. I'd been playing out for a year or so and the bookings were slowly picking up, as was my confidence. I would have turned this sort of booking down years before, but I really was starting from the bottom again. Here I was in the city that marked the start of my success, its subsequent disintegration and rebirth.

Prior to this trip I had found out that Robyn was ill again. Robyn had cancer and had suffered a brain haemorrhage. I burst into tears when I saw her. She just didn't look the same. They had to cut her head open in order to treat her. I was shell-shocked and would just burst into tears in the street when I remembered what was happening to her. Her situation just knocked me for six. I was determined that we were going to have a good time, though, while I was out there.

I got us tickets to a Broadway show and we went out for some lovely meals. We had a great time catching up, but I just kept looking at her, barely recognising her face. It really cut me up. I truly loved her as a person ever since we went on that first tour across the States. Robyn was the most beautiful person I have had the fortune to meet. She was so touched when I told her that I'd shown my daughter pictures of her; the woman she was named after. Robyn was in remission at the time and had just set up a charity for people with brain cancer. She was apparently getting better, but it was so upsetting seeing her with all her hair cut off.

I remember that towards the end of my trip to New York, we spent an entire evening watching *Law And Order* on TV in my hotel room. Cuddled up on the sofa, we just sat there watching this show. Then, she turned to face me at one point and said, 'Look at me.' I turned around. She said, 'Don't you ever, ever, ever stop DJing. Do you hear me? You have a talent, so don't waste it. Promise me.'

- 'I promise.'

That was the last time I saw her. Robyn?! If you can you hear me, wherever you are right now, I just want to reassure you… I haven't given up. I miss you darling. God bless and rest in peace. XXX

CH. 42

A Promise Kept

I made a promise to Robyn that I wouldn't turn away from music and I hope that she is proud of me. If you are looking down at me, I hope you see a stronger man.

Robyn's final words to me rang in my ears for some time, as I wrestled with the idea of getting back on track with my music. Then in 2007, I was contacted by a friend of mine, Laura Roper. Laura put me in contact with these two sisters Emma and Claire Lydon who were putting together a benefit party for their dear friend Nikki who was very ill.

I had played a few gigs around this time, but nothing serious and I wanted to help the girls so much, that I agreed to play this night for free. If I couldn't play for myself then I would play for others. It was a very emotional night and Nikki actually died on the day of the party, but I was so happy to be able to help those girls out. In fact, Claire (aka 'The Normalist') and her sister Emma are still close friends with me to this day.

Seeing the love in that room really touched me and once again, people were urging me to continue playing out. I love you both and rest in peace Nikki. XXX.

I knew I couldn't keep away for ever and so I decided to get back in the game for real, having seen how much joy music can deliver. I was lucky to have this job and I would have been a fool to let things slide. Life is too short, mate. Life is far too fucking short.

So, it took a while to get my confidence back, but with help and support from all my friends and family, I started to get back to where I was. The first few sets were hard and nervy affairs, but once you've seen what's over the edge, you have no intention of ever going back there.

I have been lucky enough to travel the world again, playing the music I love. Every city has a group of friends that welcome me in, making every town a second home.

We have lost a few souls along the way, and I just wanted to pay some respect.

2010 was a sad time. Kirsty Rogers was a good mate who I met through my close friends Tom Parker and Lucy Gaynor. When she passed we were all in a state of shock. I was at Tom and Lucy's house sitting on the end of their bed enjoying a good laugh with Kirsty, while Tom and Lucy were on the decks. Sadly, that was the last time I saw her and I just want to say, 'Keep smiling, darling!'

The very same year, we lost someone very close to me, Emily Borau. She was such a lovely spirit and I am so proud to have been in her life. I was so devastated when she passed away. Emily, her friend Demetria and I, had some great weekends raving it up. 'Keep on dancin', love!' XXX

I want to say thank you to all my friends and family (love you Mum and Dad) and was so glad to get back in contact with my brother Alva. Also big love and hugs to my brother Gary and sisters Yolanda and Samantha. Big love to my kids, grandkids and girlfriend Rachel (see, you did make the book!).

Rachel and I had a testing time in 2010 when my girl was diagnosed with breast cancer. That was a hard time, right there, but it brought us closer together. I remember her kids and I shaving her hair off for her rather than seeing it eventually fall out. I have lost a few friends to cancer, but luckily we won this battle and I am so grateful. Rachel's remission also coincided with an upturn in fortunes for me, which was perfect timing really. It was almost as if music was waiting until I was ready to go again. After that, gigs went through the roof and I was back on the road.

I started my own clothes line www.team-frost.com and have been fortunate enough to have designed my own range of personalised earphones, thanks to Adam Blair from Pump Audio.

I got my dog Blue around this time, too. I love you Blue! And thanks to Chyna who has Blue's sister Star. XXX

In 2011, I was properly made up to be a mentor to young people by the then Mayor of London Boris Johnson. It's so hard for young kids growing up in inner cities these days, where you can get yourself whacked just for entering the wrong postcode. It was just a brief stint, but I want to do more to help the younger generation.

I visited my ancestral home for the first time in 2015 when my sister Yolanda got married in Guyana. That was such a special time and it was great to see where my family's roots were formed.

I still love radio and have a show on Mi-soul.com run by former Mr Kiss himself Gordon Mac. Bailey and I co-host a show on Mi-soul, where I'm joined by many of my old colleagues from my days at Kiss. It's like one big happy family again. I also cover for people like Uncle Dugs on Rinse. Big love!

BIG LOVE TO NEW YORK CITY! I still get about a bit and when I'm in my second home of NYC, I try to bump into all my friends there, including Mr Public Enemy/Bomb Squad Hank Shocklee. Thank you from the bottom of my heart for the foreword, sir. Also, big shout out to Will, Valerie and Filipe (BP family) as well as Trigon, Eric and Digger Bruckshot. Plus, my girls Vanessa and Mickael.

In 2014, I was awarded Best Jungle DJ at the National Drum And Bass Awards, which was a top, top honour. I then received a Lifetime Achievement Award in 2017, too, so thank you to everyone who voted for me.

Finally, I have written a book. I can't quite believe that. What would my teachers say about this?

I had known Billy 'Daniel' Bunter for quite a while as a fellow DJ on the scene, albeit in that happy hardcore strand. Then, when the old-skool scene became a thing, we all started playing together on the same line-ups again. Thank you, Dan and Sonya, for believing in me so much that you were willing to publish my book.

Bryan Gee… well, what can I say? I love you, man. If it wasn't for you, then I don't where I'd be right now. V Recordings is a testament to all your hard work. And thank you to Shirley and Jaime who have helped me so much too.

Sadly, we have lost a few brothers in this journey and it was so sad to hear of the passing of Tenor Fly in 2016. I had known this guy since we were kids and I felt honoured to have played alongside this great man. I first met Tenor (Jonathan Sutter) as a fellow cub scout in 1975.

The drum and bass community is doing a benefit gig for Tenor's family and I am hoping to see all the familiar faces from our pasts at what is set to be an emotional night. When the drum and bass community comes together, it goes BIG! It's a shame that it often takes something like this to get us all under the same roof, but when called upon, we're there. Together we're strong.

I also want to say thank you to music. Without music, I wouldn't be here talking to you now. A life on the streets would have led one way and one way only.

I still have a lot of love for Brixton; the place where it all started. Now, I get snobs looking down their noses at me as I walk around town. 'What am I doing here? What are you doing here?!' FFS.

I have hurt so many people in my life and I just want to put all that behind me by going forward. I am nearly 50 and I just want to live a peaceful life and I wish the same for every one of you.

Finally, I want to thank you for giving me the time to tell my story. And for buying the book! I can't claim to be a model citizen throughout my life, but I like to think that I will be a better person tomorrow than I am today.

I would also like to encourage anybody who feels that they might be depressed, to seek help. Please don't ignore these feelings or simply try and bury them with drugs or drink. Make contact with a professional, who really can help turn your life around. You are not alone, bruv.

www.mind.org.uk
www.thecalmzone.net
www.Team-frost.com
www.vrecordings.com

Psalm 23

The L<small>ORD</small> is my shepherd, I lack nothing.
He makes me lie down in green pastures,
he leads me beside quiet waters,
he refreshes my soul.
He guides me along the right paths
for his name's sake.

Even though I walk
through the darkest valley,
I will fear no evil,
for you are with me;
your rod and your staff,
they comfort me.

You prepare a table before me
in the presence of my enemies.
You anoint my head with oil;
my cup overflows.
Surely your goodness and love will follow me
all the days of my life,
and I will dwell in the house of the L<small>ORD</small>
forever.

CH. 43

A Few Final Words

Congo Natty

"Jungle has always been very underrated as a British musical art-form and because of that jungle has been a giant middle finger to the industry that wrote it off. I am still playing sold-out dances all over the world, mashing up the place with grime artists and garage MCs. Jungle is unique. Jungle has saved souls and continues to do so. If it wasn't for music where would Frost and I, be?

    Frost and I shared a mutual friend in Tenor Fly; Nigel went to school with him. We travelled the world playing on the same bills and recording music together. Tenor Fly was an original Brixton MC from Sir Coxone Sound and in 2016 we lost a brother. That was a wake-up call. Life has no guarantees to no man.

    We have organised a tribute to Tenor Fly and Frost will play at that. It will be a special occasion and will serve as a memorial, tribute and fundraiser for Tenor Fly's daughter. This night will keep the name Tenor Fly in people's minds and hearts."

DJ Ron

"There are various sides to him (Frost). When he is with his family, little children or brother, there's that aspect to him that many people don't see. Nigel is the only one that I 'talk family' to on the circuit. Because I know his family and he knows my children. So, it's genuine, as we are real friends. When I say, 'How's your mum?' it means something because I know his mum. There is a sense of bravado that people put on in this game. Like perhaps Nigel did. He took no prisoners back then.

In terms of being a DJ, I've noticed how driven he is with it now. He's not just going through the motions. He's not just playing out either and is doing radio again. That enthusiasm is rare. He has an energy now like when he first started. He does so many different types of sets: house, funk and rare groove. He tapes them as well. Nobody does that anymore.

Frost can move into many types of society, but he will never actually change. He's a chameleon who doesn't change his colours."

Kenny Ken

"The first time I saw Frost was while raving. We snuck through this hole in the wall, behind some corrugated iron in Whitechapel to get into this warehouse. It was 1987 and it was nights like this that led me to become a DJ. Then, when I started DJing in 1988, I got to know Frost a little bit better.

I remember going to Switzerland with Frost and MC Det to work for this German promoter in 1991 and when we arrived, the promoter wouldn't meet us, thus we couldn't get our money. 'Well, if he doesn't pay, I ain't playing. That is disrespectful. I want my money!'

We didn't play and just stood around having a go on the arcade machines. After a while, we decided to go up and see this bloke, as he certainly wasn't coming down to see us.

Now, the stairs up to his office were guarded by these massive security guys and we just rushed them. It was madness. We were embroiled in a right old scrap now. It was quite comical. While we were rolling around, giving as good as we got, one of the guards yelled, 'Freeze! Call the police!' I don't know why, but at that point, we all froze. All of us. It was like someone had flipped a switch and time stood still. We certainly didn't want to end up in a Swiss jail and so we legged it. We eventually got paid when we got back home. But having Frost behind you, gave you confidence.

We've had some good times touring the world, but it's not all glamour, you know. I started dyeing my hair when I was in my thirties and I remember Frost and Det banging on my hotel door in Canada *while I was in the middle of turning my grey hair black. God, the shit I got for that! 'Ha ha! You grey fucker!' Even I found it amusing. Three members of the jungle community acting like kids while one of them dyed his hair.*

I won the Jungle Soundclash in 1994 and Bryan Gee and Frost properly hooked me up with some great tunes for that. Rebel MC as well. I will never forget that. Frost got this speshy done for me, which is an old sound system dubplate, which repeats your name over and over. I was well impressed by this. He got this guy to sing my name the following day and then took it to the studio to finish it off. Saxon fixed it up as a proper speshy and I was made up, mate. I love you brother."

Nick Halkes (XL, Positiva)

"I saw that there was this rave exhibition (organised by Music Mondays) going on at Old Street (2017) and having missed the first one, I thought I'd drop by for a drink and a look, as it was a really interesting initiative. So, I walked into this club and bumped straight into Frost. 'Oi Nick!' he bounded over in classic Frost style and we had a big hug. 'Mate, you'll have to come on stage to join this panel thing I'm doing…'

- 'What? I was just coming in for a look around.'
- 'I will call you up on stage.'

Fifteen minutes later, Frost introduces me. 'Meet the man who set up XL and signed The Prodigy and SL2…' I'm on stage with a microphone in my hand just talking about my experiences… no prep as such. Ha ha. That is Frost all over."

Fabio

"Just like that line from GoodFellas, I have known Frost for as far back as I can remember. I was about 9 when we used to play on the same adventure playground. We were not that tight back then, but we shared the same friends. Later, I knew of Boga by association, because of the crew he ran with.

Nigel has always been a character and the dance scene needs that. Frost made dnb so special. There are not so many personalities now; just like football. Frost is a flawed character, just like the rest of us.

Flawed, in a lovely way. Frost is never spiteful or horrible and he is a great storyteller. His name crops up in conversation and a smile usually creeps across the other guy's face. That says it all, mate."

Jazzie B

"The brother is writing a book? Dear me! This kid, who used to cause trouble at my nights, is doing a book. Ha ha! Seriously, though, well done Nigel!"

The Love Dove Generation

BILLY 'DANIEL' BUNTER
with ANDREW WOODS

'One of the most entertaining histories of rave I've ever read...' **Ian McQuaid, Ransom Note**

'The Love Dove Generation, one of the most honest — and indispensable — accounts of the early 90s rave scene you will ever read...' **Mark Kavanagh, Buzz.ie**

'An instant classic...' **Kirsty Allison, DJ Mag**

'Britain's biggest raver Billy 'Daniel' Bunter on a life of thrills, pills and more pills...' **Tom Fenwick, Fact Magazine**

The Love Dove Generation centres around the east London rave scene of the late '80s/early'90s and is the autobiography of Daniel Light, professionally known as Billy 'Daniel' Bunter who started out as Britain's youngest rave DJ aged just 15. Daniel rose to the top of the pile at the legendary Labrynth, 12 Dalston Lane, E8 before embarking on a global career in music that continues to this day.

Signed hardback books available from
www.musicmondays.co.uk

The Man Behind The Mask

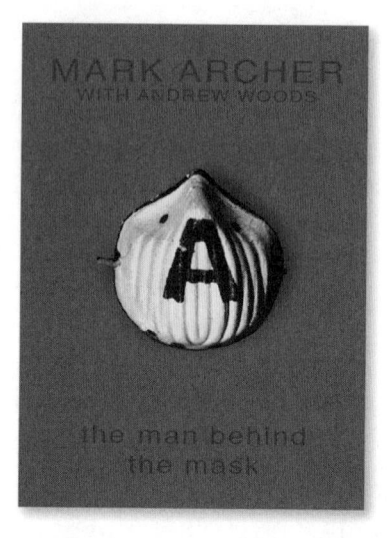

'Altern 8 occupy a unique position in dance music history...' **Moby**

'One of the top three music memoirs this year, alongside New Order bassist Peter Hook and the legendary Bruce Springsteen. **Mark Kavanagh, Buzz.ie**

The Man Behind The Mask tells the incredible story of Mark Archer who, along with Chris Peat, were those mysterious Men In Masks from the West Midlands otherwise known as Altern 8 – one of the most successful British rave acts of all time. A jaw-dropping account of some incredible highs – smash-hit singles and tours around the globe – with comedowns just as mind-blowing, this is a tale of one man's all-consuming passion for making music under a host of different personas: Bizarre Inc, Nexus 21, Altern 8, Slo Moshun, DJ Nex and Xen Mantra to name but a few.

Signed hardback books available from
www.musicmondays.co.uk

Rave Diaries And Tower Block Tales

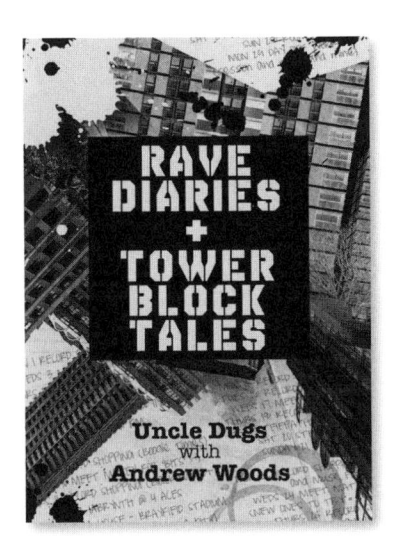

POLICE RAIDS!

GUNFIGHTS!

AND ENOUGH DRUGS TO KNOCK AN ELEPHANT OUT!

Rave Diaries And Tower Block Tales is a compelling account of one man's journey through music. Bred on a diet of rave and jungle the young Uncle Dugs had a dream: to play his beloved music on the pirate airwaves of London Town and on the main stages of the UK's biggest raves. In his pursuit of this goal Uncle Dugs became a legend of the illegal airwaves and a champion of the emerging street sounds. From rave and jungle through to grime, dubstep and beyond, Dugs has become one of the most important cogs in the UK underground.

**Signed hardback books available from
www.musicmondays.co.uk**

Big Bad & Heavy

Thank you all so much for your love and support over the last 30 years. Without all of you there's no way I could have done it. God bless you all and thank you from the bottom of my heart.

A Lincoln Biggs
Aaron Day
Acid Ash & Lady Lou
Acid Bunny
Adam "Fatz" Russell
Adam Blowers
Adi Day
Adrian Spires
Ads Pooley
Ady Bird
Ady Brown
Afeni Neville
Aisha Spence
AK1200
Al Crew
Alan Dixon
Alex Hagley
Alex Kearns
Alex Lawrence - respect to J J Frost
Alex Neil
Alex Reynolds
Alex Stubbs
Alex 'Super Don' Dawes
Alex Wright
Alison Foster
Alistair Arani
Allan Little & Kevin Jackson
Allan Mustafa

Allison Aniska
Amanda Nash
Amina Deen
Ander Wilson
Andrea Potkonjak
Andreas Thanassoulas
Andrew - Frosts fast driver
Andrew Araniello
Andrew Dawes
Andrew Pennell
Andy "DJ AYBEE" Brown
Andy Bubbles
Andy Gunn aka DJ Gunna
Angelko Rezo
Anna Foggy & Lewis Brown
Antony Fernandez
Archie Kay
Arfa G & Roachman
Ash Clayton
Ashley Scott Smith
Aurindam Majumdar
Barry Holland
Bas Buckland (Bucky)
Beau Ingleby-Lewis
Beck The Rez Crew
Ben (B-J-T) Tully
Ben Day
Ben Habitat Panks

Big, Bad & Heavy

Ben Phillips
Ben York
Big Dave Beaumont
Big Vinny Tildesley
Brad Barnett
Brian 'Dektek' Spence
Brian Nicholson
Carl Palmer
Carl Willis
Carlos, Happy Christmas! love Ems x
Carni Carn
Caroline
CassDubWild
Charlie Grey
Charlie Lane Fox
Cherisse Richarde
Chris Beardsley
Chris Coomer
Chris KeeZee
Chris Marshionist Marsh
Chris McCarthy
Chris Thurston aka "Chrissy Slim"
Chris Williams
Chrissy Lewis
Christopher Neale Mason
Clive 'OJ' Wilkinson
Clivey - B
Colin Bauld
Colin Brookfield
Colin Jones and the basement crew
Conrad Koziol
Cornerstone Drum & Bass
Craig Palmer (Kryme)
Curtis Wilson (DJ DIGIX)
D' Vinyl
Dafydd Jones
Damian Spall
Damien Crowe
Dan Corsi
Dan Kew
Dan Sharp aka DJ Frantic
Dan Whittle
Dani Todd
Daniel and India Salewski

Daniel Fraser
Daniel Nazareth
Daniel 'NO $ D' Williams
Daniel Parham
Danny Carter
Danny Drive Thru
Danny Ramzee
Darren "REDLINE" Angel
Darren E Cowley - Isotonik Studios
Darren Griffin
Darren Pizzy
Darren Pizzy
Darren Winch
Dave "Beatman" Wright
Dave Dawson Barn Owl
David Bubb
David Llewellyn & Andy Malone
David Miller
David Richard Baker
David Todd
Dean Lander (West Bletchley)
Dean Merrick
Dean peters
Deano Williams
Debbie Woods
Deborah McNally
Delroy Ford & Vicky smith
Derek Holder aka Kaom
Di Patterson (Friend)
Dimitrios Riglis
Dione Mizzi
DJ Ash Boodhoo
DJ Dara
DJ H
DJ Kryptonn
DJ LX
DJ Mosh
DJ Ollie
DJ Perky
DJ Poison
DJ Pulse
DJ Shoolace
DJ Step One
DJ Steve Riley

Big, Bad & Heavy

DJ Stretch aka Mr Papa Lover
Dj Terrorist
DJ Trubalsom
Dominik Just
DX Beats
Dylan Llewellyn
ED "DJ Ed-Strong" Brown
Ed Steerment
Edan Trigon
Eddie Szymandera
Edward Farr
Elsta - Murky D&B
Emlyn
Emma Brennan aka Bat Bren
Emma Gildy
Emz
Emz Griffin
English Matt aka Matt Pearson
Enno "Kingsley" Huebner
Eric BiG E Bridgewater
Eric Tesainer
Flint & Steel
Francis Cooper
Frank Hawes
Gareth Hughson
Gary Kingsmill
Gary Mr. Symbiote Crockford
Gary Munnery
Gary Strife
Gavin 'DJ Face' Mills
Gaz Frost
Gaz P
George Ankrett
George Crawford, Toronto Junglist since 94, till I die!
George Mahood
Georgia Brown
Georgina Leanne
Giles 'Massive G' McIntyre
Glenn McPherson
Glyn Lowercase Allaway
Grace Everill-Spencer
Graham Coomber
Gregg "Shifty" Knott
Guy Harwood

Heidi 'Fairy Rave Mother' Haynes
Helen Roberts
Huck Finn
Iain Sansome
Ian Hicks
J Marshall
JABO
Jacob Woods
James and Gareth Cotton (Cambridge WWG Crew)
James Austin
James Bohn
James Casey
James Daglish
James Hunt
James Morgan
James Parker
James Popplewell
James Smith
James White
James Wilson
James Faulkner
Jamie Caring
Jamie Rovira
Jamie Technique Clark
Jane Crockett aka Mrs Stickywings
Jason Walden
Jay Frenzic
Jay Palmer
Jen Jenny B
Jenna D'Mellow
Jerry Phillip
Jim Shreim
Jimmy Mackinners Mackinlay
JJ Pooley
Jodi 'MinXxy' Hamm
Joe 90
Joe Leeming
Joe Watson
John 'FG' Morgan
Jon O'Hare
Jon Small
Jonny H
Jose Fernandez
Josh Bigears BP2/Konkrete Jungle NYC

JP Hutton
Judge Dredd
Julian Harrison
June O'Connell
Justin Grant
Karen Hadfield
Karen Ray
Karen Salih
Kate Murdoch
Keith Hill
Kellie Croasdell
Kerry O'Brien
Kevin Rushman aka Ted (shout to my lady Donna-Marie Blake)
Kevlar
King Jim
Koostos Nigel
Kris Morrison
Kurt Edmonds
Latibroevad
Laura Clarke
Laura Codina
Lee Coulson
Lee Hammond
Lee Holt
Lee Taylor
Leone Joe Fusione
Levela
Lindsay 'Penners' Pennington
Linz Randall
Lisa Hennessy
Lisa Kitchingham
Lisa Palmer
Lizzie Covey
Lori Sapio
Louise Dalmedo
Louise Robinson
Lucas (Top Drawer Digital)
Luke Duffell
Luke Harding
Luke McGlone
Luke Vortex Agacy
Luke Whiteacre
Lydia Edwards
M.C. Express

Manuel Lema Romero
Marc Woodward
Mark & Nikki - 'The Archers'
Mark A Bamford
Mark Daniels from Birmingham
Mark E Brich (NuClear)
Mark Jackson
Mark Keal 'Steppa Magazine'
Mark Lee
Mark Moore
Mark original raver Onza
Mark Ronayne
Mark Spinks
Mark 'STRYDER' Whitehouse
Mark Turner – DJ Mark T
Mark Upshall
Mark Warn
Martin Bere
Marvellous Marvia
Mary Joseph
Mat Robinson
Matt Iron Palm Bass
Matt Sealy
Matthew Craig
Matthew Eaton
Matthew French & Donald Elliot
Matthew Haughton
Matty Kore Parry
Matty Slabz
Mayanayse
Maydine
Melly J Hunter
Mervyn Phillips
Michael Heiker
Michael Hoare
Michael Farrell
Michelle
Michelle Smith
Mike Fleet
Miss Lexx
Mitchell Hartrop
Mookie
Mr. Deepz
Naji

Natasha White
Nate Sharpe
Neil Hearne
Neil 'Neillydan' McCann
NEILIO \o/ The BoxRoom Raver
Nic Serpell-Rand
Nic 'St1x' Whatmore
Nicholas Rawlinson
Nick 'Bionick' Davidson
Nick 'Chooch' Stratton
Nick longman
Nick Sincere Porter
Nigel Davidson
Nina - Smiley Smiley Crew
Nokesy77
Oli Bee
Oliver Fletcher
Ollie Hurford
Ollie Morgan
Ollie Twist
Omar Russell
Onkar Bhamber
Pat and Jane
Par
Patrick Oldham
Patrick Williams
Paul "Snuff the Ablist" Robinson
Paul "Spikey" Haslam
Paul & Anna Whyatt
Paul Collings
Paul 'DJ AKA' Francombe
Paul Edwards
Paul EJay
Paul Hateley
Paul Osmond
Paul Wheatley
Paul Woolford
Pawel Bob
Pete Devnull
Pete 'FreQuenCee' Cairns
Pete Knowles
Peteee, The Lucky Giant
Phil "Noizee B" Evans
Phil Horner

PHIL STARLING
Phil Waples Junglist est.1994
Philip Buckley
Philip William Farmer
Phillip Cadwallader
Phillip Kearney
Raffa 'D' Voelker (GJD)
Rahul Savani
Randhir Verma
Random Raver Rich
Raymond Bamford
Rehka Chelvendra
Reidy
Renny Glynn
Rhumble
Richard Belton - aka Indesign Soldier
Richard Langton
Richard Tustin
Richard Fowler
Richie "Rollin" Swift & Blin
Ricky "50 and still 'avin' it" Gee
Rob Blanchette
Rob Bril - Toronto, Canada
Rob Homer
Rob Humber
Rob Picton aka Joe Blow
Robert Nichols
Robert Vary
Robin Gray
Rodge
Roger Mitchell
Roon Rehfeld
Ross Glithro
Roxie Webb
Roy Edmunds
Russ G
Russell Besta
Russell Coe
Russell Norris (X-Static)
Ryan Best of British
Ryan Dale
Ryan Powell
Ryck
Sam Connoley

Big, Bad & Heavy

Sam Dubzilla Leach
Sam Earl DJ SE
Sam Kinsley
Sam Maskall
Samas Sayer
Sammy Goat Ruff
Sander Zegveld
Sarah McIlroy (Sarah UK)
Sarah Tunnicliffe
Sascha Pacco
Satyan Shah
Scott "Dead Bonsai" Smith
Scott Cattell
Scott King aka Scott3
Scott M. Brewer
Sean
Shai Prendergast
Shai Shah
Shannon S
Shanti B2B Skinty
Shaz ' Exmoor Junglist' Down
Shazaboom aka Sharon Taylor x To my Bestie, Christian McCall, love Shazaboom x
Sherrie 'Shez.B' Baker
Shola Famodimu
Simon Campbell
Simon Connell
Simon Harding
Simon Harris-Jones
Simon Kenway
Simon Tappenden
Simon van der Burg
Simon Zeus Laver
SK2
Skinz
Slashdot "Davis" Dashdot
Smiler love Chesh x
Sophia Campbell
Stephen Bailey
Stephen Launchbury
Stephen Moss
Stephen Nicol
Stephen Wright
Steve Frame
Steve Franklin
Steve Holian
Steve Maskell
Steve Wilkins
Steven Gardner
Stuart Hayes
Stuart Panter
Stuart Parkins
Suzie Morgan
Taku & Hayley
Tamara Flowers
Tammy Fevrier
Tanya aka The Rollin-Raver & Steve E
Tanya Thompson
Tanz - Worcester
Tarnjit Bharaj
Taz "Major Bizzle" Benson-West (PROTOKOL)
Tennessee Van der Vyver
Terry 'DJ Harness' Haynes
Terry The Hat Hylton
The Brother Rusty
The Bunglist
The Double K
The Smithy
Tim Derudder
Tina Carlsson-Woods
Tom 3rd Door
Tom Bishop
Tom 'Pinny' Moore
Tom 'The Don' Gudgeon
Tommy Rendall
Tommy Zelkin
Tony T Hayles
Tony 'The Rhythm' Casales
Triga
Umesh 'Mac Monkee' Patel
Umran Khan
Vinnie Rice Aka Basshead
Warren Bradbury
Wayne Greyson
Wesley l'Oeuille
Will Bartlett
Will BP² NYC
Will 'Q' Morton